Cognitive-Behavioral Case Formulation and Treatment Design

A Problem-Solving Approach

Arthur M. Nezu, PhD, ABPP, is Professor of Psychology, Medicine, and Public Health at Drexel University in Philadelphia, as well as Co-Director of the Center for Behavioral Medicine and Mind/Body Studies. He is a Fellow of the American Psychological Association, the American Psychological Society, the Society for Behavior Medicine, and the American Academy of Behavioral Psychology. Dr. Nezu was previously President of the Association for Advancement of Behavior Therapy, as well as Chair of the Behavioral Psychology Specialty Council. He currently is President of the American Board of Behavioral Psychology, Chair of the World Congress of Behavioural and Cognitive Therapies, and Board Member of the American Academy of Behavioral Psychology. Dr. Nezu has contributed to over 150 scientific and professional publications on a wide variety of topics in mental health and behavioral medicine. He serves on the editorial boards of several prestigious psychology journals and has been a grant reviewer for both the National Institutes of Health and the National Institute of Mental Health.

Christine Maguth Nezu, PhD, ABPP, is Professor of Psychology, Associate Professor of Medicine, Co-Director for the Center for Behavioral Medicine and Mind/Body Studies, and Director for Assessment and Treatment Services for Sexual Aggression at Drexel University. She has coauthored over 75 professional publications across a range of topics including behavioral medicine, cognitive-behavioral assessment and treatment, mind/body psychotherapy interventions, aggressive and violent behavior, clinical decision making, integration of spiritual and psychological techniques, mental retardation, and psychopathology. Dr. Maguth Nezu currently is a Trustee of the American Board of Professional Psychology and on the Board of Directors for both the American Board of Behavioral Psychology and the American Academy of Behavioral Psychology. She also serves on the editorial boards of several leading psychology journals and is a Fellow of the American Academy of Behavioral Psychology.

Elizabeth R. Lombardo, PhD, was a practicing physical therapist for the Baltimore Veteran's Affairs Medical Center and adjunct faculty member in physical therapy at the University of Maryland before pursuing her career in psychology. Since obtaining her doctorate in clinical psychology, Dr. Lombardo has completed a postdoctoral fellowship in clinical health psychology at the University of Texas Southwestern Medical Center in Dallas and is currently in private practice.

Cognitive-Behavioral Case Formulation and Treatment Design

A Problem-Solving Approach

Arthur M. Nezu, PhD, ABPP
Christine Maguth Nezu, PhD, ABPP
Elizabeth Lombardo, PhD

 Springer Publishing Company

Springer Publishing Company, Inc.
536 Broadway
New York, NY 10012-3955

Acquisitions Editor: Sheri W. Sussman
Production Editor: Pamela Lankas
Cover design by Joanne Honigman

04 05 06 07 08/54321

Library of Congress Cataloging-in-Publication Data

Nezu, Arthur M.
Cognitive-behavioral case formulation and treatment design : a
  problem-solving approach / Arthur M. Nezu, Christine Maguth
  Nezu, Elizabeth R. Lombardo.
    p. cm.
  Includes index.
  ISBN 0-8261-2285-X
  1. Cognitive therapy. 2. Psychiatry—Case formulation.
  3. Psychiatry—Differential therapeutics. 4. Problem-solving
  therapy. I. Nezu, Christine M. II. Lombardo, Elizabeth R.
  III. Title.
RC489.C63N497 2004
616.89'142—dc22   2004003611

Printed in the United States of America by Maple-Vail Book
Manufacturing Group.

To Christine, for the beauty in her heart,
mind, and soul.
                                              —A.M.N.

To Arthur, my love, life partner, and soulmate.
                                              —C.M.N.

To Jeffrey, for his dedicated love and support.
                                              —E.R.L.

Contents

Preface

Although empirically supported interventions have been developed for specific psychological disorders, all practicing therapists would agree that it is the rare patient who is the "classic textbook case." In other words, because of huge variations regarding both patient- and environment-related factors (e.g., race, age, religion, socioeconomic status, co-morbid diagnoses, severity of symptoms, etc.) even among persons coming to outpatient therapy with the same presenting problem or receiving the same diagnosis, clinicians realize that they need to tailor their treatment plans to the unique characteristics and circumstances of a given patient. Too often, especially when dealing with pressures emanating from managed care policies, we are frustrated because the patient before us appears quite different from those we read about in the research studies, leaving us at times wondering what to do.

Because of this frustration, we decided to write a book that can help guide the therapist through the process of cognitive–behavioral case formulation and treatment design that takes such variability into account. As such, we will first present a model of clinical decision-making based on a problem-solving paradigm. This model suggests that the therapist engage in a more "problem-solving, scientific thinking-based process" when developing treatment plans in order to more effectively apply the nomothetic information from the research literature on an idiographic basis in clinical practice.

We will then provide step-by-step guides in treatment planning. Specifically, within the context of the problem-solving model, and based on the empirical literature, we will delineate (a) short-term goals, (b) long-term goals, (c) treatment targets, and (d) potential interventions for treatment targets regarding each of 11 common disorders and psychological problems (e.g., major depressive disorder, generalized anxiety, borderline personality disorder, anger problems). Therefore, this book provides for a structured reference to aid the process of case formulation and treatment design. In particular, we emphasize the link between an accurate case formulation and effective treatment planning.

In seeing this book to fruition, we would like to thank Sheri Sussman at Springer for her patience, support, and confidence; and to Susie Chen for her substantial help in library research.

I

From Case Formulation to Treatment Planning: Using a Problem-Solving Model

1

One Size Does Not Fit All: The Cognitive-Behavioral Therapist as Problem Solver

> What treatment, by whom, is most effective for this individual, with that specific problem, under which set of circumstances?
>
> —G. L. Paul

PURPOSE OF THIS BOOK

This book is written for the practicing mental health professional who is interested in applying cognitive–behavior therapy (CBT) interventions in an outpatient setting. Our goal is to provide a user-friendly guide that can help the clinician develop CBT treatment plans for 11 common psychological problems. To accomplish this objective, we focus on two major clinical tasks involved in this process: (a) case formulation; and (b) treatment design. However, because "complex problems require complex solutions" (Hersen, 1981; Nezu & Nezu, 1989), we also provide a model of clinical decision making in CBT to help the clinician more easily apply idiographically to clinical practice that set of relevant nomothetic information found in the research literature.

Why the Need for a Model
of Clinical Decision Making?

Although the movement toward developing empirically supported interventions for specific psychological disorders to some degree has become successful in identifying a group of highly efficacious clinical protocols (Chambless & Hollon, 1998), most practicing CBT therapists would agree that it is the rare patient who is the "classic textbook case." In other words, very few, if any, individuals who seek outpatient treatment fit nicely into the set of inclusion and exclusion criteria set forth by highly controlled experimental outcome studies (cf. Fensterheim, 1993).

In addition, as the famous quote by Paul posed over 30 years ago suggests, clinical work does not simply concern itself with identifying an effective treatment approach. Rather, successful CBT generally first entails case formulation, and second, based upon such a formulation, designing a treatment plan *tailored* to a given patient. In essence, unlike medical therapies which treat diseases, CBT treats people. And people can vary greatly both with regard to the manner in which they experience the same psychological problem and with regard to the reasons why such a problem initially emerged and continues to persist.

As such, it would be impossible for anyone at the present time to develop this outpatient guide in the form of a comprehensive CBT "cookbook," where the reader could easily locate in the index a treatment of choice to apply for a given patient who is experiencing a specific problem under a set of unique circumstances. Such a book would be abnormally long! For example, we previously noted the difficulties in providing simple answers to such complex questions as:

> What should be offered to the man in his mid-thirties, appearing depressed, with a distressed marriage, interpersonal problems at work, and a 6-year-old son with attention deficit disorder? Or what intervention would be most efficacious for a developmentally disabled adult with an aggressive behavior disorder and personality disorder, living in a group residence where the staff is poorly trained in contingency management or other behavioral procedures? (Nezu & Nezu, 1995, pp. 8–9)

On the other hand, this is not to suggest that the lists of empirically supported interventions or research-based practice guidelines have nothing to offer to clinicians. In fact, it is this very set of research data that clinical cognitive–behavior therapy is based upon. Yet, because of huge variations regarding both patient- and environment-related factors (e.g., race, age, religion, SES, co-morbid diagnoses, severity of symptoms, marital status, career, family, level of social support) even among persons coming to therapy with the same presenting problems, clinicians generally need to tailor their interventions to the unique characteristics and circumstances of a given patient.

In addition, unlike a disease model would suggest, psychological problems are rarely caused by a singular variable. The very reason why differing theories of a particular disorder have all been found to be valid speaks to the issue of the multicausal nature of human behavior. Major depression, for example, has been found to be causally related to a wide variety of psychosocial variables, including cognitive distortions, ineffective social skills, deficient problem-solving ability, reduced positive reinforcement, and poor self-control skills (Nezu, Nezu, Trunzo, & Sprague, 1998). However, studies have also demonstrated that no one cause ubiquitously characterizes all people experiencing depression (Nezu & Nezu, 1993). This lack of consistency for any given clinical disorder leaves substantial room for error when attempting to articulate idiographically a case formulation for a specific patient.

Collectively, this state of affairs suggests that *one size does not fit all!* Therefore, the CBT therapist frequently needs to apply his or her best clinical judgment in bridging the gap between the research literature (i.e., therapy as a "science") and its application to a given patient (i.e., therapy as an "art"). Put differently, the therapist needs to effectively answer the type of question posed by Paul (1969) for *each* patient he or she encounters, even if two of them are seemingly experiencing the same problem.

Errors in Clinical Reasoning: Problems in the Artful Application of Science

How then to best translate empirically based nomothetic information into effective idiographic applications in clinical practice? Kanfer and Phillips (1970) suggested early on that personal ingenuity and experience were the primary sources that behavior therapists have for selecting treatment approaches. Unfortunately, similar to human decision making in general, clinical decisions made by mental health professionals are vulnerable to errors in reasoning, making the outcome of such decisions potentially questionable (Arkes, 1981; Nezu & Nezu, 1989).

For example, Tversky and Kahneman (1974) identified three judgmental heuristics or information processing strategies that can *negatively* affect the veracity of the reasoning process when people make decisions. The *availability heuristic* is invoked when people attempt to estimate the frequency of a class or the probability of an event based on the *facility or ease* with which instances of that class or event come to mind. As an example related to clinical assessment, the availability heuristic might affect a therapist's prediction of a new patient's risk for suicide, if a recent case involved a person who actually committed suicide when the initial risk was thought to be low.

The *representativeness heuristic* occurs when people attempt to assess the degree to which certain events are related to each other (e.g., "What is the probability that A is associated with B or that A is a member of class B?" "What is the likelihood that event A caused event B or that B caused A?"), but base their decision on the *perceived* degree to which A *resembles* B. A major problem caused by representativeness thinking occurs when a schema is accessed by a given characteristic to the exclusion of other constructs. For example, if a particular diagnostic schema (e.g., major depression) is accessed automatically as a function of this heuristic on the basis of a given symptom (e.g., feelings of sadness), once this particular schema is accessed, the search for new information is likely to cease. The probability of viewing a given patient's problems from the perspective of other conceptual or diagnostic schemas (e.g., bipolar illness, medically related mood difficulties, personality disorder) becomes reduced, thus restricting the range of possible causal hypotheses that might be considered.

The third heuristic, that of *anchoring*, occurs when a shortcut method of estimation or prediction is used whereby ultimate decisions are based more on initial impressions than on subsequent information, even though this new information is conflicting. For example, two thirds of a sample of more than 300 behavior therapists indicated that fewer than two sessions were required to conceptualize a patient's problem (Swan & MacDonald, 1978). Thus, if the depressed patient only discusses issues of interpersonal difficulties during these two sessions, unless the therapist ensures that a broad spectrum of other problem areas are explored, the anchoring heuristic might influence the clinician to select poor social skills as the predominant reason why this patient is depressed, without the benefit of a more extensive case formulation.

In addition to those heuristics identified by Tversky and Kahnemann (1974), other problems in clinical reasoning have been identified (see Nezu & Nezu, 1989; Nezu & Nezu, 1995). First, the strategy itself used to obtain information when making decisions often inadvertently leads to erroneous conclusions. For example, *selective attention* to certain types of information can lead to biased perceptions of the degree of covariation between two events. Second, *confirmatory search strategies* have been shown to be ubiquitous means by which people attempt to verify inferences and make predictions. These strategies involve procedures that seek only to obtain information that supports one's initial impressions; attempts to seek disconfirming evidence become limited. Further, being *overconfident* in one's abilities can serve as a source of systematic error in clinical reasoning, as confidence has been found to be unrelated to clinical accuracy.

These judgmental biases collectively can lead to a situation, for example, in which a patient who complains of depressive feelings is automatically taught to change his or her negative cognitions (or to cope with stressful problems, or to increase positive experiences, or to become more assertive) without the benefit of a more detailed and comprehensive case formulation. Put another way, how a clinician conceptualizes a patient's problems may depend to a large degree on these heuristics rather than on a careful case formulation. Because such conceptualizations can influence the therapist's behavior (e.g., which problems become targeted, which assessment procedures are applied, which interventions become implemented), formal guidelines to help the process of case formulation and treatment design become crucial.

Given this context, one of the prime purposes of this book is to provide a model of clinical decision making in the practice of CBT that can foster the effectiveness and validity of CBT case formulation and treatment design. In essence, our model characterizes the CBT clinician as "an active problem solver" (Nezu & Nezu, 1989; 1993; Nezu, Nezu, Peacock, & Girdwood, 2004).

CBT CLINICIAN AS PROBLEM SOLVER

In the role of problem solver, behavioral clinicians are faced with a series of "problems to solve" whenever conducting assessment and treatment. Therapy represents problems due to the inherent discrepancy between a patient's *current* state (i.e., presence of complaints, problems, symptoms) and his or her *desired* state (i.e., achievement of his or her goals). In other words, it is the clinician's task, in providing therapy, to help the patient get from "A" to "B."

According to this problem-solving framework, numerous obstacles exist that prevent individuals from reaching their goals without the therapist's professional help. Such variables may be related to the patients themselves (e.g., behavioral, cognitive, affective, or physiological excesses or deficits) or to the environment (e.g., lack of resources, presence of aversive stimuli).

Cognitive-behavioral treatment, therefore, represents the therapist's attempt to "solve these problems." To achieve such goals, we advocate adopting a *problem-solving model of case formulation and treatment design*. Put simply, this model recommends using various problem-solving operations in order to effectively address such clinical problems.

The Problem-Solving Process

Our approach to cognitive-behavioral case formulation and treatment design draws heavily from the prescriptive model of social problem-solving developed by D'Zurilla, Nezu, and their colleagues (e.g., D'Zurilla & Nezu, 1999; Nezu, in press; Nezu, Nezu, & Lombardo, 2003). Adapted for the current purpose, this model of case formulation and treatment design focuses on two major problem-solving processes—problem orientation and rational problem solving.

Problem Orientation

Problem orientation refers to the set of orienting responses (e.g., general beliefs, assumptions, appraisals, and expectations) one engages in when attempting to understand and react to problems in general. In essence, this represents a person's *world view* regarding problems. World views refer to underlying conceptual frameworks that represent a person's understanding of "how the world works" (Pepper, 1942). In the present context, a *clinician's world view* would involve the cohesive framework that guides his or her attempts to understand, explain, predict, and change human behavior.

Depending on one's therapeutic orientation, the overarching world view that would be adopted would be one that is in keeping with that particular therapeutic perspective, in this case, a cognitive-behavioral framework. Elsewhere, we defined cognitive-behavior therapy as falling " . . . within an experimental-clinical framework and incorporates a broad definition of behavior that includes overt actions, internal cognitive phenomena, and the experience of affect or emotions. These components range in complexity from molecular (i.e., lower-level) events (e.g., smoking a cigarette, hyperventilation, a critical comment in a dyadic interaction) to molar (i.e., higher-level) pluralistic and multidimensional constructs (e.g., complex social skills, solving a difficult calculus problem, major depressive disorder)" (Nezu, Nezu, Friedman, & Haynes, 1997; pp. 368–369). This will be the definition of CBT that will be adopted in the present context.

Rational Problem Solving

Whereas problem orientation is primarily a cognitive activity, *rational problem solving* entails a set of specific cognitive and behavioral operations that are helpful in solving problems effectively. These include: (a) defining problems; (b) generating alternatives; (c) making decisions; and (d) evaluating the solution outcome. The goal of *problem definition* is to delineate the reasons why a given situation is a problem (e.g., the presence of obstacles), as well as to specify a set of realistic goals and objectives to help guide further problem-solving efforts. The purpose of the *generation-of-alternatives* task is to create, using various brainstorming principles, a large pool of possible solutions in order to increase the likelihood that the most effective ideas will be ultimately identified. The goal of *decision making* is to conduct a systematic cost-benefit analysis of the various alternatives by identifying and then weighing their potential positive and negative consequences if carried out, and then, based on this evaluation, to develop an overall solution plan. Finally, the purpose of *solution evaluation* is to monitor and evaluate the effectiveness of a solution plan and troubleshoot if the outcome is unsatisfactory. In other words, if the solution is not effective, the problem solver needs to re-cycle through the various problem-solving tasks in order to determine where renewed efforts should be directed in order to solve the problem successfully. Although each problem-solving operation may not always be directly relevant to every decision related to CBT case formulation and treatment design, we encourage their use when addressing *any* difficult clinical decision encountered during the course of treatment.

SUMMARY AND DESCRIPTION OF THE REMAINDER OF THE BOOK

Although efforts to develop empirically supported CBT interventions have been partially successful, due to the ubiquitous heterogeneity among populations of patients experiencing the same problem or having the same diagnosis, the ready applicability of such strategies to actual clinical practice remains limited. In addition, because therapy can be conceptualized as a series of "problems to be solved," another concern that emerges is the potential for various judgmental heuristics and biases to impact negatively on the veracity of the clinical decision-making process. As such, we advocate that the processes of developing an accurate case formulation and designing an effective treatment plan specific to a given patient can be enhanced by the use of a problem-solving model of clinical judgment.

In the next chapter, we describe how to apply such a model to the process of CBT case formulation. In part, this application underscores the importance of evaluating the relevance of a *range* of psychosocial variables that have been found to be causally related to a given disorder with regard to a specific patient. In chapters 5–15, for each of the 11 psychological disorders that are included, we provide descriptions of such causal variables, as well as how to measure them.

In chapter 3, we focus on the process of treatment design and how to use the problem-solving model for this clinical task. We further advocate considering the *range* of CBT treatment strategies that have been identified through research and clinical practice that are effective in addressing a particular causal factor. Moreover, in the chapters in Section II that focus on specific psychological problems, we provide the reader with a description of a range of treatment strategies for each causal variable as a basis for developing a unique treatment plan tailored for a specific patient.

In chapter 4, we briefly describe how to use this CBT outpatient treatment guide, whereas in Appendix A there is a series of "quick guides to CBT treatment planning" for the 11 disorders. Last, in Appendix B, we briefly describe selected major CBT clinical intervention strategies noted throughout the chapters.

REFERENCES

Arkes, H. R. (1981). Impediments to accurate clinical judgment and possible ways to minimize their impact. *Journal of Consulting and Clinical Psychology, 49,* 323–330.

Chambless, D. L., & Hollon, S. D. (1998). Defining empirically supported therapies. *Journal of Consulting and Clinical Psychology, 66,* 7–18.

D'Zurilla, T. J., & Nezu, A. M. (1999). *Problem-solving therapy: A social competence approach to clinical intervention* (2nd ed.). New York: Springer Publishing Co.

Fensterheim, H. (1993). Letter to the editor. *Behavior Therapist, 16,* 149.

Hersen, M. (1981). Complex problems require complex solutions. *Behavior Therapy, 12,* 15–29.

Kanfer, F. H., & Philips, J. S. (1970). *Learning foundations of behavior therapy.* New York: Wiley.

Nezu, A. M. (in press). Problem solving and behavior therapy revisited. *Behavior Therapy.*

Nezu, A. M., & Nezu, C. M. (Eds.). (1989). *Clinical decision making in behavior therapy: A problem-solving perspective.* Champaign, IL: Research Press.

Nezu, A. M., & Nezu, C. M. (1993). Identifying and selecting target problems for clinical interventions: A problem-solving model. *Psychological Assessment, 5,* 254–263.

Nezu, A. M., Nezu, C. M., Friedman, S. H., & Haynes, S. N. (1997). Case formulation in behavior therapy: Problem-solving and functional analytic strategies. In T. D. Eells (Ed.), *Handbook of psychotherapy case formulation* (pp. 368–401). New York: Guilford.

Nezu, A. M., Nezu, C. M., & Lombardo, E. (2003). Problem-solving therapy. In W. O'Donohue, J. E. Fisher, & Hayes, S. C. (Eds.), *Cognitive behavior therapy: Applying empirically supported techniques in your practice* (pp. 301–307). New York: Wiley.

Nezu, A. M., Nezu, C. M., Peacock, M. A., & Girdwood, C. P. (2004). Case formulation in cognitive-behavior therapy. In M. Hersen (Series Ed.), S. N. Haynes, & E. Heiby (Vol. Eds.), *Behavioral assessment.* Vol. 3 of the *Comprehensive Handbook of Psychological Assessment* (pp. 402–426). New York: Wiley.

Nezu, A. M., Nezu, C. M., Trunzo, J. J., & Sprague, K. S. (1998). Treatment maintenance for unipolar depression: Relevant issues, literature review, and recommendations for research and clinical practice. *Clinical Psychology: Science and Practice, 5,* 496–512.

Nezu, C. M., & Nezu, A. M. (1995). Clinical decision making in everyday practice: The science in the art. *Cognitive and Behavioral Practice, 2,* 5–25.

Paul, G. L. (1969). Behavior modification research: Design and tactics. In C. M. Franks (Ed.), *Behavior therapy: Appraisal and status* (pp. 29–62). New York: McGraw-Hill.

Pepper, S.C. (1942). *World hypotheses.* Berkeley: University of California Press.

Swan, G. E., & McDonald, M. L. (1978). Behavior therapy in practice: A national survey of behavior therapists. *Behavior Therapy, 9,* 799–807.

Tversky, A., & Kahnemann, D. (1974). Judgment under uncertainty: Heuristics and biases. *Science, 185,* 1124–1131.

2

Applying the Problem-Solving Model to Cognitive-Behavioral Case Formulation

WHAT IS CASE FORMULATION?

Case formulation can be viewed as a set of hypotheses, generally framed by a particular personality theory or psychotherapy orientation, regarding what variables serve as causes, triggers, or maintaining factors of an individual's emotional, psychological, interpersonal, and behavior problems (Eels, 1997). It is a description of a patient's complaints and symptoms of distress, as well as an organizing mechanism to help the clinician understand how such complaints came into being, how various symptoms co-exist, what environmental or intrapersonal stimuli trigger such problems, and why such symptoms persist (Nezu, Nezu, Peacock, & Girdwood, 2004). In this chapter, we describe how to apply the problem-solving model of clinical decision making to the process of CBT case formulation.

Goals of CBT Case Formulation

During this process, it can be said that the therapist begins to develop a "patient story." This story provides for a description of the various factors within the individual's life that are involved in both the emergence and maintenance of a given set of distressing symptoms. For the therapist, this story includes a proposed ending that represents a set of treatment objectives and goals. Having such a story provides for a concrete structure within which the therapist begins to think about *how* to reach such goals (i.e., what is the treatment plan?).

In general, the goals of CBT case formulation are to:

- Obtain a detailed understanding of the patient's presenting problems,
- Identify those variables that are functionally related to such difficulties, and
- Delineate treatment targets, goals, and objectives.

Ultimate Versus Instrumental Outcome Goals

In thinking of treatment goals, it is very useful to distinguish between ultimate outcome goals and instrumental outcome goals. Rosen and Proctor (1981) describe *ultimate outcomes* as general therapy goals or outcomes "for which treatment is undertaken and reflect the objectives toward which treatment efforts are to be directed" (p. 419). Such goals may include ameliorating depression, improving one's marital relationship, or decreasing phobic behavior. These are differentiated from *instrumental outcomes,* which are those changes or effects that "serve as the instruments for the attainment of other outcomes" (p. 419). Instrumental outcomes, depending on their functional relationships to other variables, may have an impact on ultimate outcomes (e.g., increasing one's self-esteem can reduce the severity of depressive affect) or on other instrumental outcomes within a hypothesized causal chain (e.g., improving a patient's coping ability can increase his or her sense of self-efficacy, which in turn may decrease depressive severity).

Clinically, instrumental outcomes (other terms being intermediate goals or mechanisms of action) reflect the therapist's hypotheses concerning those variables that are believed to be causally related to the ultimate outcome(s). Using language from the research lab regarding treatment outcome investigations, instrumental outcomes can be viewed as *independent variables* (IVs), whereas ultimate outcomes represent *dependent variables* (DVs). Instrumental outcome variables can serve as *mediators,* which are those elements that account for or explain the relationship between two other variables, similar to a causal mechanism (i.e., the mechanism by which the IV impacts or influences the DV). They can also serve as *moderators*, or those types of factors that can influence the strength and/ or direction of the relationship between two or more other variables (Haynes & O'Brien, 2000). In this manner, instrumental outcome variables denote potential targets for clinical interventions.

Making the distinction between instrumental and ultimate outcomes can also help guide the process of treatment planning, implementation, and evaluation (Nezu, Nezu, Friedman, & Haynes, 1997). In addition, it can help to identify when treatment is *not* working. Mash and Hunsley (1993), for example, suggest that within the context of clinical practice, a primary goal of assessment is early corrective feedback, rather than a simple evaluation at an endpoint of the successful or unsuccessful achievement of a patient's ultimate goal. For example, if a cognitive restructuring intervention is found to be ineffective in engendering actual changes in a depressed patient's negative thinking, then such information provides for immediate feedback that this particular treatment, as implemented, may not be working. Therefore, in order to reduce the likelihood of treatment failure, assessment of success in achieving instrumental outcomes (e.g., change in negative thinking) should *precede* an evaluation of whether one's ultimate goals were attained (e.g., decrease in depression).

APPLYING THE PROBLEM-SOLVING MODEL TO CASE FORMULATION: PROBLEM ORIENTATION

Relevant to case formulation, our problem-solving model of clinical decision making advocates adopting a problem orientation that emphasizes two particular perspectives:

1. Behavior can be multiply caused, and
2. Behavior occurs within various systems.

Multiple Causality Framework

The multiple causality framework advocated here is based in part on a *planned critical multiplism* philosophy (Shadish, 1993). This methodological approach to the conduct of science advocates the use of multiple operations in order to guard against systematic bias. In the context of clinical assessment, this approach suggests that there are numerous paths by which the same set of symptoms can emerge among different individuals. Further, within a multiple causality framework, variables that serve to act and interact in the initiation and maintenance of an individual's symptoms may be biological, psychological, or social. Moreover, these factors may contribute to the presence of a symptom or disorder in either a *proximal* (i.e., immediate antecedent, such as the presence of a phobic object) or a *distal* (i.e., developmental history, such as the occurrence of a traumatic event) manner.

In the context of treatment design, this perspective suggests that "there are multiple roads that lead to Rome." In other words, with regard to the treatment goal of enhancing one's ability to better manage stress-related arousal, several different CBT strategies exist (e.g., progressive muscle relaxation, autogenic training, visualization, deep breathing exercises) allowing for the therapist to apply differing strategies based on the unique needs of a given patient (Nezu & Nezu, 1993).

Systems Approach

A second orientation element that we advocate adopting involves a *systems perspective*. This perspective emphasizes the notion that instrumental and ultimate outcome variables can relate to each other in mutually interactive ways, rather than in a simple unidirectional and linear fashion (Kanfer, 1985; Nezu et al., 1997). For example, elsewhere, we described how various biological, psychological, and social factors can interact with each other in initiating and maintaining various non-biologically caused distressing physical symptoms (e.g., noncardiac chest pain, fibromyalgia) (Nezu, Nezu, & Lombardo, 2001). For example, early imitative learning within a family, where a parent responds to stress with undue physical symptoms, can serve as a psychological vulnerability factor that influences the manner in which a child interprets the experience of physical symptoms (i.e., gastrointestinal distress) under stressful circumstances. Such cognitive factors then can influence his or her behavior (e.g., avoiding stress, seeking out his or her parents' reassurance, focusing undue attention on the distress "caused" by the symptoms). This in turn can lead to parental reinforcement of the behavior and an exacerbation of the symptoms, which can then lead to an intensification of the child's beliefs concerning appropriate behavior under certain circumstances, and so forth. In this manner, the reciprocal relationships among the various cognitive, affective, behavioral, environmental, and biological factors can comprise a constellation of causal chains within an overall network, unique to a given individual.

This model, then, advocates assessing the manner in which such pathogenically involved variables reciprocally interact with one another in order to obtain a more complete and comprehensive picture of a patient's *unique network or set of behavioral chains*. Using a systems perspective allows the CBT clinician to better identify those instrumental outcome variables that play a key role in order to prioritize such variables as initial treatment targets. In other words, those instrumental outcome variables that appear to be either functionally related to a *wide* range of other instrumental outcome variables in the network, or related to ultimate outcome variables in a *significant* manner (i.e., the strength of the relationship is strong, as in a high correlation coefficient), are likely to be important *initial* treatment targets, as changes in such key variables can engender maximal change in both intermediate and ultimate outcome goals. An additional advantage of identifying the interacting variables in an individual's system in such a manner is that it enables the therapist to delineate *numerous* potential targets simultaneously (e.g., changing negative thinking, decreasing maladaptive behavior, improving negative mood), thereby increasing the likelihood of success if a group of such variables all become targets of effective interventions.

APPLYING THE PROBLEM-SOLVING MODEL TO CASE FORMULATION: DEFINING PROBLEMS

In general, this problem-solving task involves the following activities:

- Gathering information,
- Separating facts from assumptions, and
- Identifying the factors that contribute to the problem situation.

Identifying Ultimate Outcomes

With regard to the case formulation process, the first step in applying the problem-definition task is to investigate a broad range of areas of the patient's life (e.g., interpersonal relationships, job, finances, sex, physical health, etc.) in order to obtain a more complete understanding of his or her current functioning. This leads to the delineation of various ultimate outcome goals. Note that whereas ultimate outcomes are often *patient-defined* (e.g., "I'm feeling really sad and I want to feel better;" "I have a lot of difficulty having good relationships with the opposite sex"), at times they will become the *therapist's* translations of the patient's presenting complaints. Such translations can be in the form of formal diagnostic categories (e.g., obsessive-compulsive disorder, major depression) or a series of statements regarding specific problem situations (e.g., "improve interpersonal relationships," "increase self-confidence and self-esteem," "reduce pain"). Further, as changes occur due to treatment, certain ultimate outcome goals may be discarded, modified, or new ones added by the patient or the therapist.

Identifying Instrumental Outcomes

Next, the therapist begins to identify those instrumental outcome variables that are likely to be causally related to the stated ultimate outcome goals for a given patient. In concert with the multiple causality orientation, during this process, it is important to access the *entire* extant universe or domain of potentially relevant instrumental outcome variables that can be identified in the research literature. In other words, rather than rely on a *preferred* model of a given disorder, due to omnipresent individual differences among patients across a variety of factors (e.g., gender, age, symptom severity, ethnicity), the CBT clinician should attempt to review the relevance of a *range* of empirically derived, potentially relevant, instrumental outcome variables.

Search Guides

To help facilitate the search for these domains, two guides exist that can be used by the therapist to identify a range of relevant causal variables—a theory-driven strategy and a diagnosis-driven strategy. A *theory-driven strategy* recommends that the empirically based literature linking various instrumental outcomes to ultimate outcomes be used to guide the therapist's search for meaningful clinical targets. For example, if one ultimate goal is to reduce anger, the empirical literature containing *multiple* theories attempting to explain, for example, why people get angry or have difficulty controlling anger, would be an important source to search for potentially important instrumental outcome variables. This pool of nomothetically derived instrumental outcome variables can then be evaluated regarding its idiographic applicability to a particular patient.

A *diagnosis-driven strategy* may also facilitate the identification of treatment targets. Diagnostic guidelines, such as the *Diagnostic and Statistical Manual of Mental Disorders, Fourth Edition Text Revision* (DSM-IV-TR; American Psychiatric Association, 2000), may provide a useful means of understanding response clusters and response covariations. Symptoms of clusters that have been found to covary, and that have been categorized within particular diagnostic categories, can guide the therapist's assessment. In other words, this type of search would be guided by a patient's diagnosis; for example, generalized anxiety disorder (GAD), whereby the literature on the etiopathogenesis and treatment of GAD can serve to identify potentially relevant causal variables.

Whereas theory-driven and diagnosis-driven approaches can foster the identification of relevant instrumental outcome variables, we advocate that the therapist be guided by the multiple causality philosophy previously described. For example, exclusive use of a *single* specific theory to guide one's assessment strategy can increase the likelihood of judgmental errors and poor treatment outcome. Likewise, labeling and categorizing patients into a diagnostic category may erroneously imply that their behavior problems are always related to similar underlying variables.

As a major purpose of this book is to provide for a user-friendly case formulation and treatment design guide, we have already completed such a search for the reader regarding 11 common disorders encountered in an outpatient setting. These will be found in Section II of this book.

Multidimensional Framework of Assessment

To increase the likelihood that the CBT clinician is able to conduct a comprehensive review of the representative domain(s) of relevant instrumental outcome variables, we recommend using the following categories and dimensions:

- Patient-related variables
- Environment-related variables
- Temporal dimension
- Functional dimension

Patient-Related Variables

This category refers to factors relating to the patient, including behavioral, affective, cognitive, biological, and socio/ethnic/cultural background variables. For the purposes of the case formulation process, problem *behaviors* can be globally categorized as either behavioral deficits or excesses. Examples of behavioral *deficits* include poor social skills, deficits in daily living skills, or poor self-control. Behavioral *excesses* might include compulsive behavior, avoidance of anxiety-provoking stimuli, frequent negative self-evaluation, or aggressive actions. Problematic *affect* involves the wide array of negative emotions and mood states, such as anxiety, depression, hopelessness, fear, anger, and hostility.

With regard to psychopathology-related *cognitive* factors, it is useful to distinguish between cognitive *deficiencies* and cognitive *distortions* (Kendall, 1985). Cognitive deficiencies are absences in one's thinking processes (e.g., failure to realize the consequences of one's actions). Cognitive distortions refer to errors in cognitive processing (e.g., misinterpretations of certain events based on dichotomous thinking).

Biological variables include the wide range of physiological, medical, and physical factors that can be problems by themselves or variables that are functionally related to a patient's psychosocial problems or goals. These can include medical illness, physical limitation or disability, side effects of medication, or a biological vulnerability to heightened arousal under stress. On another level, this category includes one's actual gender and age, especially when such factors play an etiologic role in the prevalence or manifestation of a particular disorder or set of symptoms.

Socio/ethnic/cultural variables include a range of potentially important background variables, including ethnicity, sexual orientation, sex roles, culture, and socioeconomic status. The importance of considering ethnic background when conducting a diagnostic interview is emphasized in the most recent version of the *Diagnostic and Statistical Manual of Mental Disorders (Fourth Edition, Text Revision*; DSM-IV-TR; American Psychiatric Association, 2000). For example, the DSM-IV-TR recommends that the clinician consider five categories when working with multicultural environments: (a) the cultural identity of the individual (e.g., what is the person's self-identified cultural group, his or her degree of acculturation, as well as his or her current involvement in the host culture?); (b) the cultural explanation of the individual's disorder (e.g., what are the causal attributions and significance of the "condition" that is promulgated by the individual's culture?); (c) cultural factors related to psychosocial environment and levels of functioning (e.g., what is the availability of social support? what is the cultural interpretation of social stressors?); (d) cultural elements of the relationship between patient and clinician (e.g., what are the differences in both culture and social status between the clinician and the patient?); and (e) overall assessment for diagnosis and care (e.g., what are the cultural factors that might impact upon the patient's diagnosis and treatment?).

Coming from a cognitive-behavioral perspective, Tanaka-Matsumi, Seiden, and Lam (1996) suggest a similar approach when conducting a "culturally informed functional analysis." Specifically, they suggest the following eight concrete steps:

- Assess cultural identity and degree of acculturation,
- Assess and evaluate a patient's presenting problems with reference to his or her cultural norms,
- Evaluate patients' causal attributions regarding their problems,
- Conduct a functional analysis,
- Compare one's case formulation with a patient's belief system,
- Negotiate treatment objectives and methods with the patient,
- Discuss with the patient the need for data collection to assess treatment progress, and
- Discuss treatment duration, course, and expected outcome with the patient.

We would argue that a similar perspective be adopted (i.e., focus on how one perceives his or her problems within the context of being a member of a "minority group") when working with gay and lesbian individuals, persons who identify strongly with a particular religious or spiritual philosophy (be it traditional or non-traditional), and individuals of extreme SES backgrounds (either poor or wealthy). In this manner, we are better able to understand what might be considered "normal" within the parameters of a given patient's "world," as well as to identify problems that might exist simply due to differences between the person's socio/ethnic/cultural status and other groups in society, whether dominant or minority.

Environment-Related Variables

This category includes those instrumental outcome variables that emanate either from one's physical or social environment. *Physical environmental variables* can include housing, crowding, climate, and physical living conditions. *Social environmental factors* can include a patient's relationships with friends and family, spouse, and other members of one's social and work communities. This latter category also addresses a variety of socio/ethnic/ cultural aspects, but here focuses on the reactions of others (both within and outside of) the patient's self-identified (sub)culture.

Temporal Factors

This temporal dimension reminds us to gather information regarding a patient's current *and* past functioning in order to eventually develop a more accurate case formulation. Current or proximal factors often serve as potential stressors that can trigger various maladaptive behaviors, cognitions, and affective states. In addition, variables that are temporally distant often contribute to a patient's *current* difficulties (e.g., early trauma can engender posttraumatic stress disorder symptoms years later). In addition, obtaining an understanding of a patient's family history can provide information regarding how he or she developed certain beliefs about the world. Identifying these distal variables provides another opportunity to investigate the causal mechanisms that contribute to the patient's current symptom picture.

Functional Dimension

The function that each of these variables serves with respect to the identified ultimate outcome constitutes the final assessment dimension and is a cornerstone of CBT assessment (Haynes & O'Brien, 1990, 2000). Function here refers to the covariation that exists between two or more variables and is in keeping with the systems perspective that is part of our espoused orientation. In many cases, this association signifies causation (i.e., A "caused" B), whereas for others, there may be no need to invoke the concept of causality (i.e., A simply changes when B changes and visa versa). In this latter case, the covariation can more accurately describe a functional relationship whereby one variable serves as a maintaining factor of the second variable. For example, B may not be the original "cause" of A, but serves as the reason why A continues to persist. Possible reasons for this maintaining function can involve (1) because B serves as a stimulus leading to A (i.e., a discriminative stimulus or trigger); or (2) that B serves to increase the probability of A persisting because of its reinforcing properties in relation to A.

The acronym *SORC*, initially presented by Goldfried and Sprafkin (1974), can be a useful means to summarize various functional relationships among these variables. For example, if the presenting problem (e.g., depression) is identified as the *response* to be changed (i.e., the ultimate outcome), then assessment can determine which variables function as the *antecedents*, which serve as *consequences*, and which function as organismic *mediators or moderators* of the response. In this framework, a variable can be identified as a *stimulus* (*S*; intra-personal or environmental antecedents), *organismic variable* (*O*; biological, behavioral, affective, cognitive, or socio/ethnic/cultural variables), *response* (*R*), and *consequence* (*C*; intrapersonal, interpersonal, or environmental effects engendered by the response) (see also Goldfried & Davison, 1994).

In keeping with both the multiple causality and systems framework orientation espoused earlier, given the complexity of human behavior, it is likely that several important and relevant *SORC* chains within a larger causal network can be identified that collectively help to explain the initial emergence and continued persistence of a patient's problems. Moreover, these chains are likely to interact with each other, whereby within one particular causal chain, a given variable may serve as a stimulus, whereas in another chain, the same variable serves as a consequence. For example, a particular consequence may not only increase the probability that a behavior will recur in the future (via positive reinforcement), but may also increase the likelihood that a particular stimulus will be elicited (i.e., serving as a trigger or discriminative stimulus).

However, changes in a particular variable can lead to changes in the functional relationship between two other variables. For example, positive changes in coping ability (an "*O*" variable), which can serve as a moderator of the relationship between stressful events (an "*S*" variable) and depressive affect (an "*R*" variable), can thus change the strength of the relationship between stress and depression such that stressful events for a given person no longer represents a major trigger. As such, a given *SORC* chain represents a "snapshot" of the manner in which certain factors are functionally related to each other at a given point in time. A comprehensive understanding of a patient's problems, as well as his or her unique obstacles to goal attainment, will likely be best described by an interacting set of *SORC* chains within an overall causal network or system (i.e., a comprehensive, but idiographic, causal model of how a series of variables are functionally related to such problems).

The Importance of the SORC

Using SORC nomenclature to identify the functional relationships certain instrumental outcome variables have with the ultimate outcome, and with each other, provides information regarding potential target problems and suggests interventions that may be used to address them. For example, intervention strategies can be identified that are geared to change the stimulus variables, the organismic mediating variables, and/or the consequential variables in order to impact on the ultimate outcome. In this manner, the importance of the integral relationship between case formulation and treatment design placed by this model becomes apparent.

APPLYING THE PROBLEM-SOLVING MODEL TO CASE FORMULATION: GENERATING ALTERNATIVES

The goal of this problem-solving task, relevant to case formulation, is to identify a meaningful range of potential target problems, thereby maximizing the probability that the most effective ones will be ultimately identified. This objective can be met by utilizing the brainstorming method of idea production, which advocates the use of three general problem-solving principles:

- Quantity principle (i.e., the more ideas that are produced, the more likely that potentially more effective ones are generated),
- Deferment-of-judgment principle (i.e., more high-quality alternatives can be generated if evaluation is deferred until after a comprehensive list of possible solutions has been compiled), and
- Strategies-tactics principle (i.e., thinking of solution strategies, or general approaches, in addition to specific tactics, increases idea production).

At this point, the therapist uses these problem-solving principles in concert with theory-driven and diagnosis-driven search strategies and within the context of the multidimensional assessment matrix to generate a list of possible instrumental outcome variables that might be selected as treatment targets for a given patient. *Note that in chapters 5–15, we provide a description of common empirically derived instrumental outcome variables for 11 common psychological disorders.*

As an example, using the above guidelines, we developed the following list of common major instrumental outcome goals for social anxiety (see chapter 9):

- Decrease heightened physiological arousal
- Decrease dysfunctional beliefs

- Enhance interpersonal skills
- Decrease general stress
- Improve specific social skills deficits
- Decrease focus on bodily sensations
- Address related co-morbid disorders

Note that we are not advocating that *all* of these instrumental outcome variables would be relevant and important for *all* patients suffering from social anxiety. Rather, this list represents the *range* of common, empirically derived instrumental outcome factors that would be important to assess across all such patients in order to minimize the possibility that *one* of these variables is overlooked (i.e., preventing judgmental heuristics to "creep into" one's case formulation).

In addition, *beyond* the set of instrumental outcome goals that we provide for each of the 11 disorders addressed in Section II, we strongly advocate that the CBT clinician generate (using the problem-solving operations described in this chapter) *additional* such variables that may be relevant to a given patient.

APPLYING THE PROBLEM-SOLVING MODEL TO CASE FORMULATION: DECISION MAKING

Selecting instrumental outcomes specific to a given patient from such a list as the one above occurs during the decision-making process. The goal of this problem-solving activity is to select instrumental outcomes that, when targeted, will maximize treatment success for a given patient.

According to the problem-solving model, effective decision making is based on an evaluation of the *utility* of the various alternatives. The alternative or group of alternatives with the highest degree of utility should then be chosen. Utility is determined by both:

- The *likelihood* that an alternative will achieve a particular goal, and
- The *value* of that alternative.

Likelihood of Goal Attainment

Using problem-solving language, *estimates of likelihood* involve assessing the probability that an alternative will, in fact, facilitate goal attainment, as well as the probability that the person implementing the alternative will be able to do so optimally. These general principles are applied to the case formulation process by taking into account the probability that:

- Addressing *this particular* instrumental outcome variable will help *this particular* patient meet his or her overall treatment goals (i.e., Will achieving this instrumental outcome lead to the desired ultimate outcome either directly or by means of achieving another related instrumental outcome goal?),
- This particular target problem is amenable to treatment (i.e., On the basis of the literature, can *this* instrumental outcome goal be achieved successfully?),
- This particular therapist is able to treat the given target problem (i.e., Do I have the expertise to implement those interventions that are geared toward changing this target problem?), and
- The treatment necessary to facilitate change for the patient is *available*.

Answers to many of these types of criteria questions (e.g., Will achieving this instrumental outcome positively impact on this patient's ultimate outcome?) require first accessing the empirical literature to determine nomothetically the *strength* of such relationships between specific instrumental outcome-ultimate outcome pairs (e.g., zero-order correlation between depressive symptom severity and cognitive distortions; percentage of suicidal patients who score high on a hopelessness scale), and second, consistent with the multiple causality orientation, to determine if such nomothetic information is *relevant* to a specific patient. In other words, if an assessment of the presence of dysfunctional thoughts regarding a given patient with social anxiety finds significant problems regarding this particular instrumental outcome variable, it is likely that such a variable would be identified as an initial treatment target. On the other hand, if such an assessment finds otherwise (i.e., only a marginal level of dysfunctional thinking is present), then this instrumental outcome factor would *not* be targeted for this patient.

Although this might appear as if we are simply stating the obvious, we emphasize that such an evaluation needs to occur within the context of assessing the relevance of all items in the *range* of instrumental outcome variables across all such patients, and not simply bypassing the case formulation process and apply treatment techniques that address one's "favorite" treatment target.

Value of an Alternative: Focus on the Consequences

The value of an idea is estimated by assessing four specific areas of criteria. Specific to case formulation, the first area includes the *personal consequences* to both therapist and patient which may include the following:

- Time, effort, or resources necessary to reach the instrumental outcome,
- Emotional cost or gain involved in reaching this outcome,
- Consistency of this outcome with one's ethical values,
- Physical or life-threatening effects involved in changing this target problem, and
- Effects of changing this problem area on other target problems.

Social consequences, the second category of value criteria, involve the effects on other people, such as

- Significant other,
- Family member,
- Friends, or
- Community (if relevant).

In addition, *short-term effects* on the patient's other problem areas, as well as short-term iatrogenic effects related to achieving the instrumental outcome, should be assessed. Finally, the *long-term effects* of changing these instrumental outcomes on future psychological functioning should be considered. Once again, answers to these questions require idiographically applying the nomothetic empirical literature to a specific patient.

By using these types of criteria to judge utility, the clinician can conduct a cost-benefit analysis for each potential target problem that was previously generated. In essence, instrumental outcomes with a high likelihood of *maximizing positive effects* and *minimizing negative effects* are then selected as initial target problems. Thus, the likelihood and value criteria are used to guide the selection of target problems and to prioritize which areas to address early in therapy.

APPLYING THE PROBLEM-SOLVING MODEL TO CASE FORMULATION: EVALUATING SOLUTION OUTCOMES

In essence, it is at this stage of the problem-solving process regarding CBT case formulation that the clinician, by applying various problem-solving activities, has been able to delineate a list of relevant treatment targets for the patient at hand. He or she is now ready to determine if this hypothesized list is "truly valid" for this particular patient. In other words, as one of the hallmarks of CBT is its allegiance to scientific reasoning, rather than simply remaining hopeful that this list of targets is in fact valid for this patient, the therapist should attempt to engage in this final problem-solving operation. Using problem-solving terminology, this operation involves the following activities:

- Implementing the solution response,
- Monitoring the outcome of this solution, and
- Evaluating the match between predicted and actual consequences.

Clinical Pathogenesis Map

Specific to case formulation, this process of our model involves first developing a *Clinical Pathogenesis Map* (CPM; Nezu & Nezu, 1989). A CPM is a graphic depiction of those variables hypothesized to contribute to the initiation and maintenance of a given patient's difficulties, specifying the functional relationships amongst each other using SORC nomenclature. It can be viewed as an example of a path analysis or causal modeling diagram idiographically developed for a particular patient (Nezu et al., 1997). In addition, the CPM offers a concrete statement of the therapist's initial causal hypotheses against which to test alternative hypotheses. As new information is obtained, and various predictions are confirmed or disconfirmed, the CPM can be altered. The development of the CPM is essentially the "implementation of the solution plan" that was the product of the decision-making process. Moreover, it provides an important basis upon which to design the unique treatment plan for a given patient.

The following are the elements that make up a CPM:

- Distal Variables
- Antecedent Variables
- Organismic Variables
- Response Variables
- Consequences

Distal Variables

These include those historic or developmental factors that may be responsible for the initial emergence of particular vulnerabilities or for the psychological disorders or distressing symptoms themselves. Examples include severe trauma (e.g., rape, combat during a war), early learning experiences, lack of appropriate social models for responsible behavior, series of negative stressful life events, and so forth. On one hand, such developmental factors can be thought of as *static* variables, in that they are not amenable to change themselves. However, they do provide a more complete understanding of a patient's problems, especially in terms of understanding various distal variable-target problem covariations. Knowing such covariations helps the clinician predict various responses to certain stimuli (e.g., early childhood experiences of being ridiculed in public might predict anxiety responses as an adult in public settings). In addition, being part of a patient's "story," distal variables are useful pieces of the puzzle which can be used to help explain the CPM to patients in order to enhance their understanding.

Antecedent Variables

This set of elements can include any of the various *patient-related* (i.e., behavioral, cognitive, affective, biological, socio/ethnic/cultural) and *environment-related* (i.e., social and physical environmental) variables that serve as proximal *triggers* or *discriminative stimuli* for other instrumental outcome factors or the distressing symptoms themselves. An example of the first type of situation involves the environmental variable of social isolation, which triggers certain negative thoughts (e.g., "I am such a loser because I am once again home alone on Saturday night having nothing to do!") that can then trigger feelings of sadness and hopelessness. An example of the latter situation is the environmental factor of "being rejected" when asking someone for a date, which serves to quickly trigger strong feelings of depression.

Organismic Variables

These include any of the various types of *patient-related* (i.e., behavioral, cognitive, affective, biological, socio/ethnic/cultural) variables. These factors represent response *mediators* (i.e., variables that help explain why a given response occurs in the presence of certain antecedent variables) or response *moderators* (i.e., variables that influence the strength and/or direction of the relationship between an antecedent factor and a response). Examples of mediating variables include poor social skills (behavioral variable), cognitive distortions related to mistrust of other people (cognitive variable), heightened arousal and fear (emotional variable), coronary heart disease (biological variable), and ethnic background concerning one's understanding of the meaning of a particular set of symptoms (socio/ethnic/cultural variable). An example of a organismic moderator variable is social problem solving ability, which has been found to decrease the likelihood of experiencing depression under circumstances of high stress (Nezu, in press).

Response Variables

This category refers to either (a) certain patient-related instrumental outcome variables that are very closely associated with one of the patient's *ultimate* outcome goals (e.g., suicide ideation is strongly associated with suicidal behavior), or (b) the set of distressing symptoms that constitute the ultimate outcomes themselves (e.g., depression, pain, substance abuse, or a distressed marriage).

Consequential Variables

These involve the full range of both patient-related and environment-related variables that occur in reaction to a given response variable. Depending on the nature and strength of the consequence, the response-consequence relationship can serve to either increase or decrease the probability of the response occurring in the future (via the process of positive and negative reinforcement and punishment). For example, avoidance behavior (the response) in reaction to a feared stimulus (antecedent variable) can serve to decrease a mediating organismic variable (heightened arousal to high places), thus leading to a decrease in fear and anxiety (consequence) via a negative reinforcement paradigm. Such consequential variables are often the major reason why various maladaptive behaviors continue to persist (e.g., a decrease in phobia-related anxiety that results from avoidance behavior serves to negatively reinforce such a response, thereby increasing the likelihood that such a response will persist in the future. Secondary gain (e.g., attention, decrease in responsibility, excuse for taking off at work) is another category of potential consequential variables that are important to assess.

The Case of Henry

Figure 2.1 provides for an example of a CPM regarding a patient, Henry, who is suffering from social anxiety. Henry, a 32-year-old single, White

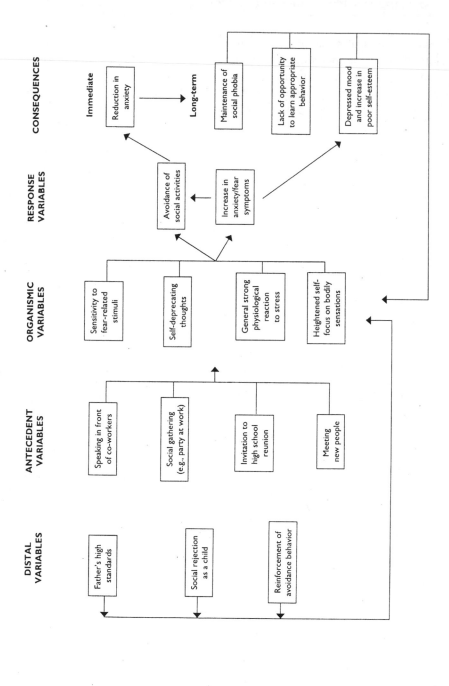

FIGURE 2.1 Example of Clinical Pathogenesis Map for "Henry," who is suffering from social anxiety.

30

male, came to outpatient therapy complaining of severe anxiety and fear in social situations. As he was progressing in his career as an accountant in a large firm, he was able to secure promotions because of his diligence and talent "with numbers." However, this career climb functioned as a double-edged sword—on the positive side, he was advancing and receiving higher salaries; yet, on the negative side, he was being asked to take on more responsibilities that entailed meeting new clients, attending social gatherings, and making presentations in front of medium-size groups. All of these new activities were very scary for Henry, hence his decision to enter therapy.

Using the problem-solving model as applied to case formulation, the initial CPM contained in Figure 2.1 was derived. Based on a broad-based assessment of Henry's past and current functioning, as the CPM indicates, there were several developmental factors (i.e., distal variables) that appear to be etiologically related to his social anxiety. These involved (a) a father who had strict and high standards for behavior in most social situations; (b) frequent rejection by other children who made fun of Henry's attempts to act "formally" (based on his father's "rules"); and (c) reinforcement of his avoidance of social situations by his mother.

Such early learning experiences served to engender the following organismic vulnerabilities: (a) heightened sensitivity to any and all social situations; (b) significant negative thinking concerning his own views and views he perceived others had of him; (c) a lowered threshold for stress in general whereby he experienced significant emotional and physical anxiety symptoms in reaction to stressful situations; and (d) intense self-focus and preoccupation with any physical symptoms that he thought made him look more anxious and awkward to others.

When certain events occurred that served as triggering stimuli (i.e., antecedent variables), such as being told by his boss that he needed to conduct a training workshop with a new group of accounting interns the following week, his anxiety and fear symptoms increased dramatically especially as it got closer to the event. Ultimately, Henry would engage in various behaviors that allowed him to avoid the feared event (e.g., call in sick that day, get someone else to take his place) (the response). Other antecedent triggers more recently included an invitation to his high school reunion and a second invitation to a party being thrown by his boss that he felt "politically" was crucial to attend. Meeting new people, whether at work or socially, always led to an increase in his anxiety.

Continued assessment further indicated that functionally, although the avoidance behavior, when successful, led to an immediate decrease in anxiety (immediate consequence), it actually negatively reinforced continued avoidance behavior and ultimately served to maintain the social anxiety symptoms. This further limited his ability to test out, for example, the tenability of his self-deprecating thoughts regarding his public speaking abilities, as well as engendering depressed mood and an increase in poor self-esteem (long-term consequences of the response). Moreover, such consequences served to reinforce and maintain the causal relationship that already existed between the various organismic and response variables, thus increasing the likelihood that without intervention, Henry's social anxiety problem would continue to persist in the future.

For other patients with social anxiety, it is possible that attempts or opportunities to successfully avoid feared social activities are ineffective or limited. In Henry's case, whereas his avoidance behavior was generally successful in the past, he did realize that his goal of continuing to rise in the company would be greatly compromised if he did not address his anxiety problem. One of the important areas of future assessment with Henry is an evaluation of such actual social and public speaking skills.

Evaluating the Validity of the CPM

Now that a CPM has been developed for a given patient, the therapist, in continuing to apply the problem-solving model of clinical decision making, seeks to determine whether the outcome of the problem-solving process thus far (i.e., the development of a CPM) is effective. This can be accomplished in two ways:

- Social validation, and
- Hypothesis testing.

Social validation involves having the clinician share the initial CPM with the patient (and significant others if they are involved). Patient feedback can be sought regarding the relevance, importance, and salience of the selected target problems and goals. Having the CPM in pictorial form makes this process much easier.

Second, *testable hypotheses* based on the original case formulation, may also be used to verify the CPM. Specifically, the therapist can evaluate the outcome by attempting to confirm or disconfirm hypotheses that are based on the CPM. For example, if a CPM, such as Henry's, indicates that his major presenting problem involves anxiety related to interpersonal difficulties and fears of social rejection, the therapist can delineate certain predictive statements. One prediction might suggest that Henry would have high scores on a self-report measure of social avoidance and distress. Another hypothesis might suggest that during a structured role play involving a social situation (e.g., meeting new people), he would experience anxiety, display visible signs of tension, and report feeling distressed. Confirmations *and* disconfirmations of such predictions can help the clinician to evaluate the veracity and relevance of the original CPM.

These two methods of evaluation, then, serve to determine if problems exist with the most current version of the CPM. If they do, the clinician must then re-initiate the problem-solving process and attempt to determine the source(s) of the mismatch (e.g., Were insufficient target problems generated? Was the cost-benefit analysis inconclusive?). If, however, the evaluation supports the veracity and relevance of the uniquely derived CPM for a given patient, the therapist may continue to the next phase of therapy, that of treatment design, as described in the next chapter.

SUMMARY

In order to develop an accurate case formulation with regard to a specific patient, we advocate applying a problem-solving model of clinical decision making. This entails adopting a particular orientation towards this process (i.e., that behavior is multiply caused and exists within a system), as well as engaging in specific problem-solving activities (i.e., problem definition, generation of alternatives, decision making, solution evaluation). A major assumption underlying this model is the notion that the therapist should conduct CBT assessment within the context of considering the relevance of a *range* of instrumental outcome variables and not by-passing the case formulation process, and apply treatment techniques that address one's "favorite" treatment targets for a given set of symptoms or psychological disorder. A major product of applying this model to case formulation is the Clinical Pathogenesis Map (CPM), which is a graphic depiction of those factors hypothesized to contribute to the initiation and maintenance of a given patient's distressing symptoms. One purpose that the CPM serves is that it provides for an important basis upon which to design a unique treatment plan for a given patient. In chapter 3, we describe how to apply the problem-solving model to this next phase of cognitive-behavioral therapy—that of treatment design.

REFERENCES

American Psychiatric Association. (2000). *Diagnostic and statistical manual of mental disorders* (ed. 4, text revision). Washington, DC: American Psychiatric Press.

Ells, T. D. (1997). Psychotherapy case formulation: History and current status. In T. D. Ells (Ed.), *Handbook of psychotherapy case formulation* (pp. 1–25). New York: Guilford Press.

Goldfried, M. R., & Davison, G. C. (1994). *Clinical behavior therapy* (expanded ed.). New York: Wiley.

Goldfried, M. R., & Sprafkin, J. (1974). *Behavioral personality assessment.* Morristown, NJ: General Learning Press.

Haynes, S. N., & O'Brien, W. H. (1990). Functional analysis in behavior therapy. *Clinical Psychology Review, 10,* 649–668.

Haynes, S. N., & O'Brien, W. H. (2000). *Principles and practice of behavioral assessment.* New York: Kluwer Academic/Plenum Publishers.

Kanfer, F. H. (1985). Target selection for clinical change programs. *Behavioral Assessment, 7,* 7–20.

Kendall, P. C. (1985). Toward a cognitive-behavioral model of child psychopathology and a critique of related interventions. *Journal of Abnormal Child Psychology, 13,* 357–372.

Mash, E. J., & Hunsley, J. (1993). Assessment considerations in the identification of failing psychotherapy: Bringing the negatives out of the darkroom. *Psychological Assessment, 5,* 292–301.

Nezu, A. M. (in press). Problem solving and behavior therapy revisited. *Behavior Therapy.*

Nezu, A. M., & Nezu, C. M. (Eds.). (1989). *Clinical decision making in behavior therapy: A problem-solving perspective.* Champaign, IL: Research Press.

Nezu, A. M., & Nezu, C. M. (1993). Identifying and selecting target problems for clinical interventions: A problem-solving model. *Psychological Assessment, 5,* 254–263.

Nezu, A. M., Nezu, C. M., Friedman, S. H., & Haynes, S. N. (1997). Case formulation in behavior therapy: Problem-solving and functional analytic strategies. In T. D. Ells (Ed.), *Handbook of psychotherapy case formulation* (pp. 368–401). New York: Guilford Press.

Nezu, A. M., Nezu, C. M., & Lombardo, E. R. (2001). Cognitive-behavior therapy for medically unexplained symptoms: A critical review of the treatment literature. *Behavior Therapy, 32,* 537–583.

Nezu, A. M., Nezu, C. M., Peacock, M. A., & Girdwood, C. P. (2004). Case formulation in cognitive-behavior therapy. In M. Hersen (Series Ed.), S. N. Haynes, & E. Heiby (Vol. Eds.), *Behavioral assessment* (pp. 402–426). Volume 3 of the *Comprehensive Handbook of Psychological Assessment.* New York: Wiley.

Rosen, A., & Proctor, E. K. (1981). Distinctions between treatment outcomes and their implications for treatment evaluations. *Journal of Consulting and Clinical Psychology, 49,* 418–425.

Shadish, W. R. (1993). Critical multiplism: A research strategy and its attendant tactics. In L. Sechrest (Ed.), *Program evaluation: A pluralistic enterprise* (pp. 13–57). San Francisco: Jossey-Bass.

Tanaka-Matsumi, J., Seiden, D., & Lam, K. (1996). The Culturally Informed Functional Assessment (CIFA) Interview: A strategy for cross-cultural behavioral practice. *Cognitive and Behavioral Practice, 3,* 215–233.

3

Applying the Problem-Solving Model to Cognitive-Behavioral Treatment Design

CBT TREATMENT DESIGN

The major task during this treatment phase is for the therapist to develop the "middle part of the patient's story," that is, the means by which to reach a patient's ultimate outcome goals. The operational definition of this means–end analysis is an efficacious treatment plan. Such a plan would contain CBT strategies geared to address those treatment targets and goals identified previously during the case formulation phase. In other words, this treatment plan, to be successful, must help the patient overcome those impediments to goal achievement as delineated in the previously developed unique CPM (Nezu & Nezu, 1993; Nezu, Nezu, Peacock, & Girdwood, 2004).

Goals of CBT Treatment Design

The goals of this major therapy activity are twofold:

1. To develop an overall treatment plan that helps the patient to achieve his or her goals, and

2. To identify those treatment components and methods that are re-
    quired for *optimal* implementation of the overall treatment plan.

With the exception of the problem-definition task, our model advocates
applying the same problem-solving operations discussed in chapter 2 to
the process of CBT treatment design (the clinician already engaged in
defining the problem during the case formulation phase). Although it might
seem that this should be a straightforward process once a CPM is developed,
given that the goals of treatment design also entail multiple clinical decisions, the potential of judgmental errors remains real. For example, a
therapist may decide to apply a specific treatment intervention with a
patient primarily on the basis of its successful use with another individual
who presented with similar problems. However, failure to consider the
unique characteristics of the patient at hand can result in implementing a
treatment strategy that might have been successful for other patients, but
due to differing circumstances (e.g., the intensity of symptoms, presence
of comorbid problems, cultural variations, etc.), it may not be an efficacious
plan for the new patient.

In addition, if the patient's presenting problems are thought to be easily
amenable to treatment, the therapist may decide erroneously to employ a
particular intervention before a comprehensive decision analysis is completed. For example, although an exposure-based treatment strategy may
be an effective intervention alternative for an individual suffering from
severe phobic symptoms in theory, it may be necessary for the therapist
to *first* implement a cognitive restructuring protocol in order to decrease the
patient's depressive symptoms (that are related to a sense of hopelessness
regarding the anxiety disorder). In such a case, it is possible that only
until after the depression lifts can the severe phobia be optimally treated
due to the depression-related lowered motivation to engage in such a
strategy. As such, the exposure treatment may be ineffective if conducted prematurely.

APPLYING THE PROBLEM-SOLVING MODEL TO TREATMENT DESIGN: PROBLEM ORIENTATION

In keeping with the planned critical multiplism framework described in
chapter 2, it is important to adopt the orientation, relevant to the treatment
design phase, that CBT should be viewed in terms of intervention strategies,
or general approaches to address certain instrumental outcomes, and not

only in terms of specific techniques. For example, behavioral stress management or anxiety reduction interventions represent one general *strategy* of treatment methods geared to address certain instrumental outcome variables related to anxiety. Under this general rubric, a variety of specific treatment *tactics* exist, including exposure, systematic desensitization, guided imagery, visualization, covert conditioning, progressive muscle relaxation, autogenic training, and mindful meditation. The efficacy of any of these techniques for a given patient is dependent on his or her unique characteristics, as well as the expertise of a given therapist. As such, it is crucial that the therapist remain cognizant of the variety of techniques and strategies from which to choose in working with a patient and his or her particular problem(s). If the therapist utilizes the first technique that comes to mind without consideration of the various alternative techniques that exist within the same strategy, the probability that the most effective technique will be chosen may decrease.

In addition, there may be multiple ways to implement each of these techniques. For example, Table 3.1 contains a *partial* list of *varying methods* that can be used to implement the intervention of "cognitive restructuring" in order to achieve the instrumental outcome variable of "decreasing self-defeating thinking" that is hypothesized to be causally related to the ultimate outcome goal of "decreasing depression." Such a listing of possible implementation methods would become necessary given that a "standard"

TABLE 3.1   Possible Differing Methods to Implement Treatment Strategy: Cognitive Restructuring

- Behavioral experiments
- Bibliotherapy
- Modeling
- Mild refutation
- Overt confrontation
- Didactics
- Homework assignments
- Use of family members as adjunct therapists
- Use of friends as adjunct therapists
- Visualization
- Use of diagrams and pictures
- Use of cartoons/humorous material
- Reversed advocacy role plays

means of achieving such an instrumental outcome goal is unsuccessful for a particular patient.

APPLYING THE PROBLEM-SOLVING MODEL TO TREATMENT DESIGN: GENERATING ALTERNATIVES

At this point, the therapist reviews the patient's unique CPM and using the various brainstorming principles outlined in chapter 2, begins to generate a list of possible treatment ideas for the patient at hand for each instrumental outcome variable that has been identified as an initial treatment target. Note that in keeping with the problem orientation espoused earlier, the clinician should consider various treatment strategies, tactics, *and* methods of implementing *each* tactic for *each* clinical target.

At this point, similar to case formulation, the clinician should attempt to access the *entire* extant universe or domain of potentially efficacious treatment strategies and tactics for a given instrumental outcome variable that can be identified in the research literature. As noted previously, rather than rely on a *preferred* treatment approach for a given set of symptoms, due to ubiquitous individual differences among patients (e.g., gender, age, symptom severity, ethnicity, presence of co-morbid problems), the CBT clinician should attempt to review the relevance of a *range* of empirically derived, potentially relevant, treatment strategies and tactics.

To help in this literature search, similar to case formulation, the therapist can use two basic search strategies—a theory-driven approach and a diagnosis-driven approach (see chapter 2). Again, we wish to caution the CBT therapist to be guided by the critical multiplism philosophy that is part of our espoused orientation. For example, exclusive use of a *single* specific therapy approach to guide one's treatment planning can increase the likelihood that he or she engages in judgmental errors and may overlook the relevance of that approach to a given patient.

As a major purpose of this book is to provide for a user-friendly case formulation and treatment design guide, we have already completed such a search for 11 common psychological problems encountered in an outpatient setting. Lists of these empirically derived clinical interventions will be found in chapters 5–15 in Section II.

As an example, using the above problem-solving guidelines, we developed a list of potentially effective intervention strategies for each of three major treatment targets for social anxiety (see chapter 9):

Treatment Target: Decrease heightened arousal

Potential Interventions:

- Exposure therapy
- Flooding
- Relaxation training

Treatment Target: Decrease dysfunctional beliefs

Potential Interventions:

- Cognitive restructuring
- Problem-solving therapy

Treatment Target: Enhance interpersonal skills

Potential Interventions:

- Social skills training
- Social effectiveness training
- Group therapy

Note that we are not advocating that *all* of the above clinical interventions would be relevant and important for *all* patients suffering from social anxiety. Rather, this list represents the *range* of *empirically derived* intervention strategies that are important to consider across all such patients in order to minimize the possibility that one of these procedures becomes overlooked (i.e., preventing the judgmental heuristics to "creep into" one's case formulation).

In addition, *beyond* the set of treatment interventions that we provide for each of the 11 disorders addressed in Section II, we strongly advocate that the CBT clinician generate (using the problem-solving operations described in this chapter) *additional* strategies and tactics that may be relevant to a given patient.

APPLYING THE PROBLEM-SOLVING MODEL TO TREATMENT DESIGN: DECISION MAKING

In applying the decision-making task to the process of treatment design, the therapist systematically evaluates each of the interventions generated previously according to specific criteria related to utility. As noted in chapter 2, the *utility* of an idea is a joint function of various *likelihood* and *value* estimates, in this case, with specific regard to the effects of a given treatment procedure. At this point, the CBT clinician has the opportunity to explore in more detail the potential interactions of such interventions with a variety of factors specific to a given patient, as well as the range of potential positive and negative effects of the interventions themselves.

In determining various likelihood estimates, the therapist asks the following questions:

- What is the likelihood that this particular intervention will achieve the specified goal(s)?
- What is the likelihood that I can optimally implement this particular treatment approach?
- What is the likelihood that the patient will be able to carry out a particular strategy in an optimal fashion?
- (If relevant) What is the likelihood that collateral or paraprofessional therapists will be able to implement a particular strategy in an optimal way?

Likelihood of a Particular Intervention Achieving the Specified Goals

In making this first judgment, the therapist assesses the effectiveness of a given therapy technique in treating a given problem or set of distressing symptoms based on the empirical literature. The therapist should rate those techniques that have been demonstrated to be effective in treating a particular problem higher than his or her preferred mode of treatment. In addition, it is important for the therapist to remain cognizant of the unique characteristics of a particular patient when reviewing the available literature and evaluating a particular tactic. That is, a given patient may be very different from the population on which the empirical literature is based. As such, the effects of a particular strategy with a patient may be quite different from those found within the population that was investigated in the research literature. Examples of relevant variables that might engender such differential treatment effects include age, gender, and ethnic background.

Likelihood of Optimal Implementation

Here, the therapist evaluates his or her own ability to apply the particular approach in question. The effectiveness of the intervention and the extent of goal attainment is strongly related to the extent to which a therapist is able to competently implement the intervention. As such, the efficacy of a given treatment technique in the literature may differ if a particular therapist has less experience or training in that technique compared with the protocol therapists included in the research investigation.

Likelihood That the Patient Can Optimally Carry Out a Particular Strategy

Patients play an integral role in CBT treatment. As such, patient-related factors need to be considered in terms of the likelihood that he or she will be able to optimally carry out a particular intervention. One factor of particular importance is the level of the individual's motivation and resistance to treatment. Because this is associated with treatment adherence, it is a factor that requires continued assessment throughout therapy. Other factors that should be considered include the patient's physical health, financial and social resources, and cognitive ability. It is possible that various interventions may need to be considered to specifically address treatment adherence issues, a type of instrumental outcome variable that was not necessarily obvious to target early during the case formulation process.

Likelihood That Collateral Therapists Are Able to Implement a Particular Strategy

At times, the competence of adjunct treatment providers may be an important component to consider when predicting overall treatment outcome for a given patient. Such providers may include caregivers, spouses, family members, and other health care providers. In addressing the likelihood that these individuals will be able to implement a particular intervention optimally, it is important for the therapist to assess who these individuals are in relation to a particular patient. In addition, it is important to assess their ability, level of involvement, and the extent to which they are invested in helping the patient achieve his or her treatment goals. An example involves the ability of the sexual partner to be an asset in the treatment of a patient's sexual dysfunction.

Estimates of Value of a Given Intervention Strategy

In assessing the *value* of treatment effects, the therapist considers the following four sets of criteria:

- Personal consequences,
- Social consequences,
- Short-term consequences, and
- Long-term consequences.

Personal Consequences

Personal consequences of a particular intervention can include:

- Amount of time and resources required of both the therapist and patient,
- Amount of effort required of both the therapist and patient,
- Emotional costs or gains that the patient may experience,
- Consistency of an intervention with the values, morals, and ethics of both the therapist and the patient,
- Physical side effects of treatment, and
- Potential positive and negative effects of treatment on other problem areas in the patient's life.

Social Consequences

Consideration of the social consequences of treatment calls for the therapist to consider the variety of ways in which a certain strategy will affect the patient's family, friends, and other significant people in his or her life. This consideration reiterates the dynamic aspect of therapy as well as the value of a multivariate approach to patients and treatment. The extent to which the patient's social environment will facilitate treatment implementation can impact the level of treatment generalization and maintenance.

Short-Term and Long-Term Consequences

In addition to the personal and social consequences that result from implementing various treatment strategies, it is also recommended that the short-term and long-term effects of interventions be considered. Specifically, it is recommended that short-term and long-term effects be evaluated in terms of each of the specific likelihood and value criteria.

Developing the Treatment Plan

It is the therapist's goal to approximate a treatment plan that is both effective in goal attainment and highly likely to be implemented optimally. Ideally, such a treatment plan would have little temporal and financial costs, would be consistent with the therapist's and patient's values and ethics, would garner reinforcement from the individual's social network, and would decrease distress and increase the patient's overall quality of life. Whereas the probability of meeting *all* of these criteria in a particular treatment plan is less than stellar, use of formal and systematic decision-making guidelines as espoused by our model can facilitate attainment of these criteria. After the therapist has evaluated each treatment tactic according to the aforementioned criteria, he or she then selects the treatment alternative(s) that look(s) most favorable with regard to the utility for goal attainment. Such criteria will also be helpful in prioritizing which interventions, for which instrumental outcome variables, should be implemented first, or whether, due to the unique circumstances of the patient, several treatment techniques should be conducted simultaneously.

APPLYING THE PROBLEM-SOLVING MODEL TO TREATMENT DESIGN: EVALUATING SOLUTION OUTCOMES

At this point, it is suggested that the therapist solicit the patient's feedback and verify the choices made during the process of decision making. This is important because it can alert the therapist to any problems and minimize treatment failure. During the treatment design phase of therapy, this problem-solving activity involves completing a Goal Attainment Map (GAM) and then comparing expected and actual outcomes.

Goal Attainment Map

Similar to the CPM, the Goal Attainment Map (GAM; Nezu & Nezu, 1989) is a graphic presentation, this time with regard to "where the patient is currently" and "where he or she wants to go." The GAM should initially include a listing of relevant instrumental outcome goals (i.e., obstacles to goal attainment, such as deficient social skills, presence of cognitive distortions) and ultimate outcome goals (i.e., treatment objectives, such as anxiety reduction) that were previously selected during the decision-making process. These outcomes are largely based on the patient's unique CPM. As such, the GAM serves as the basis upon which possible intervention strategies can be identified that ultimately lead to goal attainment. In other words, the GAM becomes the "treatment map" or plan that visually describes:

- The general treatment goals that have been mutually selected (i.e., ultimate outcomes),
- The obstacles that currently exist in reaching such goals (i.e., the targeted instrumental outcome variables), and
- The specific means (i.e., intervention strategies) by which to overcome such obstacles.

Completion of the GAM involves listing the treatment approaches selected as those that function as pathways to attaining goals. As such, the patient can have the opportunity to express concerns he or she may have with the initial treatment choices. This provides the therapist with information that can be used to eliminate or revise the particular treatment choices, so that the potential for successful treatment outcome becomes enhanced.

An example of a GAM is contained in Figure 3.1 which is one possible GAM based on the CPM of Henry, the patient introduced in chapter 2 who is experiencing social anxiety. As can be seen in this Figure, the four instrumental outcome variables that were initially identified as treatment targets were simply re-listed on the GAM. Overcoming these "obstacles to goal attainment" would hypothetically lead to attaining the two major ultimate outcome goals (i.e., decreasing avoidance behavior and decreasing anxiety and fear symptoms). For each of the four treatment targets, by applying the problem-solving model to CBT treatment design, the final piece of the GAM was able to be completed, that is, a list of empirically derived, intervention tactics geared to reach a given instrumental outcome. As can be seen, some of the treatment procedures identified are viewed as

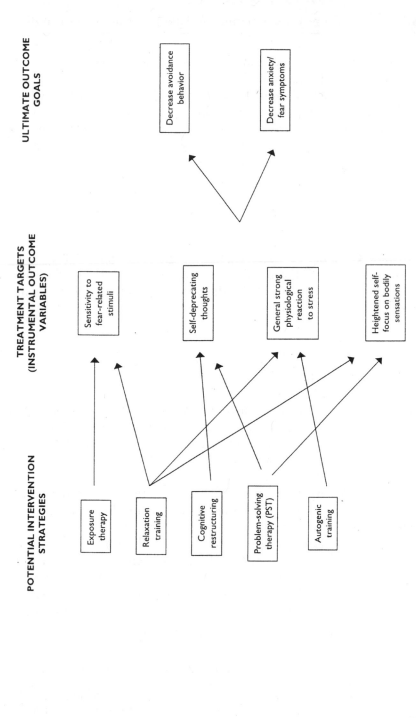

FIGURE 3.1 Example of one possible Goal Attainment Map for "Henry," who is suffering from social anxiety.

potentially addressing multiple targets, thus increasing the possibility of meaningful clinical change. Note that we are not advocating that this GAM represents the treatment of choice for social anxiety across *all* such patients. Rather, based on a unique CPM regarding Henry, in conjunction with applying the problem-solving model to the process of treatment design, this particular GAM represents the best possible (initial) treatment plan for this patient, given his particular set of unique circumstances.

Evaluating the Validity of the GAM

Now that the GAM has been developed for a given patient, the therapist, in continuing to apply the problem-solving model of clinical decision making, seeks to determine whether the outcome of the problem-solving process thus far (i.e., the development of a GAM) is effective. As noted in chapter 2, this can be accomplished in two ways:

- Social validation, and
- Hypothesis testing.

Social validation at this point involves having the clinician share the GAM with the patient (and significant others if they are involved). Patient feedback can be sought regarding the relevance, importance, and salience of the selected treatment options. Having the GAM in pictorial form makes this process much easier.

Second, *testable hypotheses* that are based on the original treatment design plan may be used to verify the GAM. This involves beginning to evaluate the actual effects of the treatment plan that are delineated in the GAM.[1] In other words, interventions that successfully achieve a particular instrumental outcome that engender positive movement toward an ultimate outcome would serve to support the validity of the GAM. Conversely, change in a given hypothesized mechanism of action that does *not* effect change in the ultimate outcome would suggest that that part of the GAM is not valid.

---

[1] To engage in such an evaluation, the clinician also must engage in another decision-making task—that of choosing which measures to use in this assessment process. It should not come as a surprise to learn that we advocate applying our problem-solving model to this process as well. However, because a detailed description of this procedure is beyond the scope of this book, we direct the reader elsewhere (Nezu, Nezu, & Foster, 2000).

TABLE 3.2   Problem-Solving Questions the Therapist Should Ask to Evaluate the Validity of the GAM

- Is CBT appropriate for this patient?
- Did I overlook any related problems?
- Is this patient motivated to change?
- Is this patient afraid to change?
- Have I overlooked any negative consequences?
- Is this treatment generally effective for this problem?
- Am I implementing this intervention properly?
- Does the patient understand this treatment?
- Does the patient agree with the use of this treatment?
- Is treatment too costly?
- Is treatment taking too long?
- Is there adequate social support for this patient?
- Was the case formulation (CPM) accurate?
- Does this treatment incur any negative effects of which I am unaware?
- Does this treatment conflict with the patient's values?
- Does the patient have unrealistic goals or expectations concerning therapy? Concerning this treatment?
- Is the patient completing homework assignments?
- Is the patient optimally practicing the technique(s) that are part of treatment (e.g., relaxation skills)?
- Are any of the patient's family members sabotaging this treatment approach?
- Should I use a different treatment approach?
- Should I change the method of using this treatment approach?
- Am I sensitive to the patient's feelings?
- Is the use of this treatment premature?
- Does this patient view me as invested in his treatment?
- Does this patient trust me as her therapist?
- Have I identified the most salient reinforcers for this patient?
- Are there conflicting problems or variables that serve to maintain the patient's difficulties, thereby controverting a successful outcome?
- Should I terminate treatment?
- Should I get opinions from other professionals?

Note. Adapted with permission from Nezu and Nezu (1989; p. 105).

These two methods of evaluation, then, serve to determine if concerns exist with the most current version of the GAM. If such problems do exist, the clinician must then re-initiate the problem-solving process and attempt to determine the source(s) of the mismatch. Table 3.2 contains a list of questions that would be important for the clinician to ask in making such a determination. If, however, the evaluation supports the validity and relevance of the GAM for a given patient, the therapist then continues to implement the treatment plan in accord with the GAM.

Summary

In this chapter, we described how to apply the various problem-solving operations to the process of CBT treatment design. An important underlying theme of this chapter involved the need to consider a *range* of treatment options for each treatment target as a means of minimizing the likelihood of judgmental errors. A major product of this application is the development of a patient's unique Goal Attainment Map, which is a graphic depiction of the treatment tactics being proposed to overcome the instrumental outcome variables identified earlier during the case formulation process as potential treatment targets. This map serves as one means to discuss the treatment plan with the patient to elicit feedback, as well as to provide useful psychoeducational material regarding the overall therapy process.

Having described how to apply the problem-solving model of clinical decision making for both CBT case formulation and treatment design in theory, the next chapter provides a guide on how to use the remainder of this book in order to conduct CBT treatment for a range of psychological disorders and problems.

REFERENCES

Nezu, A. M., & Nezu, C. M. (Eds.). (1989). *Clinical decision making in behavior therapy: A problem-solving perspective.* Champaign, IL: Research Press.

Nezu, A. M., & Nezu, C. M. (1993). Identifying and selecting target problems for clinical interventions: A problem-solving model. *Psychological Assessment, 5,* 254–263.

Nezu, A. M., Nezu, C. M., Peacock, M. A., & Girdwood, C. P. (2004). Case formulation in cognitive-behavior therapy. In S. N. Haynes & E. Heiby (Eds.), *Behavioral assessment* (pp. 402–426), Volume 3 of the *Comprehensive Handbook of Psychological Assessment*, Editor-in-Chief: M. Hersen. New York: Wiley.

Nezu, C. M., Nezu, A. M., & Foster, S. L. (2000). A 10-step guide to selecting assessment measures in clinical and research settings. In A. M. Nezu, G. F. Ronan, E. A. Meadows, & K. S. McClure (Eds.), *Practitioner's guide to empirically based measures of depression* (pp. 17–24). New York: Kluwer Academic/Plenum Publishers.

4

How to Use This Outpatient Treatment Guide

PROBLEM-SOLVING MODEL
OF CLINICAL DECISION MAKING

In chapter 1, we argued for the need for a set of guidelines that can foster the validity and idiographic relevance of CBT case formulation and treatment design. The major points behind this argument involved (a) the lack of a treatment "cookbook" that took into account all the ways that patients differ amongst each other, even those individuals who present with the same problems, (b) the ambiguity that emerges due to the discrepancies often encountered between the participants included in a particular research study and the patients seen in clinical settings, and (c) the potential problems in clinical reasoning that exist simply because we are human (i.e., the presence of common judgmental heuristics and biases).

Based on this need, we suggested that the validity of CBT case formulation and treatment design for a given patient can be fostered by applying a series of problem-solving operations. A problem-solving model strongly parallels a "scientific way of thinking" when engaged in these various clinical tasks and can help "bridge the gap" between the science and art of cognitive–behavior therapy applications (Nezu & Nezu, 1995).

Chapter 2 described how to apply this problem-solving model to the process of CBT case formulation. Table 4.1 provides a brief overview of this application in the form of questions to consider for the reader's easy use. Based on the answers to these questions, the therapist can develop a form, such as that contained in Table 4.2, to summarize the information necessary to eventually complete an initial CPM (Figure 4.1 can serve as a CPM template).

In chapter 3, we provided a similar set of guidelines with regard to CBT treatment design. Table 4.3 contains a set of questions to help the therapist apply the problem-solving model to this process in order to derive summary information to complete a form such as shown in Table 4.4. Such summary data can then serve as the basis for completing an initial GAM (Figure 4.2 can serve as a GAM template).

In addition, we offer the reader a sample template of categories to use in developing session progress notes in Table 4.5 that corresponds to the application of the problem-solving model on a session-by-session basis.

In sum, we advocate that the therapist adopt this model when conducting outpatient cognitive-behavior therapy. However, in addition to delineating this model, as noted throughout Section I, we conducted the various searches called for by our model, regarding treatment targets and treatment tactics. These are contained in Section II of this book.

Conducting CBT Outpatient Treatment

In applying the problem-solving model to the processes of CBT case formulation and treatment design, in keeping with a critical multiplism philosophy, we advocated that the clinician search the empirical literature in order to identify a *range* of:

- Instrumental outcome variables that are potentially relevant for a given patient who is experiencing a particular set of symptoms, and
- Treatment strategies and tactics that potentially can help such a patient overcome the obstacles to his or her ultimate treatment goals.

Section II contains chapters that address 11 common psychological problems and disorders that are encountered in an outpatient setting. For each problem, using the two different types of search guides (i.e., theory-driven and diagnosis-driven approaches), we have developed (a) a list of empirically derived, potentially relevant instrumental outcome variables,

TABLE 4.1   Applying the Problem-Solving Model to CBT Case Formulation: Questions to Ask

Defining the Problem and Generating Alternatives

- What is the presenting problem?
- What are possible ultimate outcome goals for this patient?
- What is the differential diagnosis?
- What procedures should I use to assess this diagnosis and to measure symptom severity?
- Based on the empirical literature, what is the range of potentially relevant instrumental outcome variables (IOVs)?
- What are additional treatment targets unique to this patient?
- What patient-related variables potentially serve as IOVs for this patient? Behavioral variables (excesses and deficits)? Affective/emotional variables? Cognitive variables (deficiencies and distortions)? Biological variables? Socio/ethnic/cultural variables?
- What environment-related variables potentially serve as IOVs for this patient? Social/cultural variables? Physical environmental variables?
- What are some important distal causal factors?
- What are current triggers or discriminative stimuli?
- What are the functional relationships amongst these key variables?
- What are some SORC chains unique to this patient?
- What variables serve as antecedents?
- What variables serve as consequences?
- What organismic variables serve as mediators?
- What organismic variables serve as moderators?

Decision Making

- What is the likelihood that addressing a given instrumental outcome variable will help *this particular* patient meet his or her overall treatment goals?
- What is the likelihood that a given instrumental outcome variable is amenable to treatment?
- What is the likelihood that I, as this patient's therapist, am able to treat this given target problem?
- What is the likelihood that the treatment necessary to facilitate change for the patient regarding this treatment target is available?
- What are the consequences if this particular IOV is targeted? The personal consequences? The social consequences? The short-term effects? The long-term effects?

Evaluating Solution Outcomes

- What does the unique CPM for this patient look like?
- What feedback does the patient (and significant others if relevant) have regarding the CPM?
- What are some predictions that this CPM is making?
- Should this CPM be revised?
- Should I begin the treatment design process?

TABLE 4.2   Summary Information Needed to Complete a Clinical Pathogenesis Map

Name: _____

Presenting Problem(s): _____

Differential Diagnosis (if relevant): _____

Ultimate Outcome Goal(s): _____

Instrumental Outcome Goal(s): (list 1, 2, 3 . . .)

Instrumental Outcome Goal #1
  Description of instrumental outcome variable:
  Relevant distal variables:
  Relevant antecedent variables:
  Relevant consequences: (immediate and long term)
  Functional relationships amongst variables (represents connections
    and directions of arrows within CPM):

Instrumental Outcome Goal #2
  Description of instrumental outcome variable:
  Relevant distal variables:
  Relevant antecedent variables:
  Relevant consequences: (immediate and long term)
  Functional relationships amongst variables (represents connections
    and directions of arrows within CPM):

Instrumental Outcome Goal #3
  Description of instrumental outcome variable:
  Relevant distal variables:
  Relevant antecedent variables:
  Relevant consequences: (immediate and long-term)
  Functional relationships amongst variables (represents connections
    and directions of arrows within CPM):

Etc.

Functional Relationships Among All Above Variables (where relevant; represents connections and directions of arrows within CPM)

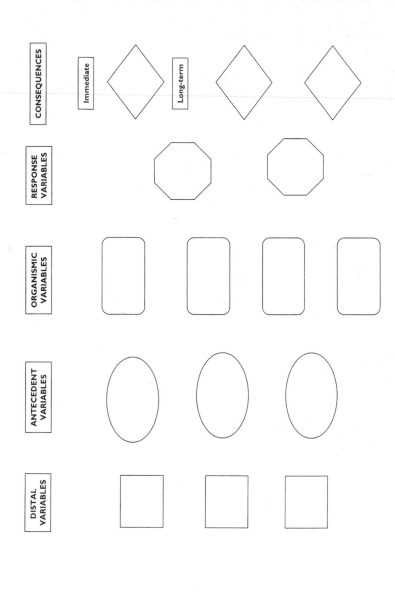

FIGURE 4.1 Sample template for Clinical Pathogenesis Map (CPM). Note that the number and shape of the boxes are arbitrary. This is only a sample template. Note that because this is a template, the lines and arrows that would need to be drawn to indicate the specific relationships (and the direction of such relationships) among variables is missing.

TABLE 4.3 Applying the Problem-Solving Model to CBT Treatment Design: Questions to Ask

Generating Alternatives

- What is the range of possible empirically derived intervention strategies and tactics that exists to address each instrumental outcome variable (IOV)?
- Are there different methods of implementing a given strategy, given the unique circumstances of this patient, that I should consider?

Decision Making

- What is the likelihood that this particular intervention will achieve the specified IOV goal(s)?
- What is the likelihood that I can optimally implement this particular treatment approach?
- What is the likelihood that this patient will be able to carry out a particular strategy in an optimal fashion?
- (If relevant) What is the likelihood that collateral or paraprofessional therapists will be able to implement a particular strategy in an optimal way?
- What are the consequences if this treatment tactic is implemented? The personal consequences? The social consequences? The short-term effects? The long-term effects?
- What are the most effective and relevant treatment tactics for this particular patient under these particular circumstances?

Evaluating Solution Outcomes

- What does the unique GAM for this patient look like?
- What is the outcome on the targeted IOV?
- What is the outcome on other IOVs?
- Are there additional positive consequences that are observed?
- Are there any unforeseen negative consequences that may occur as a function of implementing this treatment tactic?
- Do I need to revise the GAM? The CPM?
- Can I continue with the GAM as planned?
- Are there any additional problems or concerns that I need to attend to?

TABLE 4.4 Summary Information Needed to Complete a Goal Attainment Map

Name: _____

Presenting Problem(s): _____

Differential Diagnosis (if relevant): _____

Ultimate Outcome Goal(s): _____

Instrumental Outcome Goal(s): (list 1, 2, 3 . . .)

Instrumental Outcome Goal #1
   Description of Instrumental Outcome Variable (treatment target)
   Possible Treatment Strategies/Tactics (list 1, 2, 3, if relevant)

Instrumental Outcome Goal #2
   Description of Instrumental Outcome Variable (treatment target)
   Possible Treatment Strategies/Tactics (list 1, 2, 3, if relevant)

Instrumental Outcome Goal #3
   Description of Instrumental Outcome Variable (treatment target)
   Possible Treatment Strategies/Tactics (list 1, 2, 3, if relevant)

Etc.

and (b) a list of efficacious and potentially relevant treatment tactics geared to overcome such obstacles to ultimate outcome goal attainment. *Such lists can be used in conjunction with the problem-solving model in the effective idiographic application of nomothetic information to clinical cases.*

STRUCTURE OF CHAPTERS IN SECTION II

For each of the 11 chapters, we adopted a standard format to present the relevant material. Our intent is to provide relevant research and clinical information in a user-friendly manner that offers sufficient knowledge to allow the reader to make informed and effective decisions. The categories of information contained in each chapter is presented next. Although we believe these chapters will provide the reader with a solid set of guidelines in order to proceed with effective case formulation and treatment design for a range of psychological disorders, we cannot emphasize enough that we believe such information serves only as a foundation upon which to

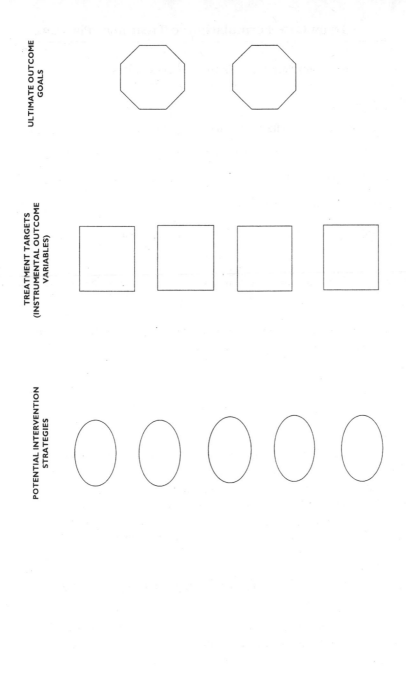

FIGURE 4.2 Sample template for Goal Attainment Map (GAM). Note that the number and shape of the boxes are arbitrary. This is only a sample template. Note that because this is a template, the lines and arrows that would need to be drawn to indicate the specific relationships (and the direction of such relationships) among variables is missing.

57

TABLE 4.5   Sample Template for Session Progress Notes

Date of session: _____

Progress since last session (e.g., effects of homework assignment): _____

_____

New information collected today: _____

Ultimate outcome goal addressed this session: _____

Instrument outcome goal/treatment target(s) addressed this session: _____

_____

Treatment tactics addressing above treatment target(s) implemented this session: ___

_____

Patient response to treatment intervention (include problems, measurement procedure, progress, relationship to ultimate outcome goal): _____

_____

Homework assigned: _____

_____

develop a treatment plan for a given patient. As mentioned repeatedly throughout the previous chapters, because of the ubiquitous differences among patients experiencing the same set of symptoms, in combination with the gap between the research literature and actual clinical practice, such information should be used in combination with the problem-solving model of clinical decision making (Nezu & Nezu, 1989).

General Description and Diagnostic Issues

This provides a description of the disorder and a brief overview of DSM-IV-TR (where relevant) diagnostic criteria.

Differential Diagnostic Issues

This section highlights various differential diagnosis concerns.

Co-Morbidity Issues

This is a brief overview of other disorders or symptoms that are commonly present along with the disorder at hand.

Assessment of the Disorder

This section contains a listing and brief description of empirically derived assessment tools to help the process of accurate diagnosis or measurement of symptom severity of the disorder. Where possible, we provide assessment tools that include clinician ratings, behavioral observation, and self-report measures.

General Therapy Goals

This section includes descriptions of:

- Ultimate outcome goals,
- Major empirically derived instrumental outcome goals (i.e., treatment targets),
- Assessment tools to measure each instrumental outcome variable, and
- A range of treatment tactics that address each treatment target.

Additional Treatment Targets

This section involves a description of various "secondary" instrumental outcome goals for the disorder.

Additional Clinical Considerations

Here, we highlight various issues that the therapist may need to consider when treating this disorder. These may include concerns related to age, gender, or ethnic background differences.

References

The literature cited in the chapter.

Appendices

In addition to this information, in Appendix A, we provide a series of "Quick Guides to Treatment Targets" for each of the 11 disorders covered in this book to foster ease of use. Moreover, in Appendix B, we briefly describe the treatment tactics noted in Section II to provide the reader with a more complete understanding of the treatment procedure itself.

REFERENCES

Nezu, A. M., & Nezu, C. M. (Eds.). (1989). *Clinical decision making in behavior therapy: A problem-solving perspective.* Champaign, IL: Research Press.

Nezu, C. M., & Nezu, A. M. (1995). Clinical decision making in everyday practice: The science in the art. *Cognitive and Behavioral Practice, 2,* 5–25.

II

Specific Disorders and Problems

5

Depression

GENERAL DESCRIPTION AND DIAGNOSTIC ISSUES

Depression is among the most prevalent of all the psychological disorders, often being referred to as the "common cold" among mental health problems (Nezu, Nezu, & Perri, 1989). However, having a *major depressive episode* is different from simply feeling sad. The hallmark difference concerns the consistency of a group of symptoms lasting for a period of at least 2 weeks duration. According to the *Diagnostic and Statistical Manual of Mental Disorders, Fourth Edition, Text Revision* (DSM-IV-TR; American Psychiatric Association, 2000), five of the following nine symptoms must be present every day during this same 2-week period, one of which needs to be one of the first two: depressed mood; decreased loss of interest or pleasure; significant weight loss or gain; insomnia or hypersomnia; psychomotor agitation or retardation; fatigue or loss of energy; feelings of worthlessness or excessive guilt; difficulties in concentration and decision making; and recurrent thoughts of death or suicidal ideation.

Although there is variability regarding the degree of impairment experienced by persons who suffer a major depressive episode, there needs to be either clinically significant distress or some decrement in social, occupational, or other areas of functioning in order for this diagnosis to be made. In extreme cases, the individual may be unable to perform minimal self-care and hygiene.

By definition, a major depressive episode is not the result of (a) the direct physiological effects of an abused substance or drug (e.g., alcohol or cocaine withdrawal), (b) the side effects of certain medications or treatments (e.g, steroids), or (c) toxic exposure.

There are two predominant types of depressive disorders, including *major depressive disorder* (MDD; presence of one or more major depressive episodes) and *dysthymic disorder* (characterized by 2 or more years of consistent depressed mood, plus other depressive symptoms, but not meeting criteria for MDD). These, in addition to the diagnosis of *depressive disorder not otherwise specified*, constitute the general category of "unipolar depression," which is distinguished from the various types of *bipolar disorder*. Bipolar illness involves both depressive and manic episodes.

Studies regarding the prevalence of MDD have varied in the range of findings. According to the DSM-IV-TR (APA, 2000), the lifetime risk for MDD in community samples has varied from 10% to 25% for women and from 5% to 12% for men. The most recent epidemiological survey conducted in the United States found a prevalence of 4.9% for current major depression and 17% for lifetime depression among adults between the ages of 15 and 54 (Kessler et al., 1994).

Depression has been more recently identified as a highly recurrent disorder (Nezu, Nezu, Trunzo, & Sprague, 1998). For example, over 75% of depressed patients have more than one depressive episode, often experiencing a relapse within a 2-year period from recovery from a previous depressive episode.

DIFFERENTIAL DIAGNOSTIC ISSUES

A major depressive episode needs to be distinguished from a *mood disorder due to a general medical condition*, where the mood disturbance is viewed as being the direct physiological result of a general medical condition such as stroke or hypothyroidism. A person with cancer or heart disease, for example, where clinical assessment and judgment determines that the mood disturbance is not biologically related to the medical condition, would more likely be diagnosed with MDD (if the episode lasts for two weeks). Other diagnostic categories that need to be distinguished from MDD include *substance-induced mood disorder* (where the mood disturbance is etiologically associated with an abused substance, a medication, or a toxin), *bipolar disorders* (which involve the presence of manic symptoms), *schizoaffective disorder* (where depressive symptoms are considered associated features of the presence of delusions or hallucinations), and *dementia* (where certain depression-like cognitive symptoms, such as disorientation and difficulty concentrating, are not due to a mood disorder).

It should be noted that a diagnosis of MDD not only requires the presence of certain symptoms, but also involves issues of severity, duration, and effects on functioning. These criteria should be used when determining differences between MDD and ubiquitous periods of sadness.

CO-MORBIDITY ISSUES

Patients experiencing a major depressive episode frequently present with additional symptoms, including anxiety, phobias, worry about physical health, obsessive rumination, irritability, and complaints of pain. The co-occurrence of anxiety disorders appears to have a negative effect on treatment outcome for depression. For example, Clayton et al. (1991) found that depressed patients with higher levels of anxiety took a longer time to recover. Marital, occupational, academic, and substance abuse problems commonly co-occur along with depression. The most serious consequence of a major depressive episode is suicide. Up to 15% of individuals with MDD die by suicide. In addition, there may be an increased rate of premature death from general medical conditions among depressed persons. For example, according to the DSM-IV-TR (APA, 2000), epidemiological evidence suggests there is a fourfold increase in death rates among individuals with MDD over the age of 55 years.

ASSESSMENT OF DISORDER

In addition to clinician ratings, a large number of self-report inventories exist to measure the severity of depressive symptoms (Nezu, Nezu, McClure, & Zwick, 2002). We include those that are more frequently applied in the research literature for general use with adults, as well as listing several that have been developed for specific populations (see Nezu, Ronan, Meadows, & McClure, 2000, for an overview of such measures).

Clinician Ratings

- *Hamilton Rating Scale for Depression* (Hamilton, 1960): commonly used 17-item rating scale that assesses the severity of depressive symptoms.

- *Schedule for Affective Disorders and Schizophrenia* (Endicott & Spitzer, 1978): provides for a means to differentially diagnose depression.

Self-Report Measures

- *Beck Depression Inventory*, Second Edition (Beck, Steer, & Brown, 1996): most widely used self-report inventory measuring depression symptom severity. The second revision, which continues to include 21 items, is based on the DSM-IV criteria.
- *Carroll Depression Scales—Revised* (Carroll, 1998): 61-item inventory assessing depressive symptomatology over the past few days.
- *Center for Epidemiological Studies Depression Scale* (Radloff, 1977): 20-item self-report inventory developed to be used with the general public.
- *Zung Depression Self-Rating Depression Scale* (Zung, 1965): 20-item self-report inventory of current depression severity.

Special Populations

- *Geriatric Depression Scale* (Yesavage et al., 1983): 30-item self-report measure of depression in adults 65 and older.
- *Hospital Anxiety and Depression Scale* (Zigmond & Snaith, 1983): 14-item self-report inventory of both depression and anxiety in medical (nonpsychiatric) outpatient populations.
- *Visual Analog Mood Scales* (Stern, 1997): self-report instrument that contains visual scales where individuals who have difficulty completing verbally demanding tasks (e.g., neurological patients) can place a mark on a line that depicts several emotions (e.g., sadness, fear, confusion).

GENERAL THERAPY GOALS

Ultimate Outcome Goals

The primary ultimate outcome goals include improvement in negative mood and loss of interest in pleasurable activities. In addition, if suicidal ideation is significant, treatment needs to focus on decreasing both ideation and active attempts. If sustained depressive mood has led to significant impairment in functioning, additional ultimate outcome goals may include improving occupational, academic, and social relationships. Improved physical health may also be considered if the depressive episode has had a deleterious effect on one's general physical well-being.

Major Instrumental Outcome Goals/Treatment Targets

- Decrease dysfunctional thinking
- Improve problem-solving ability
- Improve self-control skills
- Improve rates of positive reinforcement
- Enhance social/interpersonal skills

Goal 1: Decrease Dysfunctional Thinking

The most prevalent cognitive model of depression is that posited by Beck (e.g., Beck, Rush, Shaw, & Emery, 1979; Clark, Beck, & Alford, 1999) and is composed of three key elements: (a) negative cognitive triad; (b) negative schemas; and (c) cognitive distortions. The cognitive triad consists of three patterns of negative ideas and attitudes that characterize depressed individuals and includes negative views of the self, the world, and the future. Schemas are stable, long-standing thought patterns representing a person's generalizations about past experiences. They serve to organize information relevant to a current situation from past experiences and serve to determine the manner in which information is perceived, stored, and later recalled. Depression-prone individuals tend to respond to their environment in a fixed, negative manner and interpret new experiences in a logically inaccurate fashion. Cognitive errors include arbitrary inference, selective abstraction, overgeneralization, magnification/minimization, personalization, and dichotomous thinking.

Another major cognitive model involves a revision of Seligman's (1975) earlier model that focused on the relationship between learned helplessness and depression, whereby sustained dysfunctional thinking, such as expectancies of a lack of control over events was hypothesized to precipitate depressive symptoms. The revision, currently termed "hopelessness theory" (Abramson et al., 2002; Abramson, Metalsky, & Alloy, 1989) suggests that the pervasive expectation that highly desired outcomes will not occur or that highly aversive outcomes will occur and that one cannot change this situation serves as a proximal sufficient cause of depression.

Goal-Specific Assessment Tools

- *Automatic Thoughts Questionnaire-Revised* (Kendall, Howard, & Hays, 1989): self-report measure of both negative and positive self-statements related to depression (e.g., "I'm worthless").
- *Cognitive Triad Inventory* (Beckham, Leber, Watkins, Boyer, & Cook, 1986): self-report inventory that measures aspects of Beck's (i.e., Beck et al., 1979) cognitive theory of depression.
- *Dysfunctional Attitude Scale* (Weissman & Beck, 1978): self-report measure of depression-related dysfunctional cognitions.

Goal-Specific Potential Interventions

- Cognitive Restructuring
- Problem-Solving Therapy

Cognitive Restructuring. Conceptually, disorder-related cognitive variables can be classified into three levels: *negative automatic thoughts* (e.g., "I'm a failure"), *distorted or maladaptive assumptions* (e.g., "If I ask for a raise, I will get laughed at because I'm stupid"), and *dysfunctional self-schemas* ("I am generally inadequate when it comes to relating to people"). Intervention strategies to help decrease these dysfunctional cognitive factors are based on cognitive restructuring principles. Conceptually, cognitive restructuring can be thought of as an umbrella term that encompasses several specific therapy strategies: rational-emotive therapy (e.g., Ellis, 1994), cognitive therapy (Beck et al., 1979), and self-instructional training (Meichenbaum, 1977). Whereas differences among these three approaches exist, all involve helping patients to better identify and then alter maladaptive thoughts. Beck's Cognitive Therapy (CT) is perhaps the most recognizable and popular form of psychosocial treatment for depression. Large numbers of controlled outcome studies have been conducted during the past several decades supporting the efficacy of CT. Numerous reviews underscore its relative efficacy, its comparability to psychopharmacological approaches, and occasional superiority to other psychosocial therapies, with regard to depression (Hollon, Haman, & Brown, 2002).

Problem-Solving Therapy. A related therapy approach to CT is problem-solving therapy (PST; D'Zurilla & Nezu, 1999; Nezu, in press), which is geared to increase one's overall coping ability when dealing with stressful situations. Part of this approach involves changing those cognitive factors that negatively impinge on one's *problem orientation* or general view of problems and self-assessment regarding one's problem-solving capabilities (e.g., beliefs about why a problem occurred, attributions about who is responsible for the problem occurring in the first place, self-efficacy beliefs). A study by Nezu and Perri (1989) underscored the importance of focusing on changing depressed adults' negative problem orientation when conducting PST.

Goal 2: Improve Problem-Solving Ability

Nezu and his colleagues have suggested that deficits in one's problem-solving ability to cope with stressful life events can serve as a significant depressogenic vulnerability factor (Nezu, 1987; Nezu et al., 1989). One major problem-solving variable related to depression is *problem orientation* (i.e., set of generalized orienting responses regarding problems in living and one's ability to cope with such problems). Scores of studies have found a *negative* problem orientation (i.e., one that involves the tendency to view problems as threats, expect problems to be unsolvable, doubt one's own ability to solve problems successfully, and become frustrated and upset when faced with problems) to be significantly related to depression (Nezu, in press; Nezu, Wilkins, & Nezu, in press). In addition, specific *problem-solving skills* (e.g., understanding why a situation is a problem, setting realistic goals, generating options, making decisions, evaluating the outcome of a solution plan) have also been found to be significantly related to depression (Nezu, in press).

Goal-Specific Assessment Tools

- *Social Problem-Solving Inventory-Revised* (D'Zurilla, Nezu, & Maydeu-Olivares, 2002): self-report measure of various cognitive, affective, and behavioral aspects of real-life problem solving (e.g., problem-orientation variables, specific problem-solving skills, such as defining problems, generating solution ideas, and making decisions).
- *Problem-Solving Inventory* (Heppner, 1988): self-report questionnaire assessing problem-solving "self-appraisal."

Goal-Specific Potential Interventions

- Problem-Solving Therapy

Problem-Solving Therapy. Problem-Solving Therapy (PST) has four overall goals: (a) to help depressed individuals identify previous and current life situations that are antecedents of a depressive episode; (b) to minimize the extent to which their depressive symptoms impact negatively on current and future attempts at coping; (c) to increase the effectiveness of their problem-solving attempts at coping with current problems; and (d) to teach general skills that will enable them to deal more effectively with future problems in order to prevent future depressive episodes (Nezu et al., 1989). Research has demonstrated the efficacy of PST for depression regarding adults (e.g., Nezu, 1986; Nezu & Perri, 1989), elderly adults (Arean et al., 1993; Hussian & Lawrence, 1981); primary care patients (Mynors-Wallis, Gath, Lloyd-Thomas, & Thomlinson, 1995), and adult cancer patients (Nezu, Nezu, Felgoise, McClure, & Houts, 2003).

Goal 3: Improve Self-Control Skills

Rehm's (1977) conceptualization of depression was originally based on a general self-control model that placed major significance on an individual's ability to achieve goals through three sequential processes, namely, self-monitoring, self-evaluation, and self-reinforcement. Rehm posited that depressed individuals demonstrate deficits in each of these self-control processes. For example, Roth and Rehm (1980) compared self-monitoring in depressed and nondepressed psychiatric patients and found that when allowed to choose the type of performance feedback (e.g., correct versus incorrect responses), depressed patients more frequently selected negative feedback, whereas nondepressed patients more frequently chose positive feedback. Further, a comparison of depressed and nondepressed psychiatric patients showed that although the two groups had equivalent performances on a memory task, depressed individuals punished themselves more and rewarded themselves less than did nondepressed patients (Rozensky, Rehm, Pry, & Roth, 1977).

Goal-Specific Assessment Tools

- *Self-Control Questionnaire* (Rehm et al., 1981): self-report measure of depression-related deficits in self-control behavior.
- *Self-Control Schedule* (Rosenbaum, 1980): self-report measure of self-control methods for resolving behavior problems.

Goal-Specific Potential Interventions

- Self-Control Therapy
- Problem-Solving Therapy

Self-Control Therapy.   Self-control therapy, similar to other behaviorally oriented protocols, is structured and time-limited and focuses on overcoming the following three deficits: self-monitoring, self-evaluation, and self-reinforcement. For example, patients are taught to (a) maintain a daily record of positive experiences and their associated mood, (b) develop specific, overt, and reachable goals concerning positive activities, and (c) identify reinforcers, and to administer these rewards to themselves upon successfully achieving a goal. Studies conducted by Rehm and others based on this model of treatment demonstrate the efficacy of self-control therapy for depression (e.g., Fuchs & Rehm, 1977; Rehm, Fuchs, Roth, Kornblith, & Romano, 1979; Roth, Bielski, Jones, Paker, & Osborn, 1982).

Problem-Solving Therapy.   Aspects of problem-solving therapy (PST) are geared to help individuals better set realistic goals when coping with stressful life problems. In addition, it teaches patients to engage in appropriate self-reward when making overt attempts to solve problems. Studies that evaluated PST for depression found that in addition to decreasing depression and increasing problem-solving effectiveness, it improved depressed patients' self-control skills as well (e.g., Nezu, 1986).

Goal 4: Improve Rates of Positive Reinforcement

Lewinsohn (1974) conceptualized depression within the framework of learning theory and extended earlier behavioral formulations (Skinner, 1953) that emphasized the reduced frequency of overall activity as the primary defining characteristic of depression. The guiding theoretical assertions of Lewinsohn's work are (a) that depression is a function of the degree to which an individual's activity level is maintained by positive reinforcement, and (b) that deficits in various social skills play an influential role in determining the rate of such reinforcement for one's behavior. Research indicates, for example, that depressed persons emit fewer interpersonal behaviors than nondepressed persons and elicit minimal social reinforcement from others (Gotlib & Robinson, 1982).

Goal-Specific Assessment Tools

- *Frequency of Self-Reinforcement Questionnaire* (Heiby, 1983): measures beliefs and attitudes regarding self-reinforcement.
- *Pleasant Events Schedule* (MacPhillamy & Lewinsohn, 1982): self-report instrument that measures the frequency and subjective enjoyability of a wide range of pleasurable or reinforcing events.

Goal-Specific Potential Interventions

- Coping with Depression Course
- Behavioral Activation

Coping with Depression.   Based on his original formulation, Lewin-sohn and his colleagues developed a behaviorally oriented protocol geared to change the quality and quantity of depressed patients' interactions with their environment. Patients are taught relaxation skills, cognitive self-management, stress management skills, and provided feedback as a means of reducing the intensity and frequency of aversive events and to increase their rate of engaging in pleasant activities. A more recent revision of this behavioral approach, entitled the *Coping with Depression* course (Lewin-sohn, Antonuccio, Breckenridge, & Teri, 1987), broadened its skills train-ing to include four general domains: relaxation training, increasing pleasant activities, cognitive restructuring, and improving social interactions. Con-trolled outcome studies provide support for this program's effectiveness in reducing depression (e.g., Brown & Lewinsohn, 1984; Hoberman, Lew-insohn, & Tilson, 1988).

Behavioral Activation.   In a component analysis of cognitive therapy for depression, the behavioral activation (BA) component was found to produce as much change as the full treatment package (Jacobson et al., 1996). This surprising finding led to the development of a more comprehen-sive version based on a contextual analysis (Jacobson, Martell, & Dimidjian, 2001). BA focuses on increasing the rewarding and productive behavior of a depressed patient. This approach combines reward planning and pleasant activity scheduling in order to achieve such a goal.

Goal 5: Enhance Social and Interpersonal Skills

This conceptualization of depression identifies deficient or maladaptive interpersonal skills as being etiologically related to depression. In essence, poor social skills leads to a limited ability to obtain positive reinforcement from one's social environment. Such a formulation is part of Lewinsohn's model described previously, as well as that of Coyne (1976). Coyne suggests a strong interpersonal cyclical component to depression, whereby the de-pressed individual begins the cycle by complaining, which initially leads to an increase in social reinforcement (e.g., reassurance, empathy, attention). However, continued complaining and self-focus leads others in the person's social environment to reject the depressed individual, resulting in a de-crease in social reinforcement and support, but a confirmation of the individual's negative self-concept. As the complaining increases, so does the aversive nature of this behavior which leads to increased rejection by others.

Goal-Specific Assessment Tools

- *Interpersonal Events Schedule* (Youngren, Zeiss, & Lewinsohn, 1975): measures interpersonal activities and cognitions.
- *Social Adjustment Scale* (Paykel, Weissman, Prusoff, & Tonks, 1971): assesses various dimensions of social and interpersonal functioning and adjustment.

Goal-Specific Potential Interventions

- Social Skills Training

Social Skills Training. Becker and his colleagues (e.g., Becker & Heimberg, 1985; Becker, Heimberg, & Bellack, 1987) and Bellack, Hersen and their colleagues (e.g., Bellack, Hersen, & Himmelhoch, 1981, 1983; Hersen, Bellack, Himmelhoch, & Thase, 1984), developed treatment programs geared to improve the social skills of depressed individuals in order to decrease their emotional distress. In these treatment programs, the hypothesized mechanism of action centered around a person's ability to engage in those activities that would facilitate the quantity and quality of social interactions in order to ultimately increase the amount of response-contingent positive reinforcement (e.g., Becker & Heimberg, 1985). Several outcome studies conducted by these investigators demonstrate the efficacy of this overall approach for the treatment of depression.

McLean (1979) also viewed depression as resulting from ineffective coping and social skills and developed a 10-week program that included training in these domains (i.e., communication, behavioral productivity, social interaction, assertiveness, decision making, problem solving, cognitive self-control) as a means of developing prosocial behaviors and prevention against relapse. An evaluation of this approach conducted by McLean and Hakstian (1979) provide support for its efficacy as a treatment approach for depression.

Additional Instrumental Outcome Goals/Treatment Targets

Additional treatment targets for depression may include:

- *Decrease Suicidal Ideation.* Although not all depressed individuals experience significant suicidal ideation, there is a 50-fold increase in suicidal risk for patients with a current episode of depression as compared to the general population (Beutler et al., 2000). As such, it is extremely important to assess for the presence and meaning of suicidal thoughts and beliefs and if present, to prioritize them as a treatment target. Problem-solving therapy, by increasing a patient's ability to perceive and identify options to suicide, has been found to be one effective approach (Lerner & Clum, 1990; Salkovskis, Atha, & Storer, 1990).

- *Improve Marital Relationship.* Research has recently pointed to the strong relationship between depression and marital distress. For example, Weissman (1987) found that the 6-month prevalence rate of major depression in a community sample of women who reported marital distress was 45.5%. Hoover and Fitzgerald (1981) reported that both unipolar and bipolar patients reported greater conflict in their marriages than did nondepressed controls. A study by Gotlib and Whiffen (1989) revealed that among a sample of couples wherein the wife met diagnostic criteria for clinical depression, both husbands and wives reported greater marital dissatisfaction as compared to a group of nondepressed control couples. Based on these findings, several research teams have evaluated the efficacy of behavioral marital therapy (BMT) as a treatment for depression. For example, O'Leary and Beach (1990) demonstrated that BMT was as effective as individual cognitive therapy in reducing depression. Similar results were obtained in a study by Jacobson, Dobson, Fruzetti, Schmaling, and Salusky (1991).

- *Improve Overall Physical Health.* As noted earlier, there is an increase in the death rate from general medical conditions among depressed individuals. Depression can have a significant negative impact on one's health, both behaviorally and physiologically. For example, depression can lead to a decrease in motivation to adhere to any medical regimen for a concurrent medical condition or can have a potentially direct pathogenic effect on an existing disease, such a coronary heart disease, where depression, for example, is associated with a 3.5 fold increase in risk of mortality among patients experiencing a myocardial infarction (i.e., heart attack) (Krantz & McCeney, 2002).

- *Decrease Relapse.* Depression is better viewed as a recurrent disorder where the likelihood of experiencing another depressive episode is high (Nezu et al., 1998). Based on the type of depression-related vulnerability a patient appears to have, an inoculation component may need to be added to an overall treatment plan in order to minimize the probability of future recurrences.

ADDITIONAL CLINICAL CONSIDERATIONS

Although no single explanation can account for the significant differences in prevalence rates of depression between men and women, several biological, psychological, and social theories have been advanced (Nezu & Nezu, 1989). Nolen-Hoeksema (2002) notes the following: (a) women may have a greater biological reactivity to stress than men; (b) women, being more interpersonally oriented than men, may lead to a greater focus on others' needs at a cost to themselves; (c) women may tend to ruminate more than men when depressed, leading to increased rates of negative thinking and less effective coping with problems associated with their depression; and (d) women may be more vulnerable to depression due to a higher rate of acute and chronic stressors.

In a similar vein, Nezu and Nezu (1987; Nezu, Nezu, & Petersen, 1989) suggest that the difference in prevalence rates between men and women is more a function of *sex roles*, rather than gender per se. More specifically, they found that the sex-role dimension of *masculinity* (which is primarily defined by an active problem-solving coping style), *regardless* of one's actual gender, accounted for more of the variance in predicting depression than actual gender. Given such potential explanations, the CBT clinician should consider the above hypotheses when working with a female patient in order to determine idiographic vulnerabilities.

Cultural variations in the experience of depression (or any disorder) is always confounded by the notion that the very definition of a disorder such as depression is imbued with Western cultural assumptions. For example, rates of depression tend to be lower in Asian cultures than in Western cultures, the meaning of depression and mental health in general may be different depending on cultural background, rates of comorbidity of other disorders with depression is different across cultures, and demographic risk factors also differ across cultures (Tsai & Chentsova-Dutton, 2002). As such, it is incumbent upon the CBT clinician to view any patient's symptoms as being potentially influenced by socio-cultural-ethnic factors and attempt to overcome judgmental biases that might limit this insight.

Last, co-morbid disorders need to be assessed and factored into an overall treatment plan. Depression has a significant co-morbidity with many anxiety disorders, substance abuse, and various medical conditions.

There is also a high co-occurrence with various personality disorders as well.

REFERENCES

Abramson, L. Y., Alloy, L. B., Hankin, B. L., Haeffel, G. J., MacCoon, D. G., & Gibb, B. E. (2002). Cognitive vulnerability-stress models of depression in a self-regulatory and psychobiological context. In I. H. Gotlib & C. L. Hammen (Eds.), *Handbook of depression* (pp. 268–294). New York: Guilford Press.

Abramson, L. Y., Metalsky, G. I., & Alloy, L. B. (1989): Hopelessness depression: A theory-based subtype of depression. *Psychological Review, 96*, 358–372.

American Psychiatric Association. (2000). *Diagnostic and statistical manual of mental disorders* (ed. 4, text revision). Washington, DC: American Psychiatric Press.

Arean, P. A., Perri, M. G., Nezu, A. M., Schein, R. L., Christopher, F., & Joseph, T. X. (1993). Comparative effectiveness of social problem-solving therapy and reminiscence therapy as treatments for depression in older adults. *Journal of Consulting and Clinical Psychology, 61*, 1003–1010.

Beck, A. T., Rush, A. J., Shaw, B. F., & Emery, G. (1979). *Cognitive therapy of depression*. New York: Guilford Press.

Beck, A. T., Steer, R. A., & Brown, G. K. (1996). *Manual for the BDI-II*. San Antonio, TX: Psychological Corporation.

Becker, R. E., & Heimberg, R. G. (1985). Social skills training approaches. In M. Hersen & A. S. Bellack (Eds.), *Handbook of clinical behavior therapy with adults* (pp. 201–226). New York: Plenum Press.

Becker, R. E., Heimberg, R. G., & Bellack, A. S. (1987). *Social skills training treatment for depression*. New York: Pergamon Press.

Beckham, E. E., Leber, W. R., Watkins, J. T., Boyer, J. L., & Cook, J. B. (1986). Development of an instrument to measure Beck's cognitive triad: The Cognitive Triad Inventory. *Journal of Consulting and Clinical Psychology, 54*, 566–567.

Bellack, A. S., Hersen, M., & Himmelhoch, J. (1981). Social skills training compared with pharmacotherapy and psychotherapy in the treatment of unipolar depression. *American Journal of Psychiatry, 138*, 1562–1567.

Bellack, A. S., Hersen, M., & Himmelhoch, J. (1983). A comparison of social skills training, pharmacotherapy, and psychotherapy for depression. *Behavior Research and Therapy, 21*, 101–107.

Brown, R. A., & Lewinsohn, P. M. (1984). A psychoeducational approach to the treatment of depression: Comparison of group, individual, and minimal contact procedures. *Journal of Consulting and Clinical Psychology, 52*, 774–783.

Carroll, B. (1998). *Carroll Depression Scales-Revised (CDS-R): Technical manual*. North Tonawanda, NY: Multi-Health Systems.

Clark, D. A., & Beck, A. T., with Alford, B. A. (1999). *Cognitive theory and therapy of depression*. New York: Wiley.

Clayton, P. F., Grove, W. M., Coryell, W., Keller, M. B., Clayton, P. J., Hirschfeld, R. M. A., et al. (1991). Follow-up and family study of anxious depression. *American Journal of Psychiatry, 148,* 1512–1517.

Coyne, J. C. (1976). Toward an interactional description of depression. *Psychiatry, 39,* 28–40.

D'Zurilla, T. J., & Nezu, A. M. (1999). *Problem-solving therapy: A social competence approach to clinical intervention* (2nd ed.). New York: Springer Publishing Co.

D'Zurilla, T. J., Nezu, A. M., & Maydeu-Olivares (2002). *Social Problem-Solving Inventory-Revised (SPSI-R): Manual.* North Tonawanda, NY: Multi-Health Systems.

Ellis, A. (1994). *Reason and emotion in psychotherapy* (Rev. ed.). New York: Birch Lane Press.

Endicott, J., & Spitzer, R. L. (1978). A diagnostic interview: The Schedule for Affective Disorders and Schizophrenia. *Archives of General Psychiatry, 35,* 837–844.

Fuchs, C. Z., & Rehm, L. P. (1977). A self-control behavior therapy program for depression. *Journal of Consulting and Clinical Psychology, 45,* 206–215.

Gotlib, I. H., & Whiffen, V. E. (1989). Stress, coping, and marital satisfaction in couples with a depressed wife. *Canadian Journal of Behavioral Science, 21,* 401–418.

Hamilton, M. (1960). A rating scale for depression. *Journal of Neurology, Neurosurgery and Psychiatry, 23,* 56–62.

Heiby, E. M. (1983). Assessment of frequency of self-reinforcement. *Journal of Personality and Social Psychology, 44,* 1304–1307.

Heppner, P. P. (1988). *The Problem-Solving Inventory.* Palo Alto, CA: Consulting Psychologist Press.

Hersen, M., Bellack, A. S., Himmelhoch,, J. M., & Thase, M. E. (1984). Effects of social skills training, amitriptyline, and psychotherapy in unipolar depressed women. *Behavior Therapy, 15,* 21–40.

Hoberman, H. M., Lewinsohn, P. S., & Tilson, M. (1988). Group treatment of depression: Individual predictors of outcome. *Journal of Consulting and Clinical Psychology, 56,* 393–398.

Hollon, S. D., Haman, K. L., & Brown, L. L. (2002). Cognitive-behavioral treatment of depression. In I. H. Gotlib & C. L. Hammen (Eds.), *Handbook of depression* (pp. 383–403). New York: Guilford Press.

Hoover, C. F., & Fitzgerald, R. G. (1981). Marital conflict of manic-depressive patients. *Archives of General Psychiatry, 38,* 65–67.

Hussian, R. A., & Lawrence, P. S. (1981). Social reinforcement of activity and problem-solving training in the treatment of depressed institutionalized elderly patients. *Cognitive Therapy and Research, 5,* 57–69.

Jacobson, N. S., Dobson, K., Fruzetti, A. E., Schmaling, K. B., & Salusky, S. (1991). Marital therapy as a treatment for depression. *Journal of Consulting and Clinical Psychology, 59,* 547–557.

Jacobson, N. S., Dobson, K. S., Truax, P. A., Addis, M. E., Koerner, K., Gollan, J. K., et al. (1996). A component analysis of cognitive-behavior treatment for depression. *Journal of Consulting and Clinical Psychology, 64,* 295–304.

Jacobson, N. S., Martell, C., & Dimidjian, S. (2001). Behavioral activation treatment for depression: Returning to contextual roots. *Clinical Psychology: Science and Practice, 8,* 255–270.

Kendall, P. C., Howard, B. L., & Hays, R. C. (1989). Self-referent speech and psychopathology: The balance of positive and negative thinking. *Cognitive Therapy and Research, 13,* 583–598.

Kessler, R. C., McGonagle, K. A., Zhao, S., Nelson, C. B., Hughes, M., Eshleman, S., et al. (1994). Lifetime and 12-month prevalence of DSM-III-R psychiatric disorders in the United States: Results from the National Comorbidity Survey. *Archives of General Psychiatry, 51,* 8–19.

Krantz, D. S., & McCeney, M. K. (2002). Effects of psychological and social factors on organic disease: A critical assessment of research on coronary heart disease. In S. T. Fiske, D. L. Schacter, & C. Zahn-Waxler (Eds.), *Annual Review of Psychology, 53,* 341–604.

Lerner, M. S., & Clum, G. A. (1990). Treatment of suicide ideators: A problem-solving approach. *Behavior Therapy, 21,* 403–411.

Lewinsohn, P. M. (1974). A behavioral approach to depression. In R. J. Friedman & M. M. Katz (Eds.), *The psychology of depression: Contemporary theory and research* (pp. 157–185). New York: Wiley.

Lewinsohn, P. M., Antonuccio, D. O., Breckenridge, J., & Teri, L. (1987). *The coping with depression course: A psychoeducational intervention for unipolar depression.* Eugene, OR: Castaglia.

MacPhillamy, D. J., & Lewinsohn, P. M. (1982). The Pleasant Events Schedule: Studies on reliability, validity, and scale intercorrelation. *Journal of Consulting and Clinical Psychology, 50,* 363–380.

McLean, P. (1979). Therapeutic decision-making in the behavioral treatment of depression. In P. O. Davidson (Ed.), *The behavioral management of anxiety, depression and pain* (pp. 54–89). New York: Brunner/Mazel.

McLean, P. D., & Hakstian, A. R. (1979). Clinical depression: Comparative efficacy of outpatient treatments. *Journal of Consulting and Clinical Psychology, 47,* 818–836.

Meichenbaum, D. H. (1977). *Cognitive behavior modification.* New York: Plenum Press.

Mynors-Wallis, L. M., Gath, D. H., Lloyd-Thomas, A. R., & Tomlinson, D. (1995). Randomised controlled trial comparing problem solving treatment with amitriptyline and placebo for major depression in primary care. *British Medical Journal, 310,* 441–445.

Nezu, A. M. (1986). Efficacy of a social problem-solving therapy approach for unipolar depression. *Journal of Consulting and Clinical Psychology, 54,* 196–202.

Nezu, A. M. (1987). A problem-solving formulation of depression: A literature review and proposal of a pluralistic model. *Clinical Psychology Review, 7,* 122–144.

Nezu, A. M. (in press). Problem solving and behavior therapy revisited. *Behavior Therapy.*

Nezu, A. M., & Nezu, C. M. (1987). Psychological distress, problem solving, and coping reactions: Sex-role differences. *Sex Roles, 16,* 205–214.

Nezu, A. M., & Nezu, C. M. (1989). Cognitive-behavioral formulations of depression and gender prevalence rates: Integration or expulsion? *Canadian Psychologist, 30,* 61–62.

Nezu, A. M., Nezu, C. M., Felgoise, S. H., McClure, K. S., & Houts, P. S. (2003). Project Genesis: Assessing the efficacy of problem-solving therapy for distressed adult cancer patients. *Journal of Consulting and Clinical Psychology, 71,* 1036–1048.

Nezu, A. M., Nezu, C. M., McClure, K. S., & Zwick, M. L. (2002). Assessment of depression. In I. H. Gotlib & C. L. Hammen (Eds.), *Handbook of depression* (pp. 61–85). New York: Guilford.

Nezu, A. M., Nezu, C. M., & Peterson, M. A. (1986). Negative life stress, social support, and depressive symptoms: Sex roles as a moderator variable. *Journal of Social Behavior and Personality, 1,* 599–609.

Nezu, A. M., Nezu, C. M., & Perri, M. G. (1989). *Problem-solving therapy for depression: Theory, research, and clinical guidelines.* New York: Wiley.

Nezu, A. M., Nezu, C. M., Trunzo, J. J., & Sprague, K. S. (1998). Treatment maintenance for unipolar depression: Relevant issues, literature review, and recommendations for research and clinical practice. *Clinical Psychology: Science and Practice, 5,* 496–512.

Nezu, A. M., & Perri, M. G. (1989). Problem-solving therapy for unipolar depression: An initial dismantling investigation. *Journal of Consulting and Clinical Psychology, 57,* 408–413.

Nezu, A. M., Ronan, G. F., Meadows, E. A., & McClure, K. S. (Eds.). (2000). *Practitioner's guide to empirically based measures of depression.* New York: Kluwer Academic/Plenum Publishers.

Nezu, A. M., Wilkins, V. M., & Nezu, C. M. (in press). Social problem solving, stress, and negative affective conditions. In E. C. Chang, T. J. D'Zurilla, & L. J. Sanna (Eds.), *Social problem solving: Theory, research, and training.* Washington, DC: American Psychological Association.

Nolen-Hoeksema, S. (2002). Gender differences in depression. In I. H. Gotlib & C. L. Hammen (Eds.), *Handbook of depression* (pp. 492–509). New York: Guilford.

O'Leary, K. D., & Beach, S. R. H. (1990). Marital therapy: A viable treatment for depression. *American Journal of Psychiatry, 147,* 183–186.

Paykel, E. S., Weissman, M., Prusoff, B. A., & Tonks, C. M. (1971). Dimensions of social adjustment in depressed women. *Journal of Nervous and Mental Disease, 152,* 158–172.

Radloff, L. S. (1977). The CES-D Scale: A self-report depression scale for research in the general population. *Applied Psychological Measurement, 1,* 385–401.

Rehm, L. P. (1977). A self-control model of depression. *Behavior Therapy, 8,* 787–804.

Rehm, L. P., Fuchs, C. Z., Roth, D. M., Kornblith, S. J., & Romano, J. M. (1979). A comparison of self-control and assertion skills treatments of depression. *Behavior Therapy, 10,* 429–442.

Rehm, L. P., Kornblith, S. J., O'Hara, M. W., Lamparski, D. M., Romano, J. M., & Volkin, J. I. (1981). An evaluation of major components of a self-control therapy program for depression. *Behavior Modification, 5,* 459–489.

Rosenbaum, M. (1980). A schedule for assessing self-control behaviors: Preliminary findings. *Behavior Therapy, 11,* 109–121.

Roth, D., Bielski, R., Jones, J., Parker, W., & Osborn, G. (1982). A comparison of self-control therapy and combined self-control therapy and antidepressant medication in the treatment of depression. *Behavior Therapy, 13,* 133–144.

Roth, D., & Rehm, L. P. (1980). Relationships between self-monitoring processes, memory and depression. *Psychological Reports, 47,* 3–7.

Rozensky, R. H., Rehm, L. P., Pry, G., & Roth, G. (1977). Depression and self-reinforcement behavior in hospitalized patients. *Journal of Behavior Therapy and Experimental Psychiatry, 8,* 31–34.

Salkovskis, P. M., Atha, C., & Storer, D. (1990). Cognitive-behavioural problem solving in the treatment of patients who repeatedly attempt suicide: A controlled trial. *British Journal of Psychiatry, 157,* 871–876.

Seligman, M. E. P. (1975). *Helplessness: On depression, development and death.* San Francisco: Freeman.

Skinner, B. F. (1953). *The science of human behavior.* New York: Free Press.

Stern, R. A. (1997). *Visual Analogue Mood Scales: Professional manual.* Odessa, FL: Psychological Assessment Resources.

Tsai, J. L., & Chentsova-Dutton, Y. (2002). Understanding depression across cultures. In I. H. Gotlib & C. L. Hammen (Eds.), *Handbook of depression* (pp. 467–491). New York: Guilford.

Weissman, A. N., & Beck, A. T. (1978). *Development and validation of the Dysfunctional Attitude Scale: A preliminary investigation.* Paper presented at the meeting of the Association for the Advancement of Behavior Therapy, Chicago.

Weissman, M. M. (1987). Advances in psychiatric epidemiology: Rates and risks for major depression. *American Journal of Public Health, 77,* 445–451.

Yesavage, J. A., Brink, T. L., Rose, T. L., Lum, O., Huang, V., Adey, M., et al. (1983). Development and validation of a geriatric depression screening scale: A preliminary report. *Journal of Psychiatric Research, 17,* 37–49.

Youngren, M. A., Zeiss, A., & Lewinsohn, P. M. (1975). *Interpersonal events schedule.* University of Oregon, Eugene.

Zigmond, A. S., & Snaith, R. P. (1983). The Hospital Anxiety and Depression Scale. *Acta Psychiatrica Scandinavica, 67,* 361–370.

Zung, W. W. K. (1965). A self-rating depression scale. *Archives of General Psychiatry, 12,* 63–70.

6

Specific Phobia

GENERAL DESCRIPTION AND DIAGNOSTIC ISSUES

Specific phobia is defined by the *Diagnostic and Statistical Manual of Mental Disorders, Fourth Edition, Text Revision* (DSM-IV-TR; American Psychiatric Association, 2000), as a significant and enduring fear that is excessive or unreasonable, and cued by the actual presence or anticipation of a specific object or situation. Exposure to the phobic stimulus or thought of the stimulus almost invariably provokes an immediate anxiety response. A diagnosis of specific phobia requires that the person recognizes that the fear is excessive or unreasonable. The phobic situation is usually avoided, but may be endured with intense distress. This avoidance and/or distress interfere with the individual's normal routine, occupational (or academic) functioning, and/or social activities.

With regard to a specific phobia, one's anxiety often intensifies as proximity to the feared situation increases. The anxious response is characterized by physiological (e.g., tachycardia, sweating, shortness of breath), cognitive (e.g., catastrophic fears), and/or behavioral (e.g., avoidance) elements. As will be discussed in more detail later in the chapter, blood-injection-injury (BII) phobias differ from others regarding physiological reaction in that they may entail bradycardia and syncope.

Although fears associated with specific situations are common in the general population, they rarely result in sufficient impairment or distress

81

to warrant a diagnosis of specific phobia. For example, although at least 20% of the population in the United States reports an excessive fear of flying, there is only a 10% prevalence rate of actual flying phobia. Overall 6-month prevalence rates for specific phobia in community samples are 4.5% to 11.8%, with lifetimes rates ranging from 10% to 11.3%. Men are at the lower end and women are at the higher end of this spectrum.

The DSM-IV-TR differentiates distinct types of specific phobia into the following categories (from most to least frequent):

- Situational (e.g., airplanes, elevators, enclosed places),
- Natural environment (e.g., heights, storms, water),
- Blood-injection-injury (e.g., seeing blood, receiving injection),
- Animal (i.e., insects and animals), and
- Specific phobia, other (e.g., phobic avoidance of situations that may lead to choking, vomiting, or contracting an illness).

DIFFERENTIAL DIAGNOSTIC ISSUES

Whereas anxiety disorders share certain features (e.g., anxiety, avoidance), a differential diagnosis is made according to the specific fear. For example, in contrast to specific phobia, social phobia is characterized by fears centered on experiencing public embarrassment or humiliation in social or performance situations. Unlike *obsessive-compulsive disorder*, people with phobias neither obsess about their fears nor adopt compulsive behaviors in an effort to relieve their anxiety. In *posttraumatic stress disorder*, avoidance of stimuli is associated with a severe stressor. Contrary to specific phobia, where anxiety is cued by a specific stimulus, *agoraphobia* entails anxiety about being trapped in a variety of places or situations that might be difficult or embarrassing, or that may trigger a panic attack. Finally, although specific phobia may include situationally bound or situationally predisposed panic attacks, *panic disorder* is characterized by fear of unexpected panic attacks.

Adults with a specific phobia recognize that the phobia is excessive or unreasonable. In contrast, *delusional disorder* is characterized by the lack of this insight. Fears of having specific diseases such as cancer, heart disease, or venereal infection fall under a diagnosis of *hypochondrias*, unless they relate to specific situations where the disease might be acquired. Finally, the diagnosis of specific phobia is not warranted if the fear is reasonable, given the context of the stimuli (e.g., fear of being shot in a dangerous neighborhood).

Co-Morbidity Issues

Unlike individuals with other anxiety disorders, those with a principal specific phobia are not at a significantly elevated risk of having additional psychiatric diagnoses, except for another specific phobia. Estimates for having more than one source of fear that meet criteria for specific phobia vary from approximately 20%–75%. Having one phobia of a specific subtype tends to increase the likelihood of having another phobia from the same subtype (e.g., fear of airplanes *and* elevators). If another diagnosis is present, it is often an additional anxiety (e.g., social phobia) or mood disorder. In contrast, specific phobia is often a secondary diagnosis to individuals with other primary anxiety disorders, as is seen in 32% of patients with anxiety disorders.

ASSESSMENT OF DISORDER

In addition to a comprehensive assessment of anxiety and fears, a variety of self-report measures are listed that assess different types of a specific phobia. The reader is directed to Antony, Orsillo, and Roemer (2001) for a review of such assessment tools.

Clinician Ratings

- *Anxiety Disorders Interview Schedule for DMS-IV: Lifetime Version* (DiNardo, Brown, & Barlow, 1994): assesses current and lifetime DSM-IV diagnoses of anxiety, mood, and substance use.

Self-Report Measures

Overall

- *Fear Survey Schedule* (Greer, 1965; Wolpe & Lang, 1964): lists different objects and situations that may elicit fear.

- *Initial Fear Evaluation for Patients* (Leahy & Holland, 2000): assesses amount of fear associated with a variety of situations.

Situational Phobia

- *Acrophobia Questionnaire* (Cohen, 1977): assesses severity of anxiety and avoidance of height-related situations.
- *Claustrophobia Questionnaire* (Radomsky, Rachman, Thordarson, McIsaac, & Teachman, 2001): assesses claustrophobia and its related fear of suffocation and restriction.
- *Fear of Flying Scale* (Haug et al., 1987): assesses various aspects of fear of flying.

Dental Phobia

- *Dental Anxiety Inventory* (Stouthard, Mellenbergh, & Hoogstraten, 1993): assesses the degree to which an individual agrees with statements related to dental anxiety and the severity of dental anxiety.

Blood-Injection-Injury Phobia

- *Medical Fear Survey* (Kleinknecht, Thorndike, & Walls, 1996): assesses severity of medical fears using different subscales—injections and blood drawing, sharp objects, examinations and symptoms as indications of illness, and mutilation.

Animal Phobia

- *Fear of Spiders Questionnaire* (Szymanski & O'Donohue, 1995): assesses severity of fears related to spiders.

GENERAL THERAPY GOALS

Ultimate Outcome Goals

Reduction of fear is the ultimate goal in treating specific phobias. Additional ultimate goals are centered on increasing one's functioning that may be hindered by the phobic reactions. For example, such goals can entail enhancing occupational, academic, and social functioning damaged by the phobia. Furthermore, for patients where the phobia has prevented them from attaining optimal medical or dental care, ultimately enhancing their physical health is desirable. Finally, because individuals with a specific phobia may develop maladaptive behaviors to cope with their fears (e.g., abusing alcohol), treatment may be aimed at improving adaptive coping skills.

Major Instrumental Outcome Goals/Treatment Targets

Major instrumental outcome goals for specific phobia include:

- Decreased heightened physiological arousal
- Decreased vasovagal reactions
- Decreased dysfunctional beliefs

Goal 1: Decrease Heightened Physiological Arousal

As with all other anxiety disorders, a hallmark of specific phobias include physiological arousal. This includes a variety of sympathetic nervous responses, such as increased heart rate, sweating, and muscle tension, in response to the feared stimulus. Such responses are usually maintained by avoidance or escape behaviors. Specifically, individuals avoid the feared stimulus or escape from it when the physiological arousal becomes intolerable, thus, becoming negatively reinforced due to their resulting decrease in distress. Further, these behavioral reactions prevent the development of alternative hypotheses from being tested (e.g., contact with the feared stimulus will *not* result in feared consequences).

Goal-Specific Assessment Tools

- *Subjective Units of Distress Scale* (SUDS): assesses patients' self-reported level of physiological or psychological distress, usually on a scale from 0 (*not-at-all distressed*) to 100 (*the most distressed they have ever been*) ratings.
- *Behavioral Avoidance Test (BAT)*: patients' individually tailored hierarchy of avoided stimuli; to be used in conjunction with SUDS.

Goal-Specific Potential Interventions

- Exposure therapy
- Flooding
- Applied relaxation

Exposure Therapy.   Exposure therapy aims to extinguish conditioned fear responses to relevant stimuli. This is based on the conceptualization that specific phobias are partially maintained by the avoidance of anxiety-producing stimuli (e.g., heights, enclosed spaces, blood) and the negative reinforcement that occurs as a consequence of avoiding such stimuli. In exposure therapy, patients develop a fear hierarchy of progressively distressing situations and are then exposed to these situations in a systematic manner. Exposure can be imaginary or *in vivo*. Whereas the former is often easier to implement, there tends to be a consensus that the latter results in superior results regarding habituation.

Exposure therapy may be preceded by modeling. Modeling involves patient observation of the therapist confronted with the feared stimulus while *not* engaging in avoidance or escape behaviors. Although modeling may help decrease some anxiety and increase self-efficacy towards engaging in exposure, it appears that modeling alone is not an effective discrete treatment (Goetestam, 2002). However, coupled with direct exposure, it can help decrease treatment time. Thus, if utilized, modeling should be quickly faded to increase the patient's direct experience with the feared stimulus.

Overall, experts tend to agree that exposure therapy is the first treatment to implement for specific phobias. It has been demonstrated that matching treatments to specific symptoms (e.g., cognitive restructuring for dysfunctional beliefs, relaxation for physiological arousal) may be less effective than exposure therapy regarding cognitive, behavioral, and physiological responses (Menzies & Clarke, 1995).

In vivo exposure has been found to be efficacious in both one-session and multiple expanded-spaced treatments. One session intervention, also referred to as *massed exposure*, involves exposure during one session that lasts two to three times longer than normal. Öst and colleagues found that one massed session was as effective as five sessions of exposure in treating a variety of specific phobias (e.g., flying phobia; Öst, Brandberg, & Alm, 1997). However, long-term outcomes from massed practice may not be as beneficial. For example, for persons with spider phobias, expanded-spaced exposure over four sessions resulted in less frequent return of fear and greater generalization to novel spiders as compared to one session of mass exposure (Rowe & Craske, 1998).

Technological advances have been applied to exposure treatment of specific phobias. For example, *virtual reality* (VR) permits active participation within a computer-generated, three-dimensional virtual world, incorporating difference senses, movement, and environmental stimuli to enhance the authenticity of the stimulus. VR permits exposure therapy within the confines of the therapist's office, saving time and money. Furthermore, there is greater control over the stimulus. Studies have demonstrated the efficacy of virtual exposure to be equivalent to that of *in vivo* exposure (e.g., Emmelkamp et al., 2002).

On the down side, exposure therapy may not be effective for all patients. One reason for failure may entail the practice of safety behaviors during this intervention. For example, patients may hold their breath, search for environmental reassurances, or hold onto a table to avoid fainting. It is important that the patient be prevented from engaging in such safety behaviors in order for optimal habituation to occur.

Flooding. Flooding is an anxiety-reduction tactic similar to exposure. However, rather than a gradual encounter with the feared stimulus as conducted in exposure, flooding entails repeated exposure to stimuli identified at the top of the patient's fear hierarchy. Whereas flooding promotes habituation, the therapist needs to be cautious when implementing this intensive intervention and must ensure that the patient is properly prepared. Similar to other exposure-based treatment approaches, each session is conducted until the patient's subjective anxiety (e.g., SUDS) returns to baseline level or other appropriate criteria in order for meaningful extinction to occur.

Applied Relaxation. Applied relaxation entails using a variety of learned relaxation skills when facing a distressing situation. Such skills including diaphragmatic breathing, progressive muscle relaxation, visualization, and autogenic training. Once they have mastered these skills in controlled environments (e.g., therapist's office, at home in a quiet room), patients can apply them in real-life situations that entail being confronted with feared stimuli. Applied relaxation has been demonstrated to significantly decrease arousal regarding specific phobias (Öst, Sterner, & Fellenius, 1989).

Systematic desensitization combines relaxation with graded imaginal exposure. This intervention has been demonstrated to be effective in treating certain phobias (e.g., flying; Capafons, Sosa, & Avero, 2001). Humor desensitization, or coupling humor rather that relaxation with the feared stimulus, has also been found in one study to be as effective as traditional systematic desensitization in treating spider phobias (Ventis, Higbee, & Murdock, 2001).

Goal 2: Decrease Vasovagal Reactions

Unlike the other specific phobias, reactions to blood–injection–injury (BII) phobias often result in *vasovagal* reactions (e.g., syncope, which is a sudden brief loss of consciousness, and bradycardia, which involves atrial fibrillation). The reason for this unique phobic reaction is unknown. However, there is some evidence that BII concerns about injections are more related to fear, whereas faintness is associated with disgust and concerns about blood (Schienle, Stark, Walter, & Vaitl, 2003). In treating BII phobias, it is important to explain to patients that fainting is a response to decreased blood pressure. Consequently, treatment for BII have involved techniques aimed at increasing blood pressure in order to prevent the fainting response (e.g., applied tension).

Goal-Specific Assessment Tools

* *Blood–Injection Symptom Scale* (Page, Bennett, Carter, Smith, & Woodmore, 1997): assesses anxiety, tension, and faintness due to blood and injections.

Goal-Specific Potential Interventions

* Exposure therapy
* Applied tension
* Respiratory control

Exposure Therapy.   Exposure-based interventions have been found to be effective for blood phobias (Öst, Lindahl, Sterner, & Jerremalm, 1984), but should include cues relating to bodily mutilation, loss of control, and fears of death.

Applied Tension.   Applied tension involves having patients repeatedly tense their major muscle groups in an effort to *increase* blood pressure and, thus, prevent vasovagal reactions. Patients are first taught this skill in a relaxed environment and then directed to implement it during exposure to stimuli involving either blood, injection, or injury. Some research indicates that applied tension is more effective than exposure only (Öst, Fellenius, & Sterner, 1991), where a single, massed session is equally as effective as a 5-session intervention (Hellstroem, Fellenius, & Öst, 1996).

Another approach to applied tension involves inducing a state of anger. It has been demonstrated that patients who engage in anger imagery, and thus provoke anger in themselves, can decrease fainting (Marks, 1988).

Respiratory Control. In an effort to decrease hyperventilation that contributes to vasovagal reactions, controlled respiration may be beneficial for some patients. This technique simply entails monitoring and regulating the rate (i.e., enhance slower respiration) and depth (i.e., moderate respiration, avoiding both shallow and excessively deep inhalation) of one's breaths (Foulds, 1993). This is similar to deep breathing.

Goal 3: Decrease Dysfunctional Beliefs

Dysfunctional cognitions have also been found to be causally related to specific phobias. Distortions may be the result of phobia-specific schemas that reinforce the perceived dangerous nature of the fear stimuli. Cognitive distortions may include certain informational biases (e.g., selective attention and memory bias), exaggeration of threat, and the probability of danger. What is important to assess is the specific *meaning* that the patient attaches to the phobic stimuli, as well as the consequent experience of anxiety (e.g., "I'm going to have a heart attack if I go near the water"). Disconfirming evidence tends not to be sought or registered. Distorted thinking, including catastrophic thoughts about the consequences associated with contact with a feared stimulus, can instigate fear and avoidance. According to a cognitive model of phobias, early learning experiences tend to engender specific beliefs about the feared stimuli that lead to selective focus, evaluation, and coping strategies regarding the feared stimuli (Beck, Emery, & Greenberg, 1985).

Goal-Specific Assessment Tools

- *Dental Cognitions Questionnaire* (de Jongh, Muris, Schoenmakers, & ter Horst, 1995): assesses frequency and conviction of negative cognitions regarding dental procedures.
- *Mutilation Questionnaire* (Klorman, Hastings, Weerts, Melamed, & Lang, 1974): assesses cognitions related to blood, injury, and mutilation.
- *Spider Phobia Beliefs Questionnaire* (Arntz, Lavy, Van den Berg, & Van Rijsoort, 1993): assesses fearful beliefs about spiders.

Goal-Specific Potential Interventions

- Cognitive restructuring
- Cost-benefit analysis
- Guided positive imagery

Cognitive Restructuring. Cognitive restructuring can help alter dysfunctional beliefs related to specific phobia. With cognitive restructuring, patients learn to provide alternative interpretations regarding, for example, the consequences of being confronted with a feared stimulus (e.g., fear of "going crazy" if confronted by a spider). One specific technique that may be useful is having the patient identify the *probability* of their feared event, rather than relying on the fact that it is *possible*. Furthermore, patients can be taught to expect some anxiety and adopt a belief that they can handle such anxiety. The use of positive self-statements to modify negative automatic thoughts can also enhance self-efficacy and participation in other CBT interventions.

Cognitive restructuring can decrease the fear and panic associated with specific phobias (Booth & Rachman, 1992). However, because cognitive distortions may prevent optimal participation of the patient in other CBT interventions, cognitive restructuring aimed at changing the patients' maladaptive thoughts can also be an important adjunct to other treatments such as exposure. Altering the *perception* of threat may be an essential ingredient for effective CBT.

Cost-Benefit Analysis.   In an effort to address dysfunctional thoughts about danger and vulnerability related to the phobia, patients can be encouraged to develop a cost-benefit analysis of their beliefs and resulting behaviors. Here, the patient identifies a schema-confirming thought (e.g., "elevators can fall, so I should not get into them"). The patient then ascertains costs to this thought (e.g., "I am extremely limited in places where I can work and live"), as well as benefits (e.g., "I will save myself from falling in an elevator"). Furthermore, the patient is asked to identify the consequences of *not* abiding by this thought. By developing this discrepancy, patients are able to gain a better understanding of the impairment caused by their phobia, thus motivating change in their thinking and behaviors.

Guided Positive Imagery.   Cognitive distortions and phobic schema result in diminished perceived control or ability to cope with a feared stimulus. Positive guided imagery can help patients combat dysfunctional thoughts, as well as develop an alternative perspective toward the feared stimulus. In the induction, the therapist provides vivid imagery of the patient successfully facing the feared stimulus. Alternatively, if such a confrontation causes too much distress, the induction is based on an occasion *after* the patient has successfully faced the fear. The patient is guided through his or her thoughts, feelings, and behaviors, as well as the reactions of significant people in his or her life. This is similar to the approach advocated by Nezu and colleagues (e.g., Nezu, Nezu, Friedman,

Faddis, & Houts, 1998) with regard to the use of visualization to help individuals cope more effectively with stressful problems.

Additional Instrumental Outcome Goals/Treatment Target

Secondary treatment targets for specific phobia may include:

- *Improve Medical Health.* Certain phobias (e.g., injection or dental phobias) may result in certain health risks because of avoidance of the feared stimuli, resulting in diminished self-care. For example, injection-phobic patients with multiple sclerosis have been found initially unable to give themselves needed self-injections (Mohr, Cox, Epstein, & Boudewyn, 2002). CBT aimed at enhancing self-efficacy and decreasing anxiety assisted these individuals with overcoming their fears and avoidance. Similarly, cancer patients with claustrophobia were able to cope under radiation following CBT (Steggles, 1999).
- *Increase Self-Efficacy.* Enhancing self-efficacy will permit more confidence in individuals' ability to cope with their feared stimulus. Self-efficacy is related to better CBT outcomes for specific phobia (Zoellner, Echiverri, & Craske, 2000). It has been demonstrated that various CBT treatments including *in vivo* (Goetestam & Hokstad, 2002) and virtual reality (Botella, Banos, Villa, Perpina, & Garcia-Palacios, 2000) exposure increase self-efficacy. Furthermore, guided positive imagery and problem-solving therapy may help enhance a sense of self-efficacy.
- *Improve Social Relationships.* Fears related to specific phobia may adversely influence social relationships. For example, there may be strains between an individual with a flying phobia and his partner who wants to vacation via plane. Therapeutic interventions may entail co-joint sessions where psychoeducation regarding phobias (e.g., it is not a deliberate choice for the patient to have this phobia) is provided to both partners.
- *Decrease General Stress.* Another possible secondary treatment goal for a patient with a specific phobia includes decreasing overall general stress levels. Possible intervention approaches include various behavioral stress management strategies to reduce stress-related physical symptomatology, as well as coping skills training strategies, such

as Problem-Solving Therapy, to help the patient manage stressful negative life events more effectively.

- *Enhance Performance at Work.* A patient with a severe specific phobia may avoid certain job positions or responsibilities because of the fear (e.g., executives with a flying phobia; painters avoiding certain jobs because of fear of heights).
- *Decrease Relapse.* Relapse is more likely to occur when assessing fear to novel stimuli not specifically addressed during exposure therapy. It appears that exposure to a variety of feared stimuli, as compared to a single stimulus, results in decreased relapse (Rowe & Craske, 1998). In addition, spaced exposure may lead to less relapse than massed exposure. Conversely, distraction during exposure may result in greater relapse.

ADDITIONAL CLINICAL CONSIDERATIONS

People with specific phobias often do not seek therapeutic intervention or they belittle the negative impact it has on their lives (e.g., due to concern for how others may perceive their phobia). Thus, the clinician may identify a specific phobia in a patient who has sought therapy for another problem. To facilitate commitment to treatment for the specific phobia, the therapist may provide a rationale for specific phobias that the patient can understand. For example, explanations of the adaptive nature of certain phobias from an evolutionary sense (e.g., "cavemen who feared animals were the ones who survived and passed on their genes") can reduce the stigma associated with such fears. Predictors of CBT success include perceived credibility of the treatment, expectancy of positive outcomes, and overall motivation for therapy (Hellstroem & Öst, 1996). Further, willingness to tolerate discomfort and practice treatment tactics regularly increases overall treatment effectiveness. If motivation is low, it may be beneficial for the therapist to engage in psychoeducation of the CBT model and/or cognitive restructuring to enhance treatment expectation and motivation before commencing other interventions. In contrast, depression and medications predict worse outcomes. For example, patients who undergo exposure therapy while taking benzodiazepines often relapse when they terminate their medications. Tranquilizers may prevent the needed experience of anxiety, thus inhibiting habituation.

The effects of CBT on *co-morbidity* have also been assessed. The presence of additional specific phobias does not appear to have adverse effects on exposure therapy for a given specific phobia (Kahan, Tanzer, Darvin, & Borer, 2000) and may, in fact, benefit phobias not specifically treated. However, patients with greater overall anxiety (Muris, Mayer, & Merckelbach, 1998) or depression or agoraphobia (Nutzinger, Cayiroglu, Gruenberger, & Kieffer, 1990) appear to have less beneficial outcomes.

CBT can be effective for persons with developmental disorders. One study found the use of exposure, modeling, and differential reinforcement was effective at reducing a BII phobia in a man with mild mental retardation (Hagopian, Crockett, & Keeney, 2001). Individuals with mental retardation have also been effectively treated for dog phobias using exposure therapy (Erfanian & Miltenberger, 1990). Furthermore, systematic desensitization and modeling were effective at reducing dog phobia for persons with Down's Syndrome (Freeman, 1997).

Finally, cultural issues should be considered when working with specific phobia. For example, individuals from India are more likely to have phobias related to animals, the dark, and inclement weather, whereas those from the United Kingdom report greater agoraphobia and social phobia (Chambers, Yeragani, & Keshavan, 1988). Hispanic Americans and African Americans have higher rates of specific phobia, a consideration the clinician should take into account when working with these populations.

REFERENCES

American Psychiatric Association (2000). *Diagnostic and statistical manual of mental disorders* (ed. 4, text revision). Washington, DC: American Psychiatric Press.

Antony, M. M., Orsillo, S. M., & Roemer, L. (2001). *Practitioner's guide to empirically based measures of anxiety.* New York: Kluwer Academic/Plenum.

Arntz, A., Lavy, E., Van den Berg, G., & Van Rijsoort, S. (1993). Negative beliefs of spider phobics: A psychometric evaluation of the Spider Phobia Beliefs Questionnaire. *Advances in Behaviour Research & Therapy, 15,* 257–277.

Beck, A. T., Emery, G., & Greenberg, R. L. (1985). *Anxiety disorders and phobias: A cognitive perspective.* New York: Basic Books.

Booth, R., & Rachman, S. (1992). The reduction of claustrophobia: I. *Behaviour Research and Therapy, 30,* 207–221.

Botella, C., Banos, R. M., Villa, H., Perpina, C., & Garcia-Palacios, A. (2000). Virtual reality in the treatment of claustrophobic fear: A controlled, multiple-baseline design. *Behavior Therapy, 31,* 583–595.

Capafons, J. I., Sosa, C. D., & Avero, P. (2001). Systematic desensitization in the treatment of fear of flying. *Psychology in Spain, 2,* 11–16.

Chambers, J., Yeragani, V. K., & Keshavan, M. S. (1988). Phobias in India and the United Kingdom: A trans-cultural study. *Acta Psychiatrica Scandinavica, 74*, 388–391.

Cohen, D. C. (1977). Comparison of self-report and overt-behavioral procedures for assessing acrophobia. *Behavior Therapy, 8,* 23.

de Jongh, A., Muris, P., Schoenmakers, N., & ter Horst, G. (1995). Negative cognitions of dental phobics: Reliability and validity of the dental cognitions questionnaire. *Behaviour Research and Therapy, 33,* 507–515.

Emmelkamp, P. M. G., Krijn, M., Hulsbosch, A. M., de Vries, S., Schuemie, M. J., & van der Mast, C. A. P. G. (2002). Virtual reality treatment versus exposure in vivo: A comparative valuation in acrophobia. *Behaviour Research and Therapy, 40,* 509–516.

Erfanian, N., & Miltenberger, R. G. (1990). Contact desensitization in the treatment of dog phobias in persons who have mental retardation. *Behavioral Residential Treatment, 5,* 55–60.

Foulds, J. (1993). Cerebral circulation during treatment of blood-injury phobia: A case study. *Behavioural Psychotherapy, 21,* 137–146.

Freeman, S. (1997). Treating a dog phobia in a person with Down's syndrome by use of systematic desensitization and modeling. *British Journal of Learning Disabilities, 25,* 154–157.

Goetestam, K. G. (2002). One session group treatment of spider phobia by direct or modeled exposure. *Cognitive Behaviour Therapy, 31,* 18–24.

Goetestam, K. G., & Hokstad, A. (2002). One session treatment of spider phobia in a group setting with rotating active exposure. *European Journal of Psychiatry, 16,* 129–134.

Hagopian, L. P., Crockett, J. L., & Keeney, K. M. (2001). Multicomponent treatment for blood-injury-injection phobia in a young man with mental retardation. *Research in Developmental Disabilities, 22,* 141–149.

Haug, T., Brenne, L., Johnsen, B. H., Berntzen, D., Gotestam, K. G., & Hugdahl, K. (1987). A three-systems analysis of fear of flying: A comparison of a consonant vs. a non-consonant treatment method. *Behaviour Research and Therapy, 25,* 187–194.

Hellstroem, K., Fellenius, J., & Öst, L. G. (1996). One versus five sessions of applied tension in the treatment of blood phobia. *Behaviour Research and Therapy, 34,* 101–112.

Hellstrom, K., & Öst, L. G. (1995). One-session therapist directed exposure vs. two forms of manual directed self-exposure in the treatment of spider phobia. *Behaviour Research and Therapy, 33,* 959–965.

Hellstroem, K., & Öst, L. G. (1996). Prediction of outcome in the treatment of specific phobia: A cross validation study. *Behaviour Research and Therapy, 34,* 403–411.

Kahan, M., Tanzer, J., Darvin, D., & Borer, F. (2000). Virtual reality-assisted cognitive-behavioral treatment for fear of flying: Acute treatment and follow-up. *Cyberpsychology and Behavior, 3,* 387–392.

Kleinknecht, R. A., Thorndike, R. M., & Walls, M. M. (1996). Factorial dimensions and correlates of blood, injury, injection and related medical fears: Cross validation of the medical fear survey. *Behaviour Research and Therapy, 34,* 323–331.

Marks, I. M. (1988). Blood-injury phobia: A review. *American Journal of Psychiatry, 145,* 1207–1213.

Menzies, R. G., & Clarke, J. C. (1995). Individual response patterns, treatment matching, and the effects of behavioural and cognitive interventions for acrophobia.
Anxiety, Stress, and Coping, 8, 141–160.

Mohr, D. C., Cox, D., Epstein, L., & Boudewyn, A. (2002). Teaching patients to self-
inject: Pilot study of a treatment for injection anxiety and phobia in multiple
sclerosis patients prescribed injectable medications. *Journal of Behavior Therapy
and Experimental Psychiatry, 33,* 39–47.

Muris, P., Mayer, B., & Merckelbach, H. (1998). Trait anxiety as a predictor of behaviour
therapy outcome in spider phobia. *Behavioural and Cognitive Psychotherapy, 26,*
87–91.

Nezu, A. M., Nezu, C. M., Friedman, S. H., Faddis, S., & Houts, P. S. (1998). *Helping
cancer patients cope: A problem-solving approach.* Washington, DC: American Psychological Association.

Nutzinger, D. O., Cayiroglu, S., Gruenberger, J., & Kieffer, W. (1990). Prognosis of
cardiac phobia. *Psychopathology, 23,* 63–72.

Öst, L. G. (1996). One-session group treatment of spider phobia. *Behaviour Research
and Therapy, 34,* 707–715.

Öst, L. G., Brandberg, M., & Alm, T. (1997). One versus five sessions of exposure in
the treatment of flying phobia. *Behaviour Research and Therapy, 35,* 987–996.

Öst, L. G., Fellenius, J., & Sterner, U. (1991). Applied tension, exposure in vivo, and
tension-only in the treatment of blood phobia. *Behaviour Research and Therapy,
29,* 561–574.

Öst, L. G., Lindahl, I. L., Sterner, U., & Jerremalm, A. (1984). Exposure in vivo vs applied
relaxation in the treatment of blood phobia. *Behaviour Research and Therapy, 22,*
205–216.

Öst, L. G., Sterner, U., & Fellenius, J. (1989). Applied tension, applied relaxation, and
the combination in the treatment of blood phobia. *Behaviour Research and Therapy,
27,* 109–121.

Page, A. C., Bennett, K. S., Carter, O., Smith, J., & Woodmore, K. (1997). The Blood-
Injection Symptom Scale (BISS): Assessing a structure of phobic symptoms elicited
by blood and injections. *Behaviour Research and Therapy, 35,* 457–464.

Radomsky, A. S., Rachman, S., Thordarson, D. S., McIsaac, H. K., & Teachman, B. A.
(2001). The Claustrophobia Questionnaire. *Journal of Anxiety Disorders, 15,*
287–297.

Rowe, M. K., & Craske, M. G. (1998). Effects of an expanding-spaced vs. massed
exposure schedule on fear reduction and return of fear. *Behaviour Research and
Therapy, 36,* 701–717.

Schienle, A., Stark, R., Walter, B., & Vaitl, D. (2003). The connection between disgust
sensitivity and blood-related fears, faintness symptoms, and obsessive-compulsive-
ness in a non-clinical sample. *Anxiety, Stress, and Coping, 16,* 185–193.

Steggles, S. (1999). The use of cognitive-behavioral treatment including hypnosis for
claustrophobia in cancer patients. *American Journal of Clinical Hypnosis, 41,*
319–326.

Stouthard, M. E., Mellenbergh, G. J., & Hoogstraten, J. (1993). Assessment of dental
anxiety: A facet approach. *Anxiety, Stress, & Coping, 6,* 89–105.

Szymanski, J., & O'Donohue, W. (1995). Fear of Spiders Questionnaire. *Journal of Behavior Therapy and Experimental Psychiatry, 26,* 31–34.

Ventis, W. L., Higbee, G., & Murdock, S. A. (2001). Using humor in systematic desensitization to reduce fear. *Journal of General Psychology, 128,* 241–253.

Zoellner, L. A., Echiverri, A., & Craske, M. G. (2000). Processing of phobic stimuli and its relationship to outcome. *Behaviour Research and Therapy, 38,* 921–931.

7

Panic Disorder and Agoraphobia

GENERAL DESCRIPTION AND DIAGNOSTIC ISSUES

Panic disorder with (PDA) or without (PD) agoraphobia can be an extremely debilitating disorder that is associated with psychological, social, and occupational impairment and diminished quality of life. In essence, panic disorder can be thought of as a learned fear of certain bodily sensations, whereas agoraphobia is the behavioral reaction in anticipation of experiencing such bodily sensations or a full-blown panic attack.

Panic disorder is characterized by recurrent, unexpected panic attacks. According to the *Diagnostic and Statistical Manual of Mental Disorders, Fourth Edition Text Revision* (DSM-IV-TR; American Psychiatric Association, 2000), a panic attack is a discrete period of intense fear or discomfort in which four or more of the following symptoms develop abruptly and reach a peak within 10 minutes: palpitations; pounding heart or accelerated heart rate; sweating, trembling, or shaking; sensations of shortness of breath or smothering; feelings of choking; chest pain or discomfort; nausea or abdominal distress; feelings of being dizzy, unsteady, lightheaded, or faint; derealization or depersonalization; fear of losing control or going crazy; fear of dying; paresthesias; and chills or hot flushes. In addition, at least one of the attacks is followed by 1 month or more of the following:

persistent concern about having additional attacks; worry about the implications of the attack or its consequences (e.g., losing control, having a
heart attack, "going crazy"); or a significant change in behavior related to
the attacks.

In an effort to prevent future panic attacks, people engage in safety
behaviors, which often entails avoiding places they fear will trigger the
panic attacks. Thus, many individuals with panic disorder also experience
agoraphobia. DSM-IV-TR defines agoraphobia as significant anxiety about
being in places or situations from which escape might be difficult or
embarrassing or in which help may not be available in the event of having
a panic attack or panic-like symptoms. Agoraphobic fears typically center
on specific situations such as being outside the home alone, being in a
crowd or standing in a line, being on a bridge, or traveling in a bus, train,
or automobile. Such situations are avoided, are endured with marked
distress about having a panic attack or panic-like symptoms, and often
require the presence of a companion. Individuals' avoidance of these situations may impair their ability to travel or work or to carry out various
responsibilities (e.g., grocery shopping, taking children to the doctor). For
both panic disorder and agoraphobia, the anxiety or phobic avoidance is
not better accounted for by another mental disorder, the direct physiological effects of a substance (e.g., drugs), or a general medical condition.

Whereas panic disorder and agoraphobia frequently co-occur, they can
exist in isolation. The fundamental characteristics of agoraphobia without
accompanying panic disorder are similar to those of PDA, except that fear
is centered on the occurrence of incapacitating or extremely embarrassing
panic-like symptoms or limited-symptom attacks rather than full-blown
panic attacks. The "panic-like symptoms" include any of the 13 symptoms
listed above for panic attack or other symptoms that may be incapacitating
or embarrassing (e.g., loss of bladder control).

In over 70% of cases, a specific stressor can be identified as the precursor
to the development of PD/PDA. Most often stressors are interpersonal (e.g.,
argument with spouse) or related to physical well-being (e.g., death in
family, adverse experience with drugs). Initial panic attacks also often
occur outside the home in situations in which loss of control (e.g., driving),
adverse appraisal (e.g., job interview), perceived unsafe location (e.g.,
unknown places), or entrapment (e.g., elevators) is particularly menacing.
The panic symptoms are interpreted as dangerous and the patient develops
a fear that they will return. In an effort to decrease the likelihood of the
feared calamity, patients become hypervigilant, continually scanning their
body, or engage in certain safety behaviors that includes avoidance.

Lifetime prevalence for PD/PDA is 3.5% to 5.3% (Kessler et al., 1994).
Women are at a two-fold increased risk for developing PD/PDA compared

to men (Katerndahl & Realini, 1993). The median age of onset is 24 years, although it can occur at any age. Symptoms are typically chronic, with an overall remission rate of 39% and recurrence rate of 82% in women and 51% in men (Yonkers et al., 1998).

Differential Diagnostic Issues

Panic symptoms and avoidance are not limited to PD/PDA, as these characteristics occur within several different anxiety and mood disorders. However, outside of PD/PDA, panic attacks are often situationally bound. In particular, *specific phobia* is characterized by fear and avoidance of a particular stimulus. Fears in *social phobia* are centered on a negative evaluation from others unrelated to panic, leading to avoidance of certain social situations. *Posttraumatic stress disorder* is distinguished by fears related to a specific, life-threatening event, and avoidance is a result of attempting to decrease one's sense of impending danger. Thoughts of fear and resulting avoidance behavior to prevent the fear obsession differentiates *obsessive-compulsive disorder*. In *generalized anxiety disorder*, panic attacks are absent and anxiety is characterized by widespread worry. *Depression* can entail avoidance of situations, but this is related more to a decreased interest and depressed mood rather than fear of panic behavior or the loss of control.

Other psychiatric disorders must also be differentiated from PD/PDA. In *schizophrenia*, delusions and hallucinations may produce irrational and excessive fear of objects or situations, but these fears are not related to panic attacks. Similar to PD/PDA, *paranoid* individuals may isolate themselves and withdraw socially. However, unlike PD/PDA, this is caused by a perceived malevolent intent of another person.

Certain health conditions can present with panic-like symptoms and need to be ruled out before a diagnosis of PD/PDA becomes appropriate. Such medical ailments include endocrine disorders (e.g., hyperthyroidism, hypoglycemia, menopause), cardiovascular disorders (e.g., mitrovalve prolapse, cardiac arrhythmias), respiratory disorders (e.g., asthma, chronic bronchitis), neurological disorders (e.g., vestibular dysfunction, multiple sclerosis), and substance-related anxiety due to intoxication (e.g., cocaine, caffeine) or withdrawal (e.g., opiates, alcohol).

Co-Morbidity Issues

PD/PDA commonly occur in conjunction with other psychiatric symptomatology. Approximately 59% of patients have a comorbid mood or anxiety diagnosis, including major depressive disorder (23%), generalized anxiety disorder (16%), and social or specific phobia (15%). Non-panic disorders typically precede PD/PDA, although the reverse may also be true. For example, depression may be related to a sense of helplessness that patients feel regarding their inability to control the panic attacks. In addition, 25%–60% of people with PD/PDA also meet criteria for a personality disorder, most commonly avoidant and dependent.

ASSESSMENT OF DISORDER

A detailed evaluation is important when working with persons with PD/PDA. Below are specific psychological assessments for this disorder (see Antony, Orsillo, and Roemer, 2001, for a review of such assessment tools).

Clinician Ratings

- *Anxiety Disorders Interview Schedule for DSM-IV: Lifetime Version* (DiNardo, Brown, & Barlow, 1994): assesses current and lifetime DSM-IV diagnoses of anxiety, mood, and substance use.
- *Panic and Agoraphobia Scale* (Bandelow, 1999): assesses severity of panic disorder with and without agoraphobia; can be administered by clinician or as self-report.
- *Panic Disorder Severity Scale* (Shear et al., 1992): assesses severity of panic disorders including frequency, distress during the attack, and associated avoidance.

Self-Report Measures

- *Albany Panic and Phobia Questionnaire* (Rapee, Craske, & Barlow, 1995): assesses fear and avoidance of bodily sensations and agoraphobic situations.
- *Anxiety Sensitivity Scale* (Peterson & Reiss, 1993; Reiss, Peterson, Gursky, & McNally, 1986): assesses fear of anxiety-related symptoms.
- *Anxiety Sensitivity Index-Revised 36* (Taylor & Cox, 1998a): assesses fear of anxiety-related symptoms with numerous subscales (e.g., fear

of respiratory symptoms, publicly observable anxiety, cognitive discontrol).

- *Daily Mood Record* (Craske, Barlow, & Meadow, 2000): assesses emotional reaction to concerns about having a panic attack.
- *Panic Attack Questionnaire-Revised* (Cox, Norton, & Swinson, 1992): assesses numerous factors related to panic attacks (e.g., symptoms, cognitions, triggers, and coping).

GENERAL THERAPY GOALS

Ultimate Outcome Goals

Given the potentially severe impairment that can result from PD/PDA, ultimate outcome goals are focused on enhancing the patient's quality of life and decreasing his or her social, occupational, and functional impairment. Treatment is geared toward decreasing panic attacks and agoraphobia. Furthermore, amelioration of interpersonal relationship difficulties and associated substance abuse (e.g., prescription or nonprescription drugs) may be important ultimate goals. Finally, therapeutic strategies involve enhancing adaptive and effective coping skills.

Major Instrumental Outcome Goals/Treatment Targets

Major instrumental outcome goals for PD/PDA include:

- Decrease catastrophic interpretations of arousal
- Decrease physiological arousal
- Decrease safety behaviors

Goal 1: Decrease Catastrophic Interpretations of Arousal

PD/PDA is often characterized as "fear of fear" where patients fear the recurrence of a panic attack. Such fear develops as a result of catastrophic interpretations of physiological arousal (Beck & Emery, 1985; Clark, 1986). Specifically, *internal* (e.g., bodily sensations) or *external* (e.g., place from which escape is difficult) triggers stimulate the perception of threat. This perceived danger leads to apprehension, which stimulates somatic sensations (e.g., increased heart rate). The physiological arousal is interpreted as catastrophic, leading to greater anticipation of danger, and the sequence continues. Thus, a vicious, self-perpetuating cycle maintains the fear (Clark, 1986).

Ambiguous somatic symptoms are often interpreted as forecasting impending doom (Clark, Salkovskis, Öst, & Breitholtz, 1997). Catastrophic interpretations can take many forms. For example, heart palpitations may be interpreted as having a heart attack, dizziness as impending fainting, a lump in one's throat as choking to death, or mental blocking as going crazy (Hoffart, 1993). Beck (1988) proposed that catastrophic interpretations fall into three categories: biological (e.g., death, heart attack), mental (e.g., insanity), and behavioral (e.g., loss of control).

Patients are often unaware of the interoceptive conditioning (i.e., fear associated with internal physiological arousal such as elevated heart rate) or the misappraisal of bodily feelings, causing a perception that panic attacks occur unexpectedly and without warning. Thus, there is a lack of perceived control over the panic, which leads to further increased arousal. It has been demonstrated that change in catastrophic beliefs results in decreased panic (Hoffart, 1998).

Goal-Specific Assessment Tools

- *Agoraphobic Cognitions Questionnaire* (Chambless, Caputo, Bright, & Gallagher, 1984): assesses fearful cognitions related to panic attacks and agoraphobia.
- *Anxiety Sensitivity Profile* (Taylor & Cox, 1998b): assesses cognitive features of anxiety sensitivity (e.g., physical sensations).
- *Body Sensations Interpretation Questionnaire* (Clark, Salkovskis, Öst, & Breitholtz, 1997): assesses misinterpretations about anxiety-related somatic sensations, other body symptoms (e.g., health), social events, and other external events (e.g., general worries).
- *Dysfunctional Thought Record* (Beck, 1995): identifies situations that trigger automatic thoughts, actual automatic thoughts, emotions, adaptive counter thoughts, and emotional and cognitive consequences.
- *Agoraphobic Self-Statements Questionnaire* (van Hout, Emmelkamp, Koopmans, Boegels, & Bouman, 2001): assesses frequency of positive and negative self-statements about agoraphobia avoidance.

Goal-Specific Potential Interventions

- Cognitive restructuring
- Interoceptive exposure
- Focused cognitive therapy

Cognitive Restructuring. Intervention strategies to help decrease unfounded catastrophic thinking are based on cognitive restructuring principles. Conceptually, cognitive restructuring can be thought of as an umbrella term that encompasses several specific therapy strategies: rational-emotive therapy (e.g., Ellis, 1994), cognitive therapy (Beck et al., 1985), and self-instructional training (Meichenbaum, 1977). Whereas differences among these three approaches exist, all involve helping patients to better identify and then alter maladaptive thoughts. When treating cognitive dysfunctions in persons with PD/PDA, individuals are asked to identify those situations that serve as triggers of panic (e.g., getting on an elevator) and then to identify various fear-related negative automatic thoughts (e.g., "I cannot escape if I have a panic attack. I will die in the elevator"). They are then asked to ascertain the consequences of such thoughts (e.g., increased heart rate, heightened feelings of anxiety). Once patients learn to identify distorted thinking, they are instructed to develop alternate, more rational thoughts and beliefs. For example, alternative hypotheses are developed that entail somatic symptoms being a cause of anxiety rather than a catastrophic event.

Interoceptive Exposure. Because "actions speak louder than words," interoceptive exposure can facilitate a decrease in catastrophic interpretation of physical sensations. This therapeutic technique, in which patients are exposed to somatic cues, breaches the association between physical sensations and fear by demonstrating that such somatic sensations neither arise because of impending danger, nor result in the predicted catastrophic consequences.

In interoceptive exposure, patients experience panic-like sensations. Panic symptoms are induced that specifically mimic the patient's panic attack. Because patients often report symptoms of hyperventilation, panic may be induced by having the patient breath rapidly into a paper bag or through a straw. However, other techniques may better mirror panic symptoms, such as spinning in a chair (dizziness), physical exercise (shortness of breath), or reading or listening to distressing feared cognitions.

During the experience of panic symptoms, patients are asked questions to allow them to discover that symptoms are not, in fact, a sign of impending catastrophe. Questions may include: "How do you feel after this experience?" "What thoughts and images come to mind?" and "What conclusions can you make regarding the similarities between how you feel now and when you have a panic attack?" This allows patients to alter their catastrophic interpretations of the somatic sensations.

Focused Cognitive Therapy. Focused cognitive therapy is a manualized therapy (Beck, 1992) that specifically targets the catastrophic misinterpretations of bodily sensations. FCT uses a variety of techniques including psychoeducation, panic inductions, behavioral experiments, identifying and refuting misinterpretations, decreasing avoidant behaviors, and teaching adaptive coping skills (e.g., relaxation and controlled breathing). This specific intervention approach has been found to be effective in decreasing catastrophic misinterpretations and panic symptoms (Brown, Beck, Newman, & Beck, 1997).

Goal 2: Decrease Physiological Arousal

Patients with PD/PDA demonstrate enhanced awareness and fear of their physiological arousal, resulting in an increase in the arousal. Thus, a propagating cycle is formed. For example, as heart rate is perceived to increase, attention becomes more focused on this bodily sensation. Patients then become more anxious that something is wrong, causing an increase in heart rate. In addition, individuals with PD/PDA are often hypervigilant, continually scanning their bodies for signs of somatic problems. This heightened attention to somatic sensations serves to increase their presence and the worry that accompanies them. In an effort to stop this propelling cycle, intervention is aimed at decreasing a patient's heightened focus on and experience of physiological arousal.

Physiological arousal often involves hyperventilation. Hyperventilation results in lowered carbon dioxide levels in the blood, which can lead to feelings of dizziness. Hyperventilation has been implicated as an instigator of panic attacks.

Goal-Specific Assessment Tools

- *Body Sensation Questionnaire* (Chambless, Caputo, Bright, & Gallagher, 1984): assesses fear associated with somatic arousal sensations.
- *Body Vigilance Scale* (Schmidt, Lerew, & Trakowski, 1997): assesses level of attention on somatic sensations.

- *Panic Attack Record* (Craske, Barlow, & Meadows, 2000): assesses the severity of different somatic sensations related to panic attacks.

Goal-Specific Potential Interventions

- Distraction
- Relaxation training
- Respiratory control

Distraction. Distraction is beneficial in that it can be used both for immediate decrease in anxiety and to demonstrate patients' control over their angst. Patients are directed to use distraction when feelings of psychological and physical arousal occur. Examples include listening to or singing a song or having a conversation about a benign topic. Because attention is aimed elsewhere, distraction prevents the "downward spiral" of catastrophic thoughts, somatic sensations, and physiological arousal. Further, it provides evidence to patients that they *can* control their feared bodily sensations. It is important, however, to teach patients that distraction is not appropriate during other cognitive-behavioral techniques, such as exposure or cognitive restructuring.

Relaxation Training. Relaxation training is geared to help decrease physiological arousal in previously anxiety-provoking situations. To conduct this tactic, the patient is first taught to identify the signs and sources of physiological arousal. Then, progressive muscle relaxation is taught. Initially, patients learn to "tense–release" various muscles groups throughout the body; then "release only" these same muscle groups; and finally cued-control relaxation. Patients then practice applying the relaxation in stressful, nonphobic environments, and ultimately, in fear-related situations.

It is important to note that some patients with PD/PDA experience "relaxation-induced panic attacks" where relaxation paradoxically increases panic attacks. The reason for this is unknown. Thus, when providing relaxation training, the therapist should be attentive for the potential of this paradoxical occurrence.

Relaxation training is effective at reducing panic symptoms in both the short and long term (Öst, Westling, & Hellstroem, 1993). Moreover, relaxation also facilitates the retrieval of positive cognitions (Peveler & Johnston, 1986) which can aid other CBT interventions (e.g., cognitive restructuring).

Respiratory Control. The goal of breathing retraining, or respiratory control, is to inhibit the hyperventilation that can occur when patients feel anxious and that can lead to panic. This technique may start with interoceptive exposure via a rapid succession of short breaths to demonstrate that hyperventilation can cause panic symptoms. A discussion ensues about the erroneous catastrophic interpretations of somatic sensations. The patient then learns that controlled respiration involves slow (8–12 breaths per minute) diaphragmatic breathing. It is highlighted that such respiratory control cannot occur at the same time as hyperventilation. Diaphragmatic breathing is encouraged as a coping tool when the patient starts to feel anxious about a panic attack in an effort to decrease physiological arousal.

Goal 3: Decrease Safety Behaviors

Patients with PD/PDA often engage in safety behaviors or behaviors aimed at decreasing their anxiety. Avoidance is one type of safety behavior that is manifested as either evading internal (i.e., interoceptive) or external (e.g., agoraphobic-related situations) cues. Avoidance may be directed at particular places, as well as specific activities. For example, regarding interoceptive avoidance, behaviors that increase somatic sensations (e.g., exercise, eating heavy meals, sexual relations) may be avoided.

Regarding agoraphobia, onset of this type of avoidance is usually within a year of the initiation of repeated panic attacks. Patients with PD develop agoraphobia due to their conviction that certain situations where panic would be particularly harmful or embarrassing must be avoided. If the panic attacks are resolved, the agoraphobia often resolves as well. However, in some cases, the agoraphobia becomes chronic whether or not the person continues to experience panic attacks due to the negative reinforcement associated with the avoidance behavior.

Safety behaviors can also be seen in other forms. For example, patients often believe they are better able to confront a feared situation when accompanied by a companion. This "safe person," often a significant other, is perceived to be able to help the patient prevent the feared catastrophic events if panic symptoms develop. Additional examples of safety behaviors include clutching an object for fear of fainting, holding one's breath while walking through a crowd, carrying medication "just in case," or "white knuckling" the steering wheel while driving. These behaviors are negatively reinforced because panic usually does not occur while they are being performed. Further, magical thinking (e.g., "If I avoid public places, then I will not have a panic attack") helps to perpetuate and maintain such safety behaviors.

Treatment of these safety behaviors is important. For example, safety behaviors perpetuate catastrophic beliefs (Salkovskis, Clark, & Gelder,

1996). Furthermore, it has been demonstrated that global improvement following treatment is associated more with decreased avoidance than a reduction in panic (Basoglu et al., 1994)

Goal-Specific Assessment Tools

- *Behavioral Avoidance Test* (Craske, Barlow, & Meadows, 2000): assesses amount of avoidance and level of distress associated with confrontation of the previously avoided situations.
- *Phobic Avoidance Rating Scale* (Hoffart, Friis, & Martinsen, 1989): clinician rating that assesses severity of patient's agoraphobic avoidance.
- *Mobility Inventory for Agoraphobia* (Chambless, Caputo, Jasin, Gracely, & Williams, 1985): assesses severity of agoraphobia and panic attacks and location of perceived safety.
- *Texas Safety Maneuver Scale* (Kamphuis & Telch, 1998): assesses safety behaviors performed by individuals with panic disorder.

Goal-Specific Potential Interventions

- Exposure
- Safety signal perspective
- Guided mastery therapy
- Behavioral experiments
- Self-instructional training

Exposure.   Exposure therapy is important in the treatment of agoraphobic avoidance (Fava et al., 2001; van den, Arntz, & Hoekstra, 1994). The rationale for exposure of avoided situations lies in two-factor theory which posits that panic is paired with avoided situations via classical conditioning and then negatively reinforced via avoidance. Thus, patients do not learn to disconnect panic from these situations. Exposure for agoraphobia is usually conducted *in vivo* with systematically applied graded exposure. Patients develop a fear hierarchy that guides the exposure to progressively higher anxiety-provoking situations. Patients must remain in the fear setting until their SUDS level decreases at least 50%.

When conducting exposure, it is important for the patient to also stop performing safety behaviors. Discontinuation of safety behaviors during exposure predicts greater decreases in catastrophic thoughts and anxiety (Salkovskis, Clark, Hackmann, Wells, & Gelder, 1999).

Exposure can be conducted effectively within different contexts. For example, therapy may be implemented individually or in a group milieu. Both are equally effective at reducing agoraphobia and panic symptoms, although the former may better alleviate general anxiety and depressive symptoms (Neron, Lacroix, & Chaput, 1995). In addition, exposure can be massed, where treatment occurs in a significant block of time, or spaced, where intervention takes place over a longer period of time (e.g., 1 hour per week for several weeks). Whereas the former may be more effective, advantages of the latter include lower dropout and relapse rates.

As an important component of this intervention, patients are often assigned exposure assignments to perform on their own. Compliance with exposure homework predicts greater outcomes (Edelman & Chambless, 1993). In an effort to prevent safety behaviors, involvement in therapy from a significant other (e.g., during homework assignments) may be particularly important (Carter, Turovsky, & Barlow, 1994).

Guided Mastery Therapy.   Guided mastery therapy is based on self-efficacy theory, which posits that safety behaviors are executed because of a doubt in one's ability to cope effectively in the feared situation (Williams, 1990). That is, these safety behaviors are implemented in situations in which patients do not feel confident. Fear is conceptualized to be treated through *successful* performance-based treatment. Thus, the goal of guided mastery therapy is to enhance a sense of mastery of, or ability to effective cope with, feared situations. By encouraging patients to engage in increasingly more difficult activities, the therapist promotes proficiency in performance with the abandonment of safety behaviors. Therapist involvement needs to decrease quickly and patients are encouraged to engage in activities independently with the goal of increased self-efficacy. Guided mastery therapy has been found to be effective at decreasing safety behaviors, including avoidance (Hoffart, 1995a). Further, greater self-efficacy appears to predict less fear and avoidance following CBT (Hoffart, 1995b).

Safety Signal Perspective.   Safety signal perspective (Rachman, 1984) suggests that an overall treatment plan might be more effective if patients have perceived control over the exposure. Applying this concept in therapy, safety signals are available to patients to help decrease distress during exposure. An example entails having a patient meet a significant other inside the previously avoided shopping mall. The idea of encouraging the use of such safety signals was previously believed to hinder the benefits of exposure. However, it appears that this type of exposure is effective at decreasing agoraphobic avoidance (Sartory, Master, & Rachman, 1989). Nevertheless, it is important that the use of safety signal exposure be followed by pure exposure in order to prevent the patient's reliance on the safety signal.

Behavioral Experiments.   Behavioral experiments can be used with diverse rationale (e.g., test catastrophic thoughts), but are discussed here regarding their role in decreasing safety behaviors. Because patients are not always aware of their assumptions related to safety behaviors, this technique allows patients to identify the use and purpose of such behaviors, including agoraphobic avoidance. After identifying beliefs about what would happen in the absence of safety behaviors, patients test these hypotheses to determine if their predictions come true. For example, patients can be taught to try to *cause* a panic attack by not engaging in their safety behaviors.

Self-Instructional Training.   The goal of self-instructional training (Meichenbaum, 1977) is to replace maladaptive, self-defeating, anxiety-aggravating cognitions with more positive self-statements, which will then result in decreased reliance of safety behaviors. Patients are instructed to imagine themselves in fearful circumstances and articulate adaptive self-statements. For example a patient may imagine driving over a bridge without the accompaniment of a safety person. The therapist encourages the patient to repeat affirmations, such as "I can drive over this bridge all by myself. I will be OK." Patients then practice verbalizing these positive self-statements when engaging in the real-life feared situations. Self-instruction training aims to inhibit negative cognitions, prompting decreased arousal and safety behaviors, as well as increased adaptive coping.

Additional Instrumental Outcome Goals/Treatment Targets

Secondary treatment targets for PD/PDA may include:

- *Enhanced Interpersonal Relationships.* Significant relationships can be severely and adversely affected by PD/PDA. For example, stress associated with panic and avoidance can strain relationships. Further, sexual relations may be avoided because of the resulting somatic sensations, and there appears to be a relationship between sexual dysfunction and PD (Sbrocco, Weisberg, Barlow, & Carter, 1997). In addition, patients may be hesitant to voice interpersonal problems for fear of losing their safe person. Problematic relationships not only decrease one's quality of life, but can also hinder treatment (Carter et al., 1994). In treating PD/PDA, it has been demonstrated that brief communication skills training with significant others results in decreased agoraphobia (Arnow, Taylor, Agras, & Telch, 1985). For persons reporting marital discord, incorporating marital therapy not only decreases PD/PDA symptoms, but also enhances marital concordance (Chernen & Friedman, 1993). (See chapter 14 for interventions geared to enhance relationships.)

- *Decrease Stress.* Distress and anxious arousal can instigate panic attacks. For this reason, decreasing overall stress in the patient's life is an important additional goal. Interventions to attain this goal may include problem-solving therapy, coping skills training, engendering social support, and relaxation training.
- *Schedule Activities.* Related to the above goal, people with PD/PDA often experience pressure related to time management. In addition, as much of their time is spent around their psychopathology, pleasant events are often abandoned. Thus, scheduling activities, including time management training and commitment to participating in enjoyable events, can decrease distress and elevate mood.
- *Prevent Relapse.* Before termination, training in relapse prevention may be important. Patients are taught to identify potential future problems and how their newly learned skills can be applied to these situations. A specific plan can be developed for each patient to implement when future difficulties arise.

ADDITIONAL CLINICAL CONSIDERATIONS

CBT is an extremely effective intervention for treating PD/PDA, with 75%–90% of patients experiencing significant benefits (Clark, 1996). Further, CBT is effective at treating PD with co-morbid diagnoses (e.g., depression, generalized anxiety; Sanderson, Raue, & Wetzler, 1998; Brown, Antony, & Barlow, 1995). Although the benefits of CBT appear to be similar to psycho-pharmacological outcomes immediately following treatment, long-term follow up indicates CBT results in greater treatment gain (Clark et al., 1994; Marks, Swinson, Basoglu, & Kuch, 1994). Moreover, it is important to note that the use of medication during CBT predicts poorer outcomes (Brown & Barlow, 1996)

Panic control treatment (PCT) is a manualized therapy that incorporates many of the CBT interventions presented above (e.g., cognitive restructuring, breathing retraining, interoceptive exposure, and *in vivo* exposure;

Craske, Barlow, & Meadows, 2000). PCT is effective at decreasing PD/ PDA symptoms in both the short and long-term (Barlow, 1990).

Cultural factors may play a role in PD/PDA. For example, cultural acceptability may help to partially explain the elevated rates of this disorder in women as compared with men. That is, although it is acceptable for women to endorse fear and avoid certain situations in many cultures, it is less acceptable for men. Men appear to cope with anxiety more by using alcohol and other substances. Further, although rates of PD/PDA are similar between African Americans and European Americans, the former group tends to use healthcare more frequently and express greater concerns about death. Interestingly, Hispanic cultures have reported *ataques de nervios* (nervous attacks), similar to panic, that also often coincide with stressful events (Rivera-Arzola & Ramos-Grenier, 1997). It is important to point out, however, that *ataques de nervios* are perceived as culturally acceptable.

REFERENCES

American Psychiatric Association (2000). *Diagnostic and statistical manual of mental disorders* (ed. 4, text revision). Washington, DC: American Psychiatric Press.

Antony, M. M., Orsillo, S. M., & Roemer, L. (2001). *Practitioner's guide to empirically based measures of anxiety.* New York: Kluwer Academic/Plenum Publishers.

Arnow, B. A., Taylor, C. B., Agras, W. S., & Telch, M. J. (1985). Enhancing agoraphobia treatment outcome by changing couple communication patterns. *Behavior Therapy, 16,* 452–467.

Bandelow, B. (1999). *Panic and Agoraphobia Scale (PAS).* Seattle, WA: Hogrefe & Huber Publications.

Barlow, D. H. (1990). Long-term outcome for patients with panic disorder treated with cognitive-behavioral therapy. *Journal of Clinical Psychiatry, 51,* 17–23.

Basoglu, M., Marks, I. M., Kilic, C., Swinson, R. P., Noshirvani, H., Kuch, K. et al. (1994). Relationship of panic, anticipatory anxiety, agoraphobia and global improvement in panic disorder with agoraphobia treated with alprazolam and exposure. *British Journal of Psychiatry, 164,* 647–652.

Beck, A. T. (1988). Cognitive approaches to panic disorder: Theory and therapy. In S. Rachman & J. D. Maser (Eds.), *Panic: Psychological perspectives.* Hillsdale, NJ: Erlbaum.

Beck, A. T., & Emery, C. (1985). *Anxiety disorders and phobias: A cognitive perspective.* New York: Basic Books.

Beck, J. S. (1992). *Focused cognitive therapy (FCT) for panic disorder.* Philadelphia: Center for Cognitive Therapy, University of Pennsylvania.

Beck, J. S. (1995). *Cognitive therapy: Basics and beyond.* New York: Guilford Press.

Brown, G. K., Beck, A. T., Newman, C. F., & Beck, J. S. (1997). A comparison of focused and standard cognitive therapy for panic disorder. *Journal of Anxiety Disorders, 11,* 329–345.

Brown, T. A., Antony, M. M., & Barlow, D. H. (1995). Diagnostic comorbidity in panic disorder: Effect on treatment outcome and course of comorbid diagnoses following treatment. *Journal of Consulting and Clinical Psychology, 63,* 408–418.

Brown, T. A., & Barlow, D. H. (1996). Long-term outcome in cognitive behavioral treatment of panic disorder: Clinical predictors and alternative strategies for assessment. *Journal of Consulting and Clinical Psychology, 63,* 754–765.

Carter, M. M., Turovsky, J., & Barlow, D. H. (1994). Interpersonal relationships in panic disorder with agoraphobia: A review of empirical evidence. *Clinical Psychology: Science and Practice, 1,* 25–34.

Chambless, D. L., Caputo, G. C., Jasin, S. E., Gracely, E. J., & Williams, C. (1985). The Mobility Inventory for Agoraphobia. *Behaviour Research and Therapy, 23,* 35–44.

Chambless, D. L., Caputo, G. C., Bright, P., & Gallagher, R. (1984). Assessment of fear in agoraphobics: The Body Sensations Questionnaire and the Agoraphobic Cognitions Questionnaire. *Journal of Consulting and Clinical Psychology, 52,* 1090–1097.

Chernen, L., & Friedman, S. (1993). Treating the personality disordered agoraphobic patient with individual and marital therapy: A multiple replication study. *Journal of Anxiety Disorders, 7,* 163–177.

Clark, D. M. (1986). A cognitive approach to panic. *Behaviour Research & Therapy, 24,* 461–470.

Clark, D. M. (1996). Panic disorder: From theory to therapy. In P. M. Saklovskis (Ed.), *Frontiers of cognitive therapy* (pp. 318–344). New York: Guilford Press.

Clark, D. M., Salkovskis, P. M., Hackmann, A., & Middleton, H. (1994). A comparison of cognitive therapy, applied relaxation and imipramine in the treatment of panic disorder. *British Journal of Psychiatry, 164,* 759–769.

Clark, D. M., Salkovskis, P. M., Öst, L. G., & Breitholtz, E. (1997). Misinterpretation of body sensations in panic disorder. *Journal of Consulting and Clinical Psychology, 65,* 203–213.

Cox, B. J., Norton, G. R., & Swinson, R. P. (1992). *Panic Attack Questionnaire-Revised.* Toronto, ON: Clarke Institute of Psychiatry.

Craske, M. G., Barlow, D. H., & Meadows, E. (2000). *Master your own anxiety and panic: Therapist guide for anxiety, panic, and agoraphobia (MAP-3).* San Antonio, TX: Graywind/Psychological Corporation.

Edelman, R. E., & Chambless, D. L. (1993). Compliance during sessions and homework in exposure-based treatment of agoraphobia. *Behaviour Research and Therapy, 31,* 767–773.

Fava, G. A., Rafanelli, C., Grandi, S., Conti, S., Ruini, C., Mangelli, L. et al. (2001). Long-term outcome of panic disorder with agoraphobia treated by exposure. *Psychological Medicine, 31,* 891–898.

Hoffart, A. (1993). Cognitive treatments of agoraphobia: A critical evaluation of theoretical basis and outcome evidence. *Journal of Anxiety Disorders, 7,* 75–91.

Hoffart, A. (1995a). A comparison of cognitive and guided mastery therapy of agoraphobia. *Behaviour Research and Therapy, 33,* 423–434.

Hoffart, A. (1995b). Cognitive mediators of situation fear in agoraphobia. *Journal of Behavior Therapy and Experimental Psychiatry, 26*, 313–320.

Hoffart, A. (1998). Cognitive and guided mastery therapy of agoraphobia: Long-term outcome and mechanisms of change. *Cognitive Therapy and Research, 22*, 195–207.

Hoffart, A., Friis, S., & Martinsen, E. W. (1989). The Phobic Avoidance Rating Scale: A psychometric evaluation of an interview-based scale. *Psychiatric Developments, 1*, 81.

Kamphuis, J. H., & Telch, M. J. (1998). Texas Safety Maneuver Scale. *Clinical Psychology and Psychotherapy, 5*, 177–186.

Katerndahl, D. A., & Realini, J. P. (1993). Lifetime prevalence of panic states. *American Journal of Psychiatry, 150*, 246–249.

Kessler, R. C., McGonagle, K. A., Zhao, S., Nelson, C. B., Hughes, M., Eshleman, S. et al. (1994). Lifetime and 12-month prevalence of DSM-III-R psychiatric disorders in the United States. Results from the National Comorbidity Survey. *Archives of General Psychiatry, 51*, 8–19.

Marks, I. M., Swinson, R. P., Basoglu, M., & Kuch, K. (1994). Alprazolam and exposure alone and combined in panic disorder with agoraphobia: A controlled study in London and Toronto. *British Journal of Psychiatry, 162*, 787.

Meichenbaum, D. (1977). *Cognitive-behavioral modification: An integrative approach.* New York: Plenum Press.

Neron, S., Lacroix, D., & Chaput, Y. (1995). Group vs. individual cognitive behaviour therapy in panic disorder: An open clinical trial with a six month follow-up. *Canadian Journal of Behavioural Science, 27*, 379–392.

Öst, L. G., Westling, B. E., & Hellstroem, K. (1993). Applied relaxation, exposure in vivo and cognitive methods in the treatment of panic disorder with agoraphobia. *Behaviour Research and Therapy, 31*, 383–394.

Peterson, R. A., & Reiss, S. (1993). *Anxiety Sensitivity Index.* Worthington, OH: IDS Publishing Corporation.

Peveler, R. C., & Johnston, D. W. (1986). Subjective and cognitive effects of relaxation. *Behaviour Research and Therapy, 24*, 413–419.

Rachman, S. (1984). Agoraphobia—A safety-signal perspective. *Behaviour Research and Therapy, 22*, 59–70.

Rapee, R. M., Craske, M. G., & Barlow, D. H. (1995). Assessment instrument for panic disorder that includes fear of sensation-producing activities: The Albany Panic and Phobia Questionnaire. *Anxiety, 1*, 114–122.

Reiss, S., Peterson, R. A., Gursky, D. M., & McNally, R. J. (1986). Anxiety sensitivity, anxiety frequency and the predictions of fearfulness. *Behaviour Research and Therapy, 24*, 1–8.

Rivera-Arzola, M., & Ramos-Grenier, J. (1997). Anger, ataques de nervios, and la mujer puertorriquena: Sociocultural considerations and treatment implications. In J. Garcia & M. C. Zea (Eds.), *Psychological interventions and research with Latino populations* (pp. 125–141). Boston: Allyn and Bacon.

Salkovskis, P. M., Clark, D. M., & Gelder, M. G. (1996). Cognition-behaviour links in the persistence of panic. *Behaviour Research and Therapy, 34*, 453–458.

Salkovskis, P. M., Clark, D. M., Hackmann, A., Wells, A., & Gelder, M. G. (1999). An experimental investigation of the role of safety-seeking behaviours in the

maintenance of panic disorder with agoraphobia. *Behaviour Research and Therapy,*
37, 559–574.

Sanderson, W. C., Raue, P. J., & Wetzler, S. (1998). The generalizability of cognitive
behavior therapy for panic disorder. *Journal of Cognitive Psychotherapy, 12,*
323–330.

Sartory, G., Master, D., & Rachman, S. (1989). Safety-signal therapy in agoraphobics:
A preliminary test. *Behaviour Research and Therapy, 27,* 205–209.

Sbrocco, T., Weisberg, R. B., Barlow, D. H., & Carter, M. M. (1997). The conceptual
relationship between panic disorder and male erectile dysfunction. *Journal of Sex
and Marital Therapy, 23,* 212–220.

Schmidt, N. B., Lerew, D. R., & Trakowski, J. H. (1997). Body vigilance in panic
disorder: evaluating attention to bodily perturbations. *Journal of Consulting and
Clinical Psychology, 65,* 214–220.

Shear, M. K., Brown, T. A., Sholomskas, D. E., Barlow, D. H., Gorman, J. M., Woods,
S. W. et al. (1992). *Panic Disorders Severity Scale.* Pittsburgh, PA: Department of
Psychiatry, University of Pittsburgh Medical School.

Taylor, S., & Cox, B. J. (1998a). An expanded anxiety sensitivity index: Evidence for
a hierarchic structure in a clinical sample. *Journal of Anxiety Disorders, 12,* 463–483.

Taylor, S., & Cox, B. J. (1998b). Anxiety sensitivity: Multiple dimensions and hierarchic
structure. *Behaviour Research and Therapy, 36,* 37–51.

van den, H. M., Arntz, A., & Hoekstra, R. (1994). Exposure reduced agoraphobia but
not panic, and cognitive therapy reduced panic but not agoraphobia. *Behaviour
Research and Therapy, 32,* 447–451.

van Hout, W. J. P. J., Emmelkamp, P. M. G., Koopmans, P. C., Boegels, S. M., &
Bouman, T. K. (2001). Assessment of self-statements in agoraphobic situations:
Construction and psychometric evaluation of the Agoraphobic Self-Statements
Questionnaire (ASQ). *Journal of Anxiety Disorders, 15,* 183–201.

Williams, S. L. (1990). Guided mastery treatment of agoraphobia: Beyond stimulus
exposure. *Progress in Behavior Modification, 26,* 89–121.

Yonkers, K. A., Zlotnick, C., Allsworth, J., Warshaw, M., Shea, T., & Keller, M. B.
(1998). Is the course of panic disorder the same in women and men? *American
Journal of Psychiatry, 155,* 596–602.

8

Generalized Anxiety Disorder

GENERAL DESCRIPTION AND DIAGNOSTIC ISSUES

Generalized anxiety disorder (GAD) is characterized by pathological worry that shifts from one topic to another. People with GAD selectively attend to personally threatening stimuli and generally anticipate negative outcomes despite an actual low probability of occurrence. The intensity, duration, or frequency of the anxiety and worry is far out of proportion to the actual likelihood or impact of the feared event. Simply pointing out the unlikelihood of the feared event generally does not alter one's belief.

The *Diagnostic and Statistical Manual of Mental Disorders, Fourth Edition, Text Revision* (DSM-IV-TR; American Psychiatric Association, 2000) defines GAD as excessive anxiety and worry occurring more days than not for at least 6 months concerning various events or activities (e.g., work or school performance). The person with GAD finds it difficult to control the worry. Three or more of the following symptoms must also be present for the same duration: restlessness, fatigue, difficulty concentrating, irritability, muscle tension, and sleep disturbances. The focus of the anxiety and worry is not confined to features of an Axis I disorder and the disturbance is not due to the direct physiological effects of a substance (e.g., a drug) or general medical condition. The anxiety, worry, or physical symptoms cause clinically significant distress or impairment in social, occupational, or other important areas of functioning.

Adults with GAD often worry about everyday life circumstances, such as possible job responsibilities, finances, health of family members, misfortune to their children, and minor matters (e.g., household chores, car repairs, or being late for appointments). Although the content of worries is similar between those with GAD and nonclinical populations, the worry is more pervasive among persons with GAD. Associated features of this anxiety disorder include negative affect, somatic and/or sexual dysfunction, and anxious or dependent personality style.

In a community sample, the 1-year prevalence rate for GAD was approximately 3% and the lifetime prevalence rate was 5%. In anxiety disorder clinics, approximately 12% of the individuals present with GAD, making it the most common disorder. However, fewer than 25% of the patients with this disorder receive treatment. Women tend to be at an increased risk for GAD (ratio of 2.5:1 female to male).

Many individuals with GAD report that they have felt anxious and nervous all of their lives. Approximately half of those presenting for treatment report the onset of symptoms occurring in childhood or adolescence. However, the onset can occur during adulthood, usually following the experience of stressful life events. The course is chronic but fluctuating, worsens during times of stress, and improbably remits on its own (Yonkers, Warshaw, Massion, & Keller, 1996). Psychosocial impairment is significant in persons with GAD (Jones, Ames, Jeffries, Scarinci, & Brantley, 2001).

Differential Diagnostic Issues

Although worry is a central component to all anxiety disorders, as well as many other Axis I disorders, worry in GAD is more wide-ranging, frequent, excessive, and uncontrollable. In contrast, *panic disorder* is characterized by worry about experiencing a panic attack with more of an internal focus, as compared to GAD where the focus is on external, future events. *Social phobia* centers specifically on fears of being evaluated by or embarrassed in front of others. In *obsessive-compulsive disorder*, the obsessions are focused on a specific concern (e.g., fear of contamination). The root of the fear in *posttraumatic stress disorder* is related to a specific traumatic event that is being relived. In contrast to GAD, *anorexia nervosa* is distinguished by the fear of gaining weight. *Somatization disorder* is characterized by multiple physical complaints, whereas *hypochondriasis* entails a fear of having a serious illness. In mood disorders (e.g., *major depressive disorder*, *dysthymia*), ruminations are often negative thoughts about the past, as compared with GAD, where they are more centered on the future.

Co-morbidity Issues

In community samples, 90% of those with GAD have additional psychiatric disorders, with 75% meeting criteria for another anxiety or mood disorder. Forty-two percent meet criteria for major depression or dysthymia. Substance abuse is seen in 16% of individuals with GAD. Rates of co-morbid personality disorders are estimated at 50%, and include avoidant, dependent, and most frequently, obsessive-compulsive personality disorders.

ASSESSMENT OF DISORDER

Several different measures exist to assess various aspects of GAD. The reader is directed to Antony, Orsillo, and Roemer (2001) for a review of such assessment tools.

Clinician Ratings

- *Anxiety Disorders Interview Schedule for DSM-IV: Lifetime Version* (DiNardo, Brown, & Barlow, 1994): assesses current and lifetime DSM-IV diagnoses of anxiety, mood, and substance use.

Behavioral Assessments

- *Self-Monitoring* (e.g., Leahy & Holland, 2000): permits *in vivo* assessment of the level of anxiety and negative affect, thoughts associated with distress, cognitions during worry, and time spent worrying.

Self-Report Measures

- *Generalized Anxiety Disorder Questionnaire-IV* (Newman et al., 2002): provides diagnostic self-assessment of GAD using DSM-IV criteria.

- *Penn State Worry Questionnaire* (Meyer, Miller, Metzger, & Borkovec, 1990): assesses the intensity (but not content) of pathological worry.
- *Worry Domains Questionnaire* (Tallis, Eysenck, & Mathews, 1992): measures the degree to which an individual worries about the following areas: relationships, lack of confidence, aimless future, work, and finances.
- *Worry Scale for Older Adults* (Wisocki, 1988): assesses the extent of worry older adults experience related to social, financial, and health domains.
- *Depression Anxiety Stress Scale* (Lovibond & Lovibond, 1995): provides a specific evaluation of cognitions and stress/tension levels.

Ultimate Outcome Goals

Ultimate outcome goals when working with individuals with GAD include decreasing worry, difficulty controlling worry, and concern about worry. An important aim entails gaining a better understanding about worry, as well as the differentiation between helpful and unconstructive worry. Because coping inflexibility prevails in GAD, treatment is geared toward decreasing restrictions that such symptoms place on their lives. Thus, efforts to enhance quality of life and coping skills, including increasing an individual's awareness of alternative ways of viewing the world, are central. Attempts should also made to decrease maladaptive coping with GAD symptoms (e.g., substance abuse). Another ultimate goal may be to decrease negative affect associated with GAD. In addition, because GAD significantly and adversely affects numerous facets of the individual's life, therapy may be geared to enhance social relationships, as well as occupational and school performance.

Major Instrumental Outcome
Goals/Treatment Targets

Major instrumental outcome goals for GAD include:

- Alter maladaptive metacognitions
- Decrease intolerance of uncertainty
- Decrease avoidant behavior
- Decrease physical symptoms of anxiety

Goal 1: Alter Maladaptive Metacognitions

Wells (1995) differentiated between two different types of worries in persons with GAD. Type 1 worry refers to worrying about external (e.g., threatening situations) and internal (e.g., somatic sensations) events. In contrast, Type 2 worry signifies metacognitions about worry. These metacognitions refer to one's perceptions about the function of thoughts and feelings about worrying. The two types of worry are related, in that Type 1 worry stimulates the schema of worry (i.e., Type 2), which, in turn, results in greater Type 1 worry (e.g., distress, negative affect, somatic symptoms). Pathological worry as seen in GAD is related to Type 2 worry (Wells & Carter, 1999).

Wells (1995, 2002) describes the importance of metacognitions in perpetuating worry. Specifically, patients with GAD hold certain beliefs about the function of worry. Such beliefs may entail a negative appraisal about worry including disturbing performance, exaggerating the problem, and causing emotional distress (e.g., "I am going to go crazy with all of the worry"). However, beliefs may also be positive. Thus, schemas about worry may represent beneficial aspects of worry that include motivational influence, helping analytical thinking, helping prepare for a potentially negative event, and superstitious or magical thinking that worry will *prevent* the negative event from occurring (e.g., "if I worry, then bad things won't happen").

Goal-Specific Assessment Tools

- *Anxious Thoughts Inventory* (Wells, 1994): assesses vulnerability to anxious worry and includes a subscale on metacognitions about worry.
- *Consequences of Worrying Scale* (Davey, Tallis, & Capuzzo, 1996): assesses beliefs about the positive and negative consequences of worry.
- *Why Worry Scale* (Freeston, Rheaume, Letarte, Dugas, & Ladouceur, 1994): assesses reasons people worry (e.g., perceived protection from negative emotions should a negative event occur).

Goal-Specific Potential Interventions

- Cognitive restructuring
- Problem-solving therapy
- Mindfulness therapy

Cognitive Restructuring.   Patients with GAD are often not aware of the beliefs they hold about worry. Cognitive restructuring (e.g., Beck,

Emery, & Greenberg, 1985) centers on first identifying distorted automatic thoughts (e.g., "something terrible is going to happen") and dysfunctional assumptions (e.g., "if I worry, it won't happen"). Subsequently, core beliefs (e.g., "I am powerless") are ascertained and altered. Patients are instructed to identify cognitive distortions (e.g., catastrophizing, overgeneralizing, fortune-telling, dichotomous thinking, discounting positives) and replace them with more adaptive beliefs. Educating the patient regarding how the unchallenged thoughts actually perpetuate the worry (e.g., *"just in case* something bad does happen, I will be ready by worrying") is important. Patients should be taught to reevaluate their beliefs regarding the usefulness of their worries.

Cognitive restructuring concentrates on developing multiple alternative perspectives, rather than the sole feared negative event. This includes teaching individuals with GAD to alter distorted information processing. Patients learn it is the *interpretation* of circumstances that is threatening, rather than the circumstances themselves that cause distress. Furthermore, they are taught to rationally assess the actual *probability*, as compared to the *possibility*, that a feared event will occur.

When conducting cognitive restructuring, it is important not to try to de-catastophize the feared events. For example, if a patient fears her husband will die in a car crash on his way home from work, the therapist should not attempt to convince the patient this is not a tragedy. Rather, this treatment tactic should address the likelihood of the feared event, as well as the maladaptive assumptions about worry (e.g., "If I worry, then everything will be all right").

Homework is an important component of all CBT interventions. Leahy (2002) provides helpful suggestions on how to increase compliance with homework using cognitive restructuring techniques including facilitating the identification of automatic thoughts that may hinder homework completion, redirecting excessive focus away from negative feelings, and altering metacognitive beliefs about the benefits of worry.

Problem-Solving Therapy.   The primary means of coping in GAD is Type 1 worrying, which is perpetuated by metacognitions about worry. "Jumping from worry to worry" serves to limit the ability of the patient with GAD to clearly understand the nature of stressful problems that need to be resolved (Stoeber & Borkovec, 2002). Further, patients are often unaware of what else to do instead of worry. Thus, problem-solving therapy (D'Zurilla & Nezu, 1999; Nezu, in press), with particular emphasis on helping patients to better define problems and to generate alternative solutions, can help those with GAD establish more adaptive coping responses.

Mindfulness Therapy.   Propelled by metacognitions about worry, patients with GAD spend much time worrying about the future. Roemer and Orsillo (2002) recommend mindfulness therapy as an important component of an overall treatment plan for persons with GAD. Borrowing from Acceptance and Commitment Therapy (ACT; Hayes, Pankey, & Gregg, 2003), Roemer and Orsillo promote interventions that encourage the patient to *accept* the present rather than worry about what *might* be. They highlight the use of psychoeducation regarding beliefs about worry, relaxation training, exposure, and "mindful action" (e.g., problem solving and development of positive goals) to decrease worry and beliefs about worry, as well as to enhance the likelihood of meeting long-term positive goals.

Goal 2: Decrease Intolerance of Uncertainty

Patients with GAD report greater intolerance of uncertainty than those with other anxiety disorders (Dugas, Gagnon, Ladouceur, & Freeston, 1998). This intolerance of uncertainty guides informational processing that propagates worry (Freeston et al., 1994). Ladouceur and colleagues (Ladouceur et al., 2000) view intolerance of uncertainty as central to GAD. Although related, intolerance of uncertainty is a construct distinct from worry (Ladouceur, Talbot, & Dugas, 1997).

Patients with GAD worry in an attempt to decrease uncertainty about the future which serves to instill a false sense of control (e.g., "if I worry about my husband getting home safe, he will"). Although such individuals may recognize the low probability of the feared traumatic event, worrying serves to temporarily decrease their anxiety because it is perceived as something they can *do* about the uncertainty. Persons with GAD consistently worry about *future* events, focusing on threatening stimuli, which are interpreted as indications of upcoming peril. This future-orientation causes the patient with GAD to become prepared (e.g., emotionally and physically) for predicted danger. Thus, worry serves as a coping mechanism when experiencing an intolerance of uncertainty. As an example, a patient who has concerns (but not a phobia) about flying, despite knowledge of aviation safety, engages in worry (e.g., "I know there is a one in a million chance that the plane will crash, but if I worry, I will be prepared"). This results in chronic arousal, negative affect, and a sense of uncontrollability, which all serve to instigate the worry response. Barlow (2002) describes this phenomenon as the "anxious apprehension cycle."

Goal-Specific Assessment Tools

- *Intolerance of Uncertainty Scale* (Freeston et al., 1994): assesses intolerance of uncertainty, including emotional and behavioral consequences of uncertainty, expectations that the future will be predictable, and attempts to control the future.

Goal-Specific Potential Interventions

- Problem-solving therapy
- Self-monitoring
- Stimulus control

Problem-Solving Therapy.   Intolerance of uncertainty leads to perceiving problems when they do not actually exist and the subsequent implementation of ineffective problem-solving skills. Thus, people with GAD can be characterized by a negative problem orientation. Problem orientation refers to one's worldview about problems and one's own abilities to solve problems (Nezu, in press). For people with GAD, this mindset includes difficulty perceiving problems when they actually occur, inaccurate attributions about the causes of problems, overestimation of the threat of difficulties, perceived lack of control over problems, and a decreased commitment of time and effort devoted to effectively addressing problems.

Intolerance of uncertainty is a significant factor of a negative problem orientation (Dugas, Freeston, & Ladouceur, 1997) and both intolerance of uncertainty and a negative problem orientation differentiate people with GAD from nonclinical samples (Ladouceur, Blais, Freeston, & Dugas, 1998). A negative problem orientation has been found to be a significant predictor of worry (Dugas et al., 1997) and in general is related to maladaptive problem-solving skills (e.g., Dugas, Letarte, Rheaume, & Freeston, 1995).

Given this association between worry and a negative problem orientation, problem-solving therapy (D'Zurilla & Nezu, 1999; Nezu, in press) may be advisable for the patient with GAD.

Self-Monitoring.   In addition to its valuable role as an assessment procedure, self-monitoring is an important component of an overall treatment plan when working with patients with GAD (Brown, O'Leary, & Barlow, 2001). Patients are taught to identify those cues or stimuli that trigger anxiety, the thoughts associated with these cues, and their reactions to such cues. Cues may be internal (e.g., thoughts, physical sensations) or external (e.g., stressful events). Self-monitoring not only provides therapists with more information about the symptoms, but can also serve as a way to increase patients' understanding of their worries (e.g., how worry is related to decreased sense of tolerance). With this greater insight, there can be a decreased sense of uncertainty and an increased perception of control.

Stimulus Control.　In treating patients with GAD, a stimulus control protocol entails having them control the circumstances under which (i.e., when and where) worrying will occur. Patients are instructed to set aside a specific time period and place to worry. Worries are delayed until the scheduled time, at which point the patient is assigned the task of worrying. Postponement of worry allows patients to appreciate that worrying is not a necessary coping strategy for their intolerance of uncertainty. With stimulus control, patients often report a decreased need and enhanced ability not to worry.

Goal 3: Decrease Avoidant Behavior

Worry can serve as a (albeit maladaptive) coping mechanism for patients with GAD. Borkovec and colleagues (e.g., Borkovec, 1994; Borkovec & Inz, 1990) conceptualize worry as a method of avoidance coping. This avoidance can take the form of (a) *superstitious perceived avoidance,* or (2) *experiential avoidance.* Regarding the former, as previously discussed, individuals with GAD often engage in magical or superstitious thinking that the act of worrying will prevent future negative events.

Experiential avoidance, or avoidance of internal distress, is another way individuals with GAD use avoidant coping and can be manifested in different ways. For example, individuals may attempt to suppress worry. Ironically, however, suppressing worry has been demonstrated to *increase* distress. Shifting from worry to worry, rather than processing a specific worry, is another form of experiential avoidance. In addition, worrying about negligible events permits the individual to avoid more distressing matters such as negative cognitions and emotions about one's negative self-concept.

Despite short-term decreases in distress, in the long term, avoidance results in negative consequences. Avoidance inhibits emotional processing, an experience necessary for enduring anxiety reduction (Foa & Kozak, 1986). In addition, experiential avoidance of internal distress leads to increased chronic tension and other somatic symptoms.

Avoidance results in the negative reinforcement of worry in different manners. First, avoidance worry temporarily decreases somatic arousal and inhibits emotional processing of the feared event. Second, because worry is based on an unlikely event that usually does not occur, patients with GAD often attribute the nonoccurrence of the feared event as the successful consequence of their avoidance worry. In addition to reinforcement, worry coping is further strengthened by the cyclic relationship between worry and avoidance (i.e. avoidance can be a reaction to and an instigator of worry).

In addition to avoidance, over 50% of patients with GAD engage in certain "worry behaviors" (i.e., corrective, preventative, or ritualistic behaviors aimed at decreasing or avoiding distress; Craske, Rapee, Jackel, & Barlow, 1989). Some of these worry behaviors include avoidance, such as not listening to the radio traffic report for fear it will cause a loved one to be in an accident.

Goal-Specific Assessment Tools

- *Subjective Units of Distress Scale* (SUDS): assesses patients' self-reported level of physiological or psychological distress, usually on a scale from 0 (*not at all distressed*) to 100 (*the most distressed they have ever been*) ratings.
- *Behavioral Avoidance Test (BAT)*: patients' individually tailored hierarchy of avoided stimuli; to be used in conjunction with SUDS.

Goal-Specific Potential Interventions

- Exposure therapy
- Behavioral experiments
- Interpersonal strategies

Exposure Therapy.   Unlike other anxiety disorders where *behavioral* avoidance is more evident, avoidance among GAD patients is characterized by avoidance of *cognitions*. Exposure for those with GAD is aimed at fully contemplating the feared thoughts and experiencing the resulting anxiety. As with any exposure therapy, the patient must have a good understanding of its purpose to habituate to the troubling thoughts. Exposure is also presented as an opportunity to implement other skills that have been learned (e.g., cognitive restructuring). Exposure therapy has been demonstrated to be an effective component of treatment when working with GAD (Borkovec & Costello, 1993).

To engage in exposure for GAD, patients first identify two or three foremost worries. Vivid images (e.g., cognitions, emotions, behaviors) are identified for each situation. Patients are then asked to focus on the worry and associated images over a 25–30-minute time period, allowing themselves to experience their fears. Following exposure, debriefing occurs, where patients discuss and process that which makes them anxious. If the patient refuses exposure therapy, the clinician can increase his or her adherence by modeling the exposure protocol, encouraging the use of positive coping self-statements, and teaching the patient to use "time projection" (e.g. how will you feel in an hour after you do this?).

Behavioral Experiments. As previously reported, worries are reinforced by the *non*-occurrence of the feared catastrophic event, coupled with avoidance and magical thinking. Similar to exposure, behavioral experiments, or hypothesis testing, facilitates both the experience of fear and the disconnection between worry and non-occurrence of the feared event. Patients are taught to view their thoughts as *hypotheses*, rather than facts, for which supporting and opposing evidence is sought. Patients are instructed to clearly define their beliefs about the perceived consequences of response prevention. They are then asked to test the veracity of their beliefs while *not* engaging in their avoidance or worry behaviors. Following this, patients evaluate the actual versus predicted outcome. For example, the individual who fears that reading obituaries will actually *cause* a loved one to die is instructed to read the obituaries and then assess the consequences.

Interpersonal Strategies. Individuals with GAD often distance themselves from others in an attempt to avoid criticism or rejection that they fear would occur if they got close to people. The resulting avoidance-coping places a strain on relationships and prevents the development of other potential relationships. In GAD, it has been demonstrated that worries are often focused on interpersonal relationships (Breitholtz, Johansson, & Öst, 1999). Moreover, persistent interpersonal difficulties predict poor CBT outcomes (Borkovec, Newman, Pincus, & Lytle, 2002). Social skills, assertiveness, and communication skills training can improve interpersonal interactions. Newman and colleagues have developed a comprehensive intervention entitled Integrative Therapy. This treatment incorporates interpersonal procedures, CBT, and experiential factors (Newman, Castonguay, & Borkovec, 2003). In addition, in an effort to decrease interpersonal avoidance and enhance interpersonal relations, co-joint therapy with partners can help address strained relationships.

Goal 4: Decrease Physical Symptoms of Anxiety

Physical symptoms in GAD are less related to sympathetic nervous system arousal (e.g., elevated heart rate) and more experienced as muscular tension. Associated somatic symptoms may also include restlessness, feeling jumpy, irritability, difficulty sleeping, fatigue, and difficulty concentrating. In addition, certain medical conditions are associated with GAD, including chest pain (Carter & Maddock, 1992) and irritable bowel syndrome (Tollefson, Tollefson, Pederson, & Luxenberg, 1991). In fact, people with GAD exhibit increased healthcare utilization as compared with the general public (Roy-Byrne & Katon, 1997).

Goal-Specific Assessment Tools

* *Leahy Anxiety Checklist* (Leahy & Holland, 2000): assesses different somatic symptoms associated with anxiety.

Goal-Specific Potential Interventions:

* Relaxation training
* Self-control desensitization
* Sleep hygiene training

Relaxation Training.   Several types of relaxation skills can be taught to help clients decrease the somatic symptoms associated with GAD. Progressive muscle relaxation (PMR), diaphragmatic breathing, guided positive imagery, meditation, and biofeedback are examples of relaxation skills. Because patients with GAD often report difficulty in relaxing, diverse techniques aimed at decreasing tension should be presented and practiced frequently (i.e., both insession and outside of sessions). Relaxation training has been found to be an effective treatment for GAD symptoms (Öst & Breitholtz, 2000).

It is important to note, however, that for some patients with GAD, relaxation results in a paradoxical *increase* in anxiety. For these individuals, relaxation intensifies their perceived lack of control, prompting more worry and somatic distress. In addition, rather than being able to relax, some patients may spend the quiet time ruminating about their worries. Because individuals with GAD are often perfectionistic, worries such as "Am I doing this correctly?" can further minimize the relaxation response. To help prevent possible adverse effects of relaxation training, the therapist should proceed slowly, reminding patients of their control during inductions, and explain that relaxation is not "right" or "wrong," but rather a process that will progress over time with practice.

Self-Control Desensitization.   Goldfried's (1971) self-control desensitization entails pairing relaxation with worrying thoughts and images. Unlike traditional systematic desensitization, however, a detailed fear hierarchy is not needed. Patients identify anxiety-provoking situations and cues (e.g., physical, cognitive, behavioral, and external), which are then categorized as mild, moderate, or severe. After patients have learned progressive muscle relaxation, they are instructed to perform this stress management skill when imagining these stressful situations. Patients alternate between imagining the distressing situation and implementing the relaxation response. Self-control desensitization permits both extinction of anxiety, as well as a means of practicing newly learned adaptive coping skills.

Sleep Hygiene Training. Sleep disturbances are often associated with GAD and can result in physical complaints (e.g., muscle stiffness, difficulty concentrating). Behavioral sleep hygiene training can help restore slumber (Leahy & Holland, 2000). First, patients are instructed to develop a regular sleeping schedule (i.e., going to bed and waking at the same time each day, even on weekends). In an attempt to establish a conditioned pairing between bed and sleep, the bed is used only for sleep and sex (e.g., not a place to read or watch TV). Patients are further instructed not to *try* to fall asleep, as this will increase anxiety and paradoxically decrease the likelihood of sleep. Instead, they can concentrate on relaxing. Fluid intake restriction, particularly caffeine and alcohol, before bed is important to prevent urinary urgency from awakening the patient. If sleep has not occurred within 15 minutes of going to bed, patients are instructed to get out of bed. At this point, they are instructed to identify automatic thoughts (e.g., "I will never get to sleep and I won't be able to function tomorrow") and then challenge such cognitive distortions. Finally, patients are taught to not expect immediate results.

Additional Instrumental Outcome Goals/Treatment Target

- *Enhance time management skills.* Because patients with GAD often feel overwhelmed and "out of control" with perceived obligations brought on by worry, time management training can be a useful intervention. Patients are taught to delegate responsibilities, be assertive when appropriate (e.g., say "no"), and adhere to a predetermined schedule. In addition, patients are taught to develop a priority list of tasks (e.g., "must be completed this week" versus "to be completed if there is time").
- *Decrease general life stress.* Normal life stress can aggravate generalized anxiety. Often, people with GAD are able to function reasonably well until they experience stressful events. Self-instructional training, problem-solving therapy, relaxation training, time management, and behavioral activation can help decrease stress.
- *Increase self-efficacy.* Individuals with GAD often have low self-efficacy, which can contribute to negative affect, decreased perceived

control, and the perpetuation of pathological worry. Interventions such as cognitive restructuring, problem-solving therapy, and guided positive imagery can help increase self-efficacy and enhance benefits of other CBT interventions.

- *Decrease need for benzodiazepines.* Often patients with GAD are prescribed benzodiazepines, which are highly addictive and pose significant risks if used long-term (Persons, Mennin, & Tucker, 2001). Whereas CBT and medications both can be equally helpful in the short-term, the long-term benefits of CBT are significantly greater than medication (Gould, Otto, Pollack, & Yap, 1997). Furthermore, CBT has been demonstrated to result in significantly reduced use of this medication following intervention (Barlow, Rapee, & Brown, 1992). Thus, exposure therapy, cognitive restructuring, and problem-solving therapy can help decrease the need for benzodiazepines. Of course it is vital to work with the prescribing healthcare provider to assist the tapering and termination of any medication.

ADDITIONAL CLINICAL CONSIDERATIONS

Meta-analysis demonstrates that CBT for GAD produces significant improvements that are maintained for at least 1 year after treatment termination (Borkovec & Whisman, 2003). CBT results in 77% of participants no longer meeting diagnostic criteria for GAD (Ladouceur et al., 2000). Overall cognitive change appears to be a particularly strong predictor of beneficial treatment outcomes (Chambless & Gillis, 1993). This change can be facilitated via the cognitive and/or behavioral techniques already described.

As reported earlier, GAD often exists with co-morbid disorders and may help maintain other anxiety disorders (Roy-Byrne & Katon, 1997). Barlow (2002) conceptualizes a central component of GAD, anxiety apprehension, as contributing to all other emotional disorders. Support for this comes from the finding that CBT aimed at decreasing GAD can result in decreased symptoms of other co-morbid disorders (Borkovec, Abel, & Newman, 1995).

It is interesting to note that GAD is the most common anxiety disorder in the elderly, with prevalence rates of 4.6%–7.1%. Although GAD has the same diagnostic criteria throughout adulthood, worry in the elderly is often more focused on health. GAD is frequently under diagnosed in older adults because (a) complaints are often more centered on physical symptoms of anxiety, (b) the elderly usually seek treatment through their physician, and (c) older adults tend to be less psychologically minded, describing their anxiety as "fret" or "concern" rather than worry, and are reluctant to accept a psychological explanation and treatment for their symptoms (Stanley & Novy, 2000). Consequently, when working with older adults, interventions should focus on fostering adoption of a biopsychosocial model. In addition, it has been suggested that agitation in demented elderly patients may be an expression of GAD, where physical agitation appears to respond well to behavior interventions (Mintzer & Brawman-Mintzer, 1996).

In addition to age, cultural factors should be considered when working with patients with GAD. For example, for Chinese patients, a combination of cognitive therapy and Taoist philosophy has been found to decrease anxiety symptoms and improve coping (Zhang et al., 2002).

Last, technology may help facilitate CBT for patients with GAD. For example, a PDA-type computer can be used not only for immediate self-monitoring purposes, but also to provide relaxation, imaginal exposure, and cognitive restructuring (e.g., Newman, Consoli, & Taylor, 1999). This provides the patient with more "therapy" time without the therapist and serves as a cost effective adjunct to conventional assessment and therapy.

REFERENCES

American Psychiatric Association (2000). *Diagnostic and statistical manual of mental disorders* (ed. 4, text revision). Washington, DC: American Psychiatric Press.

Antony, M. M., Orsillo, S. M., & Roemer, L. (2001). *Practitioner's guide to empirically based measures of anxiety*. New York: Kluwer Academic/Plenum Publishers.

Barlow, D. H. (2002). *Anxiety and its disorders: The nature and treatment of anxiety and panic* (2nd ed.). New York: Guilford Press.

Barlow, D. H., Rapee, R. M., & Brown, T. A. (1992). Behavioral treatment of generalized anxiety disorder. *Behavior Therapy, 23,* 551–570.

Beck, A. T., Emery, G., & Greenberg, R. L. (1985). *Anxiety disorders and phobias: A cognitive perspective*. New York: Basic Books.

Borkovec, T. D. (1994). *The nature, functions, and origins of worry*. In G. C. L. Davey & F. Tallis (Eds.). New York: Wiley.

Borkovec, T. D., Abel, J. L., & Newman, H. (1995). Effects of psychotherapy on comorbid conditions in generalized anxiety disorder. *Journal of Consulting and Clinical Psychology, 63,* 479–483.

Borkovec, T. D., & Costello, E. (1993). Efficacy of applied relaxation and cognitive-behavioral therapy in the treatment of generalized anxiety disorder. *Journal of Consulting and Clinical Psychology, 61,* 611–619.

Borkovec, T. D., & Inz, J. (1990). The nature of worry in generalized anxiety disorder: A predominance of thought activity. *Behaviour Research and Therapy, 28,* 153–158.

Borkovec, T. D., Newman, M. G., Pincus, A. L., & Lytle, R. (2002). A component analysis of cognitive-behavioral therapy for generalized anxiety disorder and the role of interpersonal problems. *Journal of Consulting and Clinical Psychology, 70,* 288–298.

Borkovec, T. D., & Whisman, M. (2003). Psychosocial treatment for generalized anxiety disorder. In M. Mavissakalian & R. F. Prien (Eds.), *Anxiety disorders: Psychological and pharmacological treatments.* Washington, DC: American Psychiatric Press.

Breitholtz, E., Johansson, B., & Öst, L. G. (1999). Cognitions in generalized anxiety disorder and panic disorder patients: A prospective approach. *Behaviour Research & Therapy, 37,* 533–544.

Brown, T. A., O'Leary, T. A., & Barlow, D. H. (2001). Generalized anxiety disorder. In D. H. Barlow (Ed.), *Clinical handbook of psychological disorders: A step-by-step treatment manual* (3rd ed.) (pp. 154–208). New York: Guilford Press.

Carter, C. S., & Maddock, R. J. (1992). Chest pain in generalized anxiety disorder. *International Journal of Psychiatry Medicine, 22,* 291–298.

Chambless, D. L., & Gillis, M. M. (1993). Cognitive therapy of anxiety disorders. *Journal of Consulting and Clinical Psychology, 61,* 248–260.

Craske, M. G., Rapee, R. M., Jackel, L., & Barlow, D. H. (1989). Qualitative dimensions of worry in DSM-III-R generalized anxiety disorder subjects and nonanxious controls. *Behaviour Research and Therapy, 27,* 397–402.

Davey, G. C. L., Tallis, F., & Capuzzo, N. (1996). Beliefs about the consequences of worrying. *Cognitive Therapy and Research, 20,* 499–520.

Dugas, M. J., Freeston, M. H., & Ladouceur, R. (1997). Intolerance of uncertainty and problem orientation in worry. *Cognitive Therapy and Research, 21,* 593–606.

Dugas, M. J., Gagnon, F., Ladouceur, R., & Freeston, M. H. (1998). Generalized anxiety disorder: A preliminary test of a conceptual model. *Behaviour Research and Therapy, 36,* 215–226.

Dugas, M. J., Letarte, H., Rheaume, J., & Freeston, M. H. (1995). Worry and problem solving: Evidence of a specific relationship. *Cognitive Therapy and Research, 19,* 109–120.

D'Zurilla, T. J., & Nezu, A. M. (1999). *Problem-solving therapy: A social competence approach to clinical intervention* (2nd ed.). New York: Springer Publishing Co.

Foa, E. B., & Kozak, M. J. (1986). Emotional processing of fear: Exposure to corrective information. *Psychological Bulletin, 99,* 20–35.

Freeston, M. H., Rheaume, J., Letarte, H., Dugas, M. J., & Ladouceur, R. (1994). Why do people worry? *Personality and Individual Differences, 17,* 791–802.

Goldfried, M. R. (1971). Systematic desensitization as training in self-control. *Journal of Consulting and Clinical Psychology, 37,* 228–234.

Gould, R. A., Otto, M. W., Pollack, M. H., & Yap, L. (1997). Cognitive behavioral and pharmacological treatment of generalized anxiety disorder: A preliminary meta-analysis. *Behavior Therapy, 28,* 285–305.

Hayes, S. C., Pankey, J., & Gregg, J. (2003). Acceptance and commitment therapy. In R. DiTomasso & E. Gosch (Eds.), *Comparative treatments for anxiety disorders* (pp. 110–136). New York: Springer Publishing Co.

Jones, G. N., Ames, S. C., Jeffries, S. K., Scarinci, I. C., & Brantley, P. J. (2001). Utilization of medical services and quality of life among low-income patients with generalized anxiety disorder attending primary care clinics. *International Journal of Psychiatry in Medicine, 31*, 183–198.

Ladouceur, R., Blais, F., Freeston, M. H., & Dugas, M. J. (1998). Problem solving and problem orientation in generalized anxiety disorder. *Journal of Anxiety Disorders, 12*, 139–152.

Ladouceur, R., Dugas, M. J., Freeston, M. H., Leger, E., Gagnon, F., & Thibodeau, N. (2000). Efficacy of a cognitive-behavioral treatment for generalized anxiety disorder: Evaluation in a controlled clinical trial. *Journal of Consulting and Clinical Psychology, 68*, 957–964.

Ladouceur, R., Talbot, F., & Dugas, M. J. (1997). Behavioral expressions of intolerance of uncertainty in worry. *Behavior Modification, 21*, 355–371.

Leahy, R. L. (2002). Improving homework compliance in the treatment of generalized anxiety disorder. *Journal of Clinical Psychology, 58*, 499–511.

Leahy, R. L., & Holland, S. J. (2000). *Treatment plans and interventions for depression and anxiety disorders.* New York: Guilford.

Lovibond, P. F., & Lovibond, S. H. (1995). The structure of negative emotional states: Comparison of the Depression Anxiety Stress Scales (DASS) with the Beck Depression and Anxiety Inventories. *Behaviour Research and Therapy, 33*, 335–343.

Meyer, T. J., Miller, M. L., Metzger, R. L., & Borkovec, T. D. (1990). Development and validation of the Penn State Worry Questionnaire. *Behaviour Research and Therapy, 28*, 487–495.

Mintzer, J. E., & Brawman-Mintzer, O. (1996). Agitation as a possible expression of generalized anxiety disorder in demented elderly patients: Toward a treatment approach. *Journal of Clinical Psychiatry, 57*, 55–63.

Newman, M. G., Castonguay, L. G., & Borkovec, T. D. (2003). Integrative therapy for generalized anxiety disorder. In C. L. Heimber, C. L. Turk, & D. S. Mennin (Eds.), *Generalized anxiety disorder: Advances in research and practice.* New York: Guilford Press.

Newman, M. G., Consoli, A. J., & Taylor, C. B. (1999). A palmtop computer program for the treatment of generalized anxiety disorder. *Behavior Modification, 23*, 597–619.

Newman, M. G., Zuellig, A. R., Kachin, K. E., Constantino, M. J., Przeworski, A., Erickson, T. et al. (2002). Preliminary reliability and validity of the Generalized Anxiety Disorder Questionnaire-IV: A revised self-report diagnostic measure of generalized anxiety disorder. *Behavior Therapy, 33*, 215–233.

Nezu, A. M. (in press). Problem solving and behavior therapy revisited. *Behavior Therapy.*

Öst, L. G., & Breitholtz, E. (2000). Applied relaxation vs. cognitive therapy in the treatment of generalized anxiety disorder. *Behaviour Research and Therapy, 38*, 777–790.

Persons, J. B., Mennin, D. S., & Tucker, D. E. (2001). Common misconceptions about the nature and treatment of generalized anxiety disorder. *Psychiatric Annals, 31*, 501–507.

Roemer, L., & Orsillo, S. M. (2002). Expanding our conceptualization of and treatment for generalized anxiety disorder: Integrating mindfulness/acceptance-based approaches with existing cognitive-behavioral models. *Clinical Psychology: Science and Practice, 9,* 54–68.

Roy-Byrne, P. P., & Katon, W. (1997). Generalized anxiety disorder in primary care: The precursor/modifier pathway to increased health care utilization. *Journal of Clinical Psychiatry, 58*(Suppl. 3), 34–38.

Stanley, M. A., & Novy, D. M. (2000). Cognitive-behavior therapy for generalized anxiety in late life: An evaluative overview. *Journal of Anxiety Disorders, 14,* 191–207.

Stoeber, J., & Borkovec, T. D. (2002). Reduced concreteness of worry in generalized anxiety disorder: Findings from a therapy study. *Cognitive Therapy and Research, 26,* 89–96.

Tallis, F., Eysenck, M., & Mathews, A. (1992). A questionnaire for the measurement of nonpathological worry. *Personality and Individual Differences, 13,* 161–168.

Tollefson, G. D., Tollefson, S. L., Pederson, M., & Luxenberg, M. (1991). Comorbid irritable bowel syndrome in patients with generalized anxiety and major depression. *Annals of Clinical Psychiatry, 3,* 215–222.

Wells, A. (1994). A multi-dimensional measure of worry: Development and preliminary validation of the Anxious Thoughts Inventory. *Anxiety, Stress, and Coping, 6,* 289–299.

Wells, A. (1995). Meta-cognition and worry: A cognitive model of generalized anxiety disorder. *Behavioural and Cognitive Psychotherapy, 23,* 301–320.

Wells, A. (2002). Worry, metacognition, and GAD: Nature, consequences, and treatment. *Journal of Cognitive Psychotherapy, 16,* 179–192.

Wells, A., & Carter, K. (1999). Preliminary tests of a cognitive model of generalized anxiety disorder. *Behaviour Research & Therapy, 37,* 585–594.

Wisocki, P. A. (1988). Worry as a phenomenon relevant to the elderly. *Behavior Therapy, 19,* 369–379.

Yonkers, K. A., Warshaw, M. G., Massion, A. O., & Keller, M. B. (1996). Phenomenology and course of generalized anxiety disorder. *British Journal of Psychiatry, 168,* 308–313.

Zhang, Y., Young, D., Lee, S., Li, L., Zhang, H., Xiao, Z. et al. (2002). Chinese Taoist cognitive psychotherapy in the treatment of generalized anxiety disorder in contemporary China. *Transcultural Psychiatry, 39,* 115–129.

Zinbarg, R. E., Craske, M. G., & Barlow, D. H. (1993). *Therapist's guide for the mastery of anxiety and worry.* San Antonio, TX: Psychological Corporation/Graywind Publications.

9

Social Anxiety

GENERAL DESCRIPTION AND DIAGNOSTIC ISSUES

Social phobia involves debilitating fears surrounding social performance or interactions. It is the third most prevalent psychological disorder, with a 13.3% lifetime prevalence rate (Kessler et al., 1994). The mean age of onset appears to be around 15 years, where onset after the age of 25 is rare.

Social phobia is defined by the *Diagnostic and Statistical Manual of Mental Disorders, Fourth Edition Text Revision* (DSM-IV-TR; American Psychiatric Association, 2000) as a marked and persistent fear of one or more social or performance situations in which the person is exposed to unfamiliar people or to possible scrutiny by others. People with social phobia fear that they will behave in a certain manner (or show anxiety symptoms) that is humiliating or embarrassing. Exposure to the feared social situation generally provokes anxiety, which can lead to a panic attack.

Individuals with social phobia fear that other people will judge them as being inadequate. The feared stimulus is either avoided or tolerated with great psychological distress. To meet diagnostic criteria, the person must recognize this fear as "excessive or unreasonable." Social phobia adversely impacts on general functioning, causing severe impairment in occupational, academic, and interpersonal realms. The anxiety or resulting avoidance is not a direct consequence of substances or a medical condition and is not explained by other psychiatric disorders (e.g., panic disorder, separation anxiety, body dysmorphic disorder, or schizoid personality disorder).

Social phobia is a heterogeneous disorder, where individuals may fear a specific situation or more global interactions. This latter group, specified by the DSM-IV-TR as "generalized," involves general social situations and has a close association with avoidant personality disorder. In contrast, others with social phobia experience more specific, performance-based fears, such as public speaking, but are not distressed in general social interactions.

Symptoms may be centered on social interactions (e.g., talking in front of others, being introduced or asked questions, interacting with people who are deemed important, being assertive) and/or performance of activities in public (e.g., being observed engaging in any behavior, using public restrooms, giving speeches, test anxiety).

Given the interpersonal nature of society, impairment can be profound in this population. Social relationships are avoided or strained. Similarly, academic and occupational functioning may be harmed because of the distress and avoidance of specific activities (e.g., getting in front of a class, giving a business presentation).

Differential Diagnostic Issues

Differential diagnosis of social phobia from other anxiety disorders is made based on the *source* of the fear. Social phobia differs from *panic disorder* in that those with panic disorder "fear fear," fear the occurrence of a panic attack, or fear that other panic behaviors will result in embarrassment or incapacitation. Social phobia, on the other hand, is based on the fear of negative evaluation from others. Although social phobia is characterized by avoidance or heightened distress related to situations where scrutiny is expected, *agoraphobia with or without panic disorder* does not rely on this expectation. In fact, the DSM-IV-TR differentiates these disorders by the presence of a confidant. Those with agoraphobia will typically experience a *decrease* in distress in the presence of a friend, whereas those with social phobia will maintain or experience *increased* distress. *Generalized anxiety disorder* differs from social phobia in that the former entails a pervasive worry not limited to performance or social situations. Individuals with a *specific phobia* may experience distress regarding social situations (e.g., embarrassed about a fear of heights), but this fear is not central.

Other disorders need to be differentiated from social phobia. *Depression* can entail avoidance of social situations, but this is more due to decreased interest and mood rather than anxiety, as seen in social phobia. Similar to social phobia, *pervasive developmental disorder* and *schizoid personality disorder* are characterized by avoiding social situations, although in these latter two disorders, the avoidance is due to a lack of interest, instead of fear.

Avoidant personality disorder (APD) shares many features with generalized social phobia and the two often co-occur (e.g., 22% to 70% of individuals with social phobia also meet criteria for APD). This particular additional Axis II diagnosis should be considered if the anxiety is longstanding (i.e., beginning in early adulthood) and generalized to numerous settings.

Co-Morbidity Issues

Co-morbid disorders are not uncommon in persons with social phobia. Overall, close to 70% of those with social phobia have an additional Axis I diagnosis. Specific disorders include simple phobia (59%), agoraphobia (45%), alcohol abuse (19%), major depressive disorder (17%), drug abuse (13%), and dsythymia (13%). In addition, 61% of individuals with social phobia meet criteria for various Axis II disorders. Patients often present to therapy for other disorders, so it is important to assess for social phobia in those who present with other symptoms or problems (e.g., depression).

ASSESSMENT OF DISORDER

Several different measures exist to assess various aspects of social anxiety. The reader is directed to Antony, Orsillo, and Roemer (2001) for a review of such assessment tools.

Clinician Ratings

- *Anxiety Disorders Interview Schedule for DMS-IV: Lifetime Version* (DiNardo, Brown, & Barlow, 1994): assesses current and lifetime DSM-IV diagnoses of anxiety, mood, and substance use.

- *Brief Social Phobia Scale* (Davidson et al., 1991): assesses social phobia symptoms according to three subscales—fear, physiological arousal, and avoidance.
- *Liebowitz Social Anxiety Scale* (Liebowitz, 1987): assesses problems with both social interactions and performance, yielding fear and avoidance scores.

Behavioral Assessments

- *Social Situations Interaction Test* (Mersch, Ernmelkamp, Bogels, & van der, 1989): consists of four scenarios where the client role-plays potentially anxiety provoking situations with a confederate.

Self-Report Measures

- *Social Anxiety Interaction Scale* (Mattick & Clarke, 1998): measures fears regarding general social interactions.
- *Social Avoidance and Distress Scale* (Watson & Friend, 1969): assesses distress and avoidance in social situations, as well as concerns with social-evaluative threats.
- *Social Phobia and Anxiety Inventory* (Turner, Beidel, & Dancu, 1996): measures the severity of symptoms (physiological, cognitive, behavioral) associated with social anxiety and social phobia and contains two subscales—social phobia and agoraphobia.
- *Social Phobia Inventory* (Connor et al., 2000): assesses symptoms of social phobia according to three subscales—fear, avoidance, and physiological arousal.
- *Social Phobia Scale* (Mattick & Clarke, 1998): measures fears of being evaluated during routine activities.

GENERAL THERAPY GOALS

Ultimate Outcome Goals

When working with patients with social phobia, general ultimate outcome goals include decreasing the frequency and intensity of social anxiety related to performance or social situations, enhancing functioning in social or performance situations, and increasing adaptive coping skills. In addition, addressing negative self-fulfilling prophecies that may occur in this population is important. Specifically, anxiety may result in maladaptive behaviors (e.g., avoidance, less than optimal social skills), which results in a negative reaction by others, and in the eyes of an individual with social phobia, "prove" their fears.

In addition, depending on the individual, other ultimate goals may be present. Given the significant co-morbidity of those with social phobia, decreasing problems related to other psychological disorders or symptoms may be an ultimate goal. For example, individuals who "self-medicate" by using alcohol or other drugs to help decrease social phobia symptoms would benefit from interventions to address substance abuse. Because of the social nature of this disorder, relationships can be strained as a consequence. Thus, enhancing significant relationships (e.g., marriage) may be an ultimate goal. An additional general treatment goal may be to decrease impaired occupational and/or academic functioning that is a consequence of the social phobic behaviors.

Major Instrumental Outcome Goals/Treatment Targets

Major instrumental outcome goals for social phobia include:

- Decrease heightened physiological arousal
- Decrease dysfunctional beliefs
- Enhance interpersonal skills

Goal 1: Decrease Heightened Physiological Arousal

Physiological arousal is a hallmark of social phobia. Individuals suffering from this disorder experience sympathetic nervous responses (e.g., increased heart rate, sweating, muscle tension) in response to social stressors. In addition, this arousal often becomes a source of concern itself (e.g., anxiety about sweaty palms when shaking someone's hand). It is this anxiety associated with social stimuli that the individual with social phobia wishes to avoid.

Goal-Specific Assessment Tools

- *Subjective Units of Distress Scale* (SUDS): patients' self-reported level of physiological or psychological distress, usually on a scale from 0 (*not at all distressed*) to 100 (*the most distressed they have ever been*).
- *Behavioral Avoidance Test (BAT):* patients' individually tailored hierarchy of avoided social situations; to be used in conjunction with SUDS ratings.

Goal-Specific Potential Interventions

- Exposure therapy
- Flooding
- Relaxation training

Exposure Therapy. The research literature suggests that exposure therapy as a treatment for social phobia is particularly effective, more so than any other CBT strategy applied by itself (Donohue, Van Hasselt, & Hersen, 1994). Exposure therapy aims to extinguish conditioned fear responses to relevant stimuli. This is based on the conceptualization that social phobia is partially maintained by the avoidance of anxiety-producing situations (e.g., going to a party, speaking at a business function) and the negative reinforcement that occurs as a consequence of avoiding such situations. This conditioned fear response can be evoked by a variety of similar situations as a function of generalization across stimuli. Whereas many individuals with social phobia can recall the onset of symptoms with the experience of a traumatic event, a sizeable number recall vicarious learning experiences, suggesting the role of social learning in the etiology of social phobia (Öst & Hugdahl, 1981).

Exposure aims to extinguish the fear-based anxiety, where habituation occurs by having patients expose themselves repeatedly to relevant fear-provoking situations until the anxiety reduces. Often this takes the form of *guided exposure*, whereby the patient is gradually exposed to increasingly more distressing situations. This exposure can be *imaginal* (e.g., having the patient imagine themselves giving a speech in front of a large audience), in-session role-plays (e.g., therapist role plays with the patient being at a formal dinner party), or *in vivo* (e.g., patient is encouraged to attend a office party). In vivo practice is likely to have a greater impact on decreasing avoidance as it impacts on generalization.

Barlow (Barlow, 2002; Barlow, Raffa, & Cohen, 2002) suggests that some form of exposure should be a central feature of any treatment for social phobia. As in all CBT procedures, encouraging patients to practice exposure in vivo, as homework, is a critical treatment feature. For example, Edelman and Chambless (1995) found that compliance with homework predicts better outcomes.

Flooding.   Flooding is based on the same conditioning principles as exposure, but instead of beginning with less distressing situations on a fear hierarchy, the patient is exposed to an intensive flooding of a highly stressful scenario in the beginning. Similar to other exposure-based treatment approaches, each session is conducted until the patient's subjective anxiety (e.g., SUDS) returns to baseline level or other appropriate criteria in order for meaningful extinction to occur.

Relaxation Training.   This approach includes a wide range of behavioral stress management strategies geared to specifically reduce a patient's symptoms of heightened physiological arousal and anxiety. It also aims to substitute a new conditioned response (relaxation) for the previously conditioned response (anxiety and fear). Such strategies include progressive muscle relaxation, autogenic training, and visualization, and are geared specifically to reduce negative arousal. Although there is not substantial support for applying relaxation procedures *in isolation* in treating social anxiety, used in conjunction with other strategies, such tactics can enhance overall CBT-treatment effects. For example, when a patient with low self-efficacy has difficulty believing that exposure can work or is too anxious to even attempt other strategies, having the skills to reduce his or her own anxiety may provide motivation to continue in treatment regarding other clinical tools.

Goal 2: Decrease Dysfunctional Beliefs

Dysfunctional beliefs are pervasive in social phobia and include extreme standards of perfectionism in social performance (e.g., "I can't show any signs of fear"), conditional beliefs of others' reactions (e.g., "If I mess up, no one will like me"), and negative beliefs about oneself (e.g., "I am no good"). Such beliefs can enhance anxiety and anxious behaviors, thus perpetuating the patient's overall distress. Some researchers posit that dysfunctional beliefs are at the root of social phobia. For example, Beck and his colleagues (e.g., Beck, Emery, & Greenberg, 1985) theorize that extreme standards of perfectionism in social performance, conditional beliefs of others' beliefs, and negative beliefs about oneself all contribute to a self-fulfilling prophecy. Clark and Wells (1995) further attribute the development of anxiety symptoms and maladaptive coping strategies (e.g., avoidance) to self-focused attention, coupled with unrealistically high standards for social performance and the expectation for negative evaluation from others. Such thoughts and behaviors increase the perception of threats, resulting in a cyclical maintenance of social phobia.

Another theory invoking a cognitive conceptualization proposes that social phobia develops because of a discrepancy between one's sense of self and others' expected standards (Rapee & Heimberg, 1997). According to this framework, the person with social phobia focuses on negative behaviors (e.g., sweating) and the perceived menacing environment, producing an idea of how one "should" act. A comparison is then made between this "should view" and the distorted view of the patient's self-perceived behavior.

Maladaptive cognitions appear to be related to alcohol abuse in persons with social phobia. Socially anxious individuals who hold expectations of enhanced social assertiveness, decreased tension, and positive changes as a function of drinking can become future alcohol abusers. In fact, studies have demonstrated social phobia precedes alcohol abuse, perhaps due to maladaptive cognitions (e.g., Davidson, Hughes, George, & Blazer, 1993).

Goal-Specific Assessment Tools

- *Social Interaction Self-Statement Test* (SISST; Glass, Merluzzi, Biever, & Larsen, 1982): self-report measure that provides scores for both positive and negative self-statements associated with social situations and can be used to assess cognitions during role-plays of social interactions.
- *Fear of Negative Evaluation* (FNE; Watson & Friend, 1969): 30-item self-report inventory that measures the expectations and distress associated with negative evaluation from others.
- *Self-Statements During Public Speaking* (SSPS; Hofmann & DiBartolo, 2000): a 10-item self-report instrument measuring both positive and negative self-statements related to public speaking.

Goal-Specific Potential Interventions

- Cognitive restructuring
- Problem-solving therapy

Cognitive Restructuring. Conceptually, disorder-related cognitive variables can be classified into three levels: *negative automatic thoughts* (e.g., "If I talk in front of this group, I'll say something stupid"), *distorted or maladaptive assumptions* (e.g., "If I say something stupid, no one will like me and all will reject me"), and *dysfunctional self-schemas* ("I am stupid and inadequate"). Intervention strategies to help decrease these dysfunctional cognitive factors are based on cognitive restructuring principles. Conceptually, cognitive restructuring can be thought of as an umbrella term that encompasses several specific therapy strategies: rational-emotive therapy (e.g., Ellis, 1994), cognitive therapy (Beck et al., 1985), and self-instructional training (Meichenbaum, 1977). Whereas differences among these three approaches exist, all involve helping patients to better identify and then alter maladaptive thoughts. When treating cognitive dysfunctions in persons with social phobia, individuals are asked to recognize negative automatic thoughts, first related to more benign events, and then to the actual feared stimuli. Patients are next taught how to assess the accuracy of these thoughts or their use of various cognitive errors (e.g., all-or-nothing thinking, mind reading, automatically anticipating negative outcomes), and replace maladaptive cognitions with more adaptive ones. For homework, patients are asked to maintain a journal of automatic thoughts during stressful situations and appropriate rebuttals.

Problem-Solving Therapy.   A related therapy approach is problem-solving therapy (e.g., D'Zurilla & Nezu, 1999; Nezu, in press), which is geared to increase one's overall coping ability when dealing with stressful situations. Part of this approach involves changing those cognitive factors that negatively impinge on one's *problem orientation* or general view of problems and one's self-assessment regarding one's problem-solving capabilities (e.g., beliefs about why a problem occurred, attributions about who is responsible for the problem occurring in the first place, self-efficacy beliefs). One study that compared all four of these approaches to changing negative cognitions related to social phobia found no differences in outcome among any of these strategies (DiGiuseppe, McGowan, Simon, & Gardner, 1990). However, this remains the only study to investigate the efficacy of this approach for social phobia.

Goal 3: Enhance Interpersonal Skills

Whereas social phobia often entails dysfunctional thoughts related to one's social abilities, some fears may not be totally ill-founded. At times, the patient may lack appropriate interpersonal skills, which can lead to distress and perpetuate the social anxiety. Avoidance of such situations also serves to limit opportunities to learn such skills developmentally.

Goal-Specific Assessment Tools

- Clinician observations of in-session role plays that center on relevant social situations can be important tools for assessing specific interpersonal skills deficits.

Goal-Specific Potential Interventions

- Social skills training
- Social effectiveness training
- Group therapy

Social Skills Training.   This strategy is based on the idea that some individuals with social phobia are deficient in verbal and nonverbal social skills. As such, one treatment component for social phobia might involve teaching patients a wide variety of interpersonal and social skills (e.g., empathy, listening, making friends, self-disclosure).

Social Effectiveness Therapy.   This is a therapy package that combines interpersonal skills training and exposure for the treatment of social phobia (Turner, Beidel, Cooley, Woody, & Messer, 1994) and has demonstrated significant promise. For example, SET has led to 84% improvement in generalized social phobia despite Axis I and II co-morbidity.

Group Therapy.   In general, providing treatment in a group setting may be particularly beneficial for some patients in terms of enhancing interpersonal skills. While a meta-analysis demonstrated no significant differences between group and individual therapy (Taylor, 1996), a group setting does provide some unique opportunities. In addition to interpersonal interactions, group therapy permits modeling, normalization, peer encouragement, and reinforcement of skills attained. Heimberg and his colleagues (e.g., Heimberg, Salzman, Holt, & Blendell, 1993) developed a treatment approach that combines in-session exposure and cognitive restructuring specifically in a group setting and has demonstrated its efficacy both short and long term.

Additional Instrumental Outcome Goals/Treatment Target

Secondary treatment targets for social phobia may include:

- *Decrease General Stress.* Individuals with social phobia report more negative and less positive life events than those without psychological disorders, which corresponded to greater depressive symptoms and anxiety (Brown, Juster, Heimberg, & Winning, 1998). As such, a possible secondary treatment goal for a patient with social phobia includes decreasing overall general stress levels. Possible intervention approaches include various behavioral stress management strategies to reduce stress-related physical symptomatology, as well as coping skills training strategies, such as Problem-Solving Therapy, to help the patient manage stressful negative life events more effectively.

- *Improve Specific Social Skills Deficits.* If the social-phobic behavior has led to an impairment in a given social skill area unique to a given patient, then that deficit may need to be targeted as a meaningful therapy goal. Such deficits may include interpersonal communications, public speaking, or assertiveness skills.

- *Decrease Focus on Bodily Sensations.* Heightened focused attention on bodily sensations (e.g., heart rate, sweating) can have adverse effects. For example, when given information about an increase in heart rate, persons with social phobia report greater anxiety and negative cognitions, whereas the opposite occurs when participants are told their pulse had decreased (Wells & Papageorgiou, 2001). Further, patients with social phobia who interpret internal cues as "catastrophic" are more likely to relapse following intervention (Clark & Wells, 1995). In response to such data, Wells and Papageorgiou (1998) evaluated a strategy that combined exposure with training to shift attention to outside oneself, rather than on one's own physiological responses, and found it to engender greater decreases in anxiety and maladaptive cognitions.

- *Address Co-Morbid Disorders.* As noted previously, co-morbid psychological problems are not uncommon in persons with social phobia. In fact, such a patient may present with complaints associated with another disorder, where the social phobia becomes apparent only later in therapy. Although research is somewhat inconsistent regarding the effects of co-morbid disorders, when treating individuals with social phobia, it would appear that assessing for their presence and identifying them as a *potential* target makes sound clinical sense.

ADDITIONAL CLINICAL CONSIDERATIONS

Ethnic diversity considerations regarding social phobia include both culture-related differential terminology and varying foci of the fear. With regard to the first instance, African-Caribbean patients often use the term "paranoid" to refer to social anxiety. Thus, a patient with this ethnic background may report feelings of "paranoia" that are, in fact, not delusional beliefs, but rather manifestations of social phobia. For Japanese and other Eastern cultures, the source of social fears may differ from more Western cultures. A disorder exists called *Taijin Kyfusho* (TKS) experienced by some members of Eastern cultures. TKS involves social phobic symptoms centered on a fear of embarrassing *others*, rather than oneself (Dinnel, Kleinknecht, & Tanaka-Matsumi, 2002). This is an important distinction, as compared to the "Western social phobia," and would alter the therapeutic emphasis toward exposure to feared situations as they relate to embarrassing others.

Another final example of the importance of ethnicity comes from a case report of an African American woman suffering from social phobia (Fink, Turner, & Beidel, 1996). In this case, the validity of the patient's fear hierarchy was significantly strengthened when the situations incorporated racial cues (e.g., "You have to present to a group of Caucasian males who you know are judgmental both toward your skills and your race"). These authors suggest that incorporating such details can also apply to gender, sexual orientation, and other sociocultural factors.

REFERENCES

American Psychiatric Association. (2000). *Diagnostic and statistical manual of mental disorders* (ed. 4, text revision). Washington, DC: American Psychiatric Press.

Antony, M. M., Orsillo, S. M., & Roemer, L. (2001). *Practitioner's guide to empirically based measures of anxiety.* New York: Kluwer Academic/Plenum Publishers.

Barlow, D. H. (2002). *Anxiety and its disorders: The nature and treatment of anxiety and panic* (2nd ed.). New York: Guilford Press.

Barlow, D. H., Raffa, S. D., & Cohen, E. M. (2002). Psychosocial treatments for panic disorders, phobias, and generalized anxiety disorder. In P. E. Nathan & J. M. Gorman (Eds.), *A guide to treatments that work* (2nd ed., pp. 301–335). New York: Oxford University Press.

Beck, A. T., Emery, C., & Greenberg, R. L. (1985). *Anxiety disorders and phobias: A cognitive perspective.* New York: Basic Books.

Brown, E. J., Juster, H. R., Heimberg, R. G., & Winning, C. D. (1998). Stressful life events and personality styles: relation to impairment and treatment outcome in patients with social phobia. *Journal of Anxiety Disorders, 12,* 233–251.

Clark, D. M., & Wells, A. (1995). A cognitive model of social phobia. In R. G.Heimberg & M. R. Liebowitz (Eds.), *Social phobia: Diagnosis, assessment, and treatment* (pp. 69–93). New York: Guilford Press.

Connor, K. M., Davidson, J. R., Churchill, L. E., Sherwood, A., Foa, E., & Weisler, R. H. (2000). Psychometric properties of the Social Phobia Inventory (SPIN). New self-rating scale. *British Journal of Psychiatry, 176,* 379–386.

Davidson, J. R., Hughes, D. L., George, L. K., & Blazer, D. G. (1993). The epidemiology of social phobia: findings from the Duke Epidemiological Catchment Area Study. *Psychological Medicine, 23,* 709–718.

Davidson, J. R., Potts, N. L., Richichi, E. A., Ford, S. M., Krishnan, K. R., Smith, R. D. et al. (1991). The Brief Social Phobia Scale. *Journal of Clinical Psychiatry, 52*(Supplement), 48–51.

DiGiuseppe, R., Simon, K. S., McGowan, L., & Gardner, F. (1990). A comparative outcome study of four cognitive therapies in the treatment of social anxiety. *Journal of Rational-Emotive and Cognitive-Behavior Therapy, 8,* 129–146.

DiNardo, P. A., Brown, T. A., & Barlow, D. H. (1994). *Anxiety Disorders Interview Schedule for DMS-IV: Lifetime Version (ADIS-IV-L).* Albany, NY: Graywind Publications.

Dinnel, D. L., Kleinknecht, R. A., & Tanaka-Matsumi, J. (2002). A cross-cultural comparison of social phobia symptoms. *Journal of Psychopathology and Behavioral Assessment, 24,* 75–84.

Donohue, B. C., Van Hasselt, V. B., & Hersen, M. (1994). Behavioral assessment and treatment of social phobia. *Behavior Modification, 18,* 262–288.

D'Zurilla, T. J., & Nezu, A. M. (1999). *Problem-solving therapy: A social competence approach to clinical intervention* (2nd ed.). New York: Springer Publishing Co.

Edelman, R. E., & Chambless, D. L. (1995). Adherence during sessions and homework in cognitive-behavioral group treatment of social phobia. *Behaviour Research and Therapy, 33,* 573–577.

Ellis, A. (1994). *Reason and emotion in psychotherapy* (rev. ed.). New York: Birch Lane Press.

Fink, C. M., Turner, S. M., & Beidel, D. C. (1996). Culturally relevant factors in the behavioral treatment of social phobia: A case study. *Journal of Anxiety Disorders, 10,* 201–209.

Glass, C. R., Merluzzi, T. V., Biever, J. L., & Larsen, K. H. (1982). Cognitive assessment of social anxiety: Development and validation of a self-statement questionnaire. *Cognitive Therapy and Research, 6,* 37–55.

Heimberg, R. G., Salzman, D. G., Halt, C. S., & Blendell, K. A. (1993). Cognitive-behavioral group treatment for social phobia: Effectiveness at five-year follow-up. *Cognitive Therapy and Research, 17,* 325–339.

Hofmann, S. G., & DiBartolo, P. M. (2000). An instrument to assess self-statements during public speaking: Scale development and preliminary psychometric properties. *Behavior Therapy, 31,* 499–515.

Kessler, R. C., McGonagle, K. A., Zhao, S., Nelson, C. B., Hughes, M., Eshleman, S. et al. (1994). Lifetime and 12-month prevalence of DSM-III-R psychiatric disorders in the United States. Results from the National Comorbidity Survey. *Archives of General Psychiatry, 51,* 8–19.

Liebowitz, M. R. (1987). Social phobia. *Modern Problems in Pharmacopsychiatry, 22,* 141–173.

Mattick, R. P., & Clarke, J. C. (1998). Development and validation of measures of social phobia scrutiny fear and social interaction anxiety. *Behaviour Research and Therapy, 36,* 455–470.

Meichenbaum, D. H. (1977). *Cognitive behavior modification.* New York: Plenum Press.

Mersch, P. P., Emmelkamp, P. M., Bogels, S. M., & van der, S. J. (1989). Social phobia: Individual response patterns and the effects of behavioral and cognitive interventions. *Behaviour Research and Therapy, 27*, 421–434.

Nezu, A. M. (in press). Problem solving and behavior therapy revisited. *Behavior Therapy*.

Öst, L. G., & Hugdahl, K. (1981). Acquisition of phobias and anxiety response patterns in clinical patients. *Behaviour Research and Therapy, 16*, 439–447.

Rapee, R. M., & Heimberg, R. G. (1997). A cognitive-behavioral model of anxiety in social phobia. *Behaviour Research and Therapy, 35*, 741–756.

Taylor, S. (1996). Meta-analysis of cognitive-behavioral treatments for social phobia. *Journal of Behaviour Therapy and Experimental Psychiatry, 27*, 1–9.

Turner, S. M., Beidel, D. C., Cooley, M. R., Woody, S. R., & Messer, S. C. (1994). A multicomponent behavioral treatment for social phobia: Social effectiveness therapy. *Behaviour Research and Therapy, 32*, 381–390.

Turner, S. M., Beidel, D. C., & Dancu, C. V. (1996). *SPAI: Social Phobia and Anxiety Inventory*. North Tonawanda, NY: Multi-Health Systems.

Watson, D., & Friend, R. (1969). Measurement of social-evaluative anxiety. *Journal of Consulting and Clinical Psychology, 33*, 448–457.

Wells, A., & Papageorgiou, C. (1998). Social phobia: Effects of external attention on anxiety, negative beliefs, and perspective taking. *Behavior Therapy, 29*, 357–370.

Wells, A., & Papageorgiou, C. (2001). Brief cognitive therapy for social phobia: A case series. *Behaviour Research and Therapy, 39*, 713–720.

10

Obsessive-Compulsive Disorder

GENERAL DESCRIPTION AND DIAGNOSTIC ISSUES

Obsessive-compulsive disorder (OCD) is characterized by the presence of obsessions, compulsions, or both. *Obsessions* are defined as persistent ideas, thoughts, impulses, or images that are experienced as intrusive or inappropriate, viewed as unacceptable, and lead to marked anxiety and distress. The individual with OCD attempts to reduce the experienced distress by ignoring or suppressing the obsessions, avoiding certain situations, or engaging in behaviors aimed at neutralizing the obsessions. *Compulsions* refer to this latter reaction and entail a variety of repetitive behaviors (e.g., hand washing, ordering, checking) or cognitive acts (e.g., praying, counting, repeating words silently). Such behaviors are either excessive or not connected in a realistic way with what they are designed to neutralize or prevent. In most cases, the person feels driven to perform the compulsion to either reduce the distress that accompanies an obsession or prevent some dreaded event from occurring. Both avoidance and ritualistic behaviors result in decreased distress, although this reduction is temporary.

According to the *Diagnostic and Statistical Manual of Mental Disorders, Fourth Edition Text Revision* (DSM-IV-TR; American Psychiatric Association, 2000), a diagnosis of OCD requires the presence of obsessions and compulsions that are sufficiently severe to be overly time consuming (i.e., take more than 1 hour a day), cause marked distress, or result in significant impairment. Patients with OCD tend to recognize that the obsessions are a "product of their own mind." If another Axis I disorder is present, the content of the obsessions or compulsions is not restricted to it, nor is the OCD due to the direct physiological effects of a substance (e.g., use of drug) or a general medical condition.

By definition, adults with OCD have, at some point, recognized that the obsessions. or compulsions are excessive or unreasonable. However, there is a broad range of insight regarding the rationality of their symptoms. The specification "with Poor Insight" is used for diagnostic purposes if the person does not generally recognize that the obsessions and compulsions are disproportionate or irrational.

OCD has diverse manifestations and often involves more than one type of obsession and/or compulsion. The most common obsessions are repeated thoughts about *contamination* (e.g., becoming contaminated who touching a doorknob), *repeated doubts* (e.g., wondering whether one has performed an act such as turning off the stove), a need to have items in a particular *order* (e.g., intense distress when objects are disordered or asymmetrical), *aggressive or horrific impulses* (e.g., images of hurting one's child), and *sexual imagery* (e.g., a recurrent pornographic image). The most common compulsions involve *washing and cleaning, counting, checking, requesting or demanding assurances, repeating actions*, and *ordering*. Specific examples include individuals with obsessions about becoming contaminated who may wash their hands until their skin is raw, or persons distressed by unwanted profane thoughts may find relief in repeating a prayer over and over.

OCD usually begins in adolescence or early adulthood with the modal age of onset in males between 6 and 15 years and between 20 and 29 years for females. As children, boys suffer from OCD twice as often as girls, but once adulthood has been reached, rates of OCD are equal between genders. Regarding the course, the majority of individuals with OCD experience a chronic waxing and waning, with an exacerbation of symptoms usually related to stress. Although OCD was previously thought to be relatively rare in the general population, recent community studies have estimated a lifetime prevalence of 2.5% (Karno, Golding, Sorensen, & Burnam, 1988).

Differential Diagnostic Issues

OCD must be distinguished from other anxiety disorders. Unlike OCD where cognitions are the root of fear, *panic disorder* is characterized by fear associated with somatic experiences, *social phobia* is differentiated by fear of performance or evaluation, and *specific phobia* is distinguished by anxiety provoked by a specific object or situation. OCD differs from *generalized anxiety disorder* in that the latter refers to pervasive worry about numerous real-life events, whereas OCD-related fears are more unrealistic or magical and are handled by engaging in neutralizing behaviors.

Because OCD shares certain characteristics with other Axis I disorders, further differentiations must be made. *Depression* is often characterized by ruminations, but unlike OCD, these ruminations are characterized by pessimism, relate to themselves and others, and are not suppressed. Eating disorders (e.g., *anorexia nervosa* and *bulimia*) may share certain characteristics with OCD, but obsessions and compulsions are centered on body weight. *Body dysmorphic disorder* entails nearly delusional obsessions specifically about a particular perceived physical flaw and ritualistic looking at that anatomical structure (e.g., checking in mirror). In *hypochondriasis*, the obsession is related to a single event, where the individual focuses on physical symptoms which are interpreted as indications that a disease has been contracted. In contrast, those with OCD have multiple sources of distress and, when related to diseases, fear that they *will* contract an illness. *Trichotillomania* is characterized by compulsive hair pulling in an attempt to decrease distress. People with *pervasive developmental disorders* (e.g., *Asperger's disorder*) are extremely rigid and compulsive, with stereotyped behaviors that somewhat resemble very severe OCD. However, those with pervasive developmental disorders have extremely severe problems relating to and communicating with other people, problems that do not occur in OCD at that level. Moreover, although persons with OCD usually recognize their fears as unreasonable but products of their own minds, patients with *psychotic disorders* differ in that they believe that an external force has implanted the thoughts. Further, individuals with psychotic disorders generally have no compulsions.

Finally, although often confused, OCD is distinct from obsessive-compulsive personality disorder (OCPD). OCPD is characterized by an enduring preoccupation with rules, schedules, and lists and distinguishing traits such as perfectionism, an excessive devotion to work, rigidity, and inflexibility.

Co-Morbidity Issues

Over 50% of persons with OCD suffer from additional Axis I disorders, most frequently other anxiety and mood disorders. Specifically, 39% have an additional anxiety disorder (26% of persons with OCD have social phobia and 20% meet criteria for specific phobia), and 32% have mood disorders (with 28%–38% meeting criteria for major depressive disorder). Approximately 80% of persons with OCD have elevated depressive symptoms (e.g., negative affect, decreased self-esteem, guilt). Further, 10% of females with OCD have a history of anorexia nervosa. Although over half of the individuals with Tourette's disorder have OCD, only about 5%–7% of those with OCD have Tourette's disorder. Persons with OCD often meet criteria for personality disorders, particularly Cluster C (i.e., avoidant, dependent personality and occasionally obsessive compulsive personality disorders).

ASSESSMENT OF DISORDER

Several different measures exist to assess various aspects of OCD. The reader is directed to Antony, Orsillo, and Roemer (2001) for a review of such assessment tools.

Clinician Ratings

- *Anxiety Disorders Interview Schedule for DMS-IV: Lifetime Version* (DiNardo, Brown, & Barlow, 1994): assesses current and lifetime DSM-IV diagnoses of anxiety, mood, and substance use.
- *Overvalued Ideas Scale* (Neziroglu, McKay, Yaryura-Tobias, Stevens, & Todaro, 1999): provides open-ended assessment of the strength of the most prominent OCD belief over the previous week.
- *Yale-Brown Obsessive Compulsive Scale* (Goodman et al., 1989): assesses severity and types of symptoms in OCD.

Behavioral Assessments

- *Self-Monitoring* (Leahy & Holland, 2000) assesses *in vivo* obsessions, rituals, time spent engaging in obsessions and rituals, and level of distress.

Self-Report Measures

- *Maudsley Obsessional Compulsive Inventory* (Hodgson & Rachman, 1977): assesses obsessive-compulsive behaviors and rituals with the

following subscales: Checking, Washing, Doubting/Conscientiousness, and Slowness/Repetition.
- *Obsessive Compulsive Inventory* (Foa, Kozak, Salkovskis, Coles, & Amir, 1998): assesses both the frequency and distress severity related to obsessions and compulsions.
- *Obsessive Compulsive Questionnaire* (Leahy et al., 2000): assesses amount bothered by a variety of obsessions and time spent engaged in rituals.
- *Padua Inventory—Washington State University Revisions* (Burns, Keortge, Formea, & Sternberger, 1996): assesses both obsessions and compulsions, with the following subscales: Contamination, Checking, Impaired Mental Control, and Urges and Worries.

GENERAL THERAPY GOALS

Ultimate Outcome Goals

OCD has the potential to be the most debilitating of the anxiety disorders due to the heightened distress that significantly interferes with the individual's normal routine and/or occupational functioning. Thus, ultimate outcome goals include decreasing distress, decreasing time spent engaging in obsessions and rituals, and enhancing occupational/school performance. In addition, because OCD can be a significant stressor not only for the patient, but also for the patient's family and social network, improving relationships may be an important ultimate outcome. In short, ultimate outcome goals are centered on decreasing the interruptive nature of OCD and enhancing the patient's overall quality of life.

Major Instrumental Outcome Goals/Treatment Targets

Major instrumental outcome goals for OCD include:

- Decrease appraisal of intrusive thoughts
- Decrease overt neutralizing behaviors
- Decrease covert maladaptive behaviors

Goal 1: Decrease Negative Appraisal of Intrusive Thoughts

Although over 80% of the population have had intrusive thoughts at one time (Salkovkis & Harrison, 1984), OCD is not as common. What distinguishes individuals with OCD from nonclinical populations is their misinterpretation regarding the significance of the appraisal of the thoughts as threatening. This threatening appraisal causes both distress and subsequent attempts to decrease the distress.

The threatening appraisal of intrusive thoughts is centered on beliefs about both *responsibility* (e.g., "If I don't wash my hands, I could get my family sick") and *danger* (e.g., "There are noxious germs everywhere"). Salkovskis (1985) proposed that individuals with OCD have overactive schemas of responsibility (e.g., "It is my responsibility to protect myself and my loved ones") and danger (e.g., "It is highly likely that something bad will happen"), which influence their dysfunctional interpretation of intrusive thoughts. Thus, such individuals *overestimate* the probability of danger, their amount of responsibility for the predicted danger, and the consequences for being responsible.

This sense of responsibility for impending danger is key to a cognitive formulation of OCD and serves to differentiate OCD from other anxiety disorders. This appraisal of responsibility results in, and is enhanced by, selective attention to danger, adverse mood (e.g., distress, negative affect), and maladaptive coping strategies (e.g., overt neutralizing behaviors, avoidance, thought suppression) (Salkovskis, 1999; Salkovskis et al., 2000). As a consequence, a perpetuating system maintaining the OCD symptoms comes to exist.

Related to the appraisal of responsibility is the belief held by many with OCD that negative thoughts *cause* negative events. For example, the mother who has intrusive thoughts about hurting her child believes thinking about this injury will cause her to perform it. This phenomenon has been termed "thought-action fusion" (Amir, Freshman, Ramsey, Neary, & Brigidi, 2001).

Typical OCD-related beliefs are listed as follows (Obsessive Compulsive Cognitions Working Group, 2001). Because such beliefs are hypothesized to play a strong causal role in producing obsessions and compulsions, they become potentially important treatment targets.

- *Overimportance of Thoughts* (the belief that the occurrence of a thought implies something important).

- *Need to Control Thoughts* (the overevaluation of the importance of exerting complete control over intrusive thoughts, images, and impulses, as well as the belief that such control is both possible and desirable).
- *Perfectionism* (the tendency to believe [a] that there is a perfect solution to every problem, [b] that doing something perfectly is both possible and necessary, and [c] that even minor mistakes have serious consequences).
- *Inflated Responsibility* (the belief that one has the power to bring about or prevent crucial negative outcomes).
- *Overestimation of Threat* (beliefs indicating an exaggerated estimate of the probability or severity of harm).
- *Intolerance for Uncertainty* (beliefs [a] that it is crucial to be certain about events, [b] that one has a poor ability to cope with unpredictable change, and [c] that if a situation is ambiguous, it is extremely difficulty to function adequately).

Goal-Specific Assessment Tools

- *Dysfunctional Thought Record* (Beck, 1995): identifies situations that trigger automatic thoughts, actual automatic thoughts, emotions, adaptive counter thoughts, and emotional and cognitive consequences.
- *Interpretation of Intrusions Inventory* (Steketee & Frost, 2001): assesses appraisal and interpretation of intrusive thoughts.
- *Obsessional Beliefs Questionnaire* (Steketee & Frost, 2001): assesses dysfunctional assumptions and beliefs regarding items such as overimportance and control of thoughts, overestimation of threat, and responsibility.
- *Responsibility Attitude Scale* (Salkovskis et al., 2000): assesses general attitudes and beliefs about one's perceived responsibility.
- *Responsibility Interpretation Questionnaire* (Salkovskis et al., 2000): measures the frequency and conviction of specific interpretations of possible danger resulting from intrusive thoughts.
- *Thought-Action Fusion* (Shafran, Thordarson, & Rachman, 1996): assesses cognitive distortions related to OCD (e.g., belief that thinking about a troubling event will make it happen).

Goal-Specific Potential Interventions

- Cognitive restructuring
- Pie chart strategy
- Problem-solving therapy

Cognitive Restructuring. Cognitive restructuring is geared to changing the maladaptive appraisal of intrusive thoughts, particularly one's appraisal related to harm and responsibility (Emmelkamp & Beens, 1991). The first step is for patients to gain a better understanding of these thoughts. Using techniques such as guided discovery, the occurrence of intrusive thoughts can be normalized (e.g., they occur in over 80% of the population) and evaluations of these intrusions are identified. Specific targets in cognitive restructuring for OCD are dysfunctional thoughts related to responsibility and danger with the goal of "de-catastrophizing" intrusive thoughts. Thus, patients are taught to (a) alter the interpretation of intrusive thoughts as stimuli, (b) identify negative automatic thoughts, (c) challenge such negative automatic thoughts, and (d) replace these thoughts with more adaptive cognitions (van Oppen, de Haan, van Balkom, & Spinhoven, 1995). The use of *Socratic questioning* to identify and challenge dysfunctional thoughts, *cost-benefit analyses* to assess appraisals, and *homework* to promote continuity of learned skills are central components of this approach for patients with OCD. Cognitive restructuring should center more on developing less harmful explanations of intrusions rather than rebutting the beliefs (Salkovskis, 1999).

The *downward arrow technique* can be an additional useful tool in cognitive restructuring for OCD. Specifically, this procedure can assist in identifying the interpretation of intrusive thoughts, challenging the patient's assumptions, and underscoring the maladaptive consequences of obsessions. When using the downward arrow technique, the therapist asks the patient to identify "what would be so bad if" the thoughts and assumptions held were true.

Pie Chart Strategy. Because patients with OCD often overestimate their responsibility for a negative event, they are instructed to identify their true amount of responsibility. One technique to accomplish this identification entails constructing a "pie chart" (Leahy & Holland, 2000). Here, patients are asked to develop a list of people who might be responsible for a dangerous event, starting with themselves. They then assign the amount of responsibility by each individual on the list starting at the bottom. The percent of responsibility is diagrammed in a pie chart. The last amount of responsibility for the peril is then assigned to the patient. This allows a modification of all-or-nothing thinking regarding the patient's responsibility for a feared event.

Problem-Solving Therapy. Patients with OCD typically do not question the veracity of their appraisal of responsibility and danger regarding their intrusive thoughts. In addition, they continue to use maladaptive coping techniques in dealing with such thoughts (e.g., compulsive and avoidant behaviors). Problem-solving training facilitates the acquisition of a greater flexibility and appropriateness of coping skills (Nezu, in press). Here, patients might learn to generate a variety of options in dealing with the intrusive thoughts instead of engaging in their habitual compulsions. In addition, skills in decision making and solution implementation are taught. Using problem-solving therapy, patients learn to develop alternative explanations for the intrusions, as well as more adaptive ways to cope with them.

Goal 2: Decrease Overt Neutralizing Behaviors

As previously noted, OCD is characterized by overt compulsions executed in an effort to decrease distress and increase control over intrusive thoughts. Compulsions are effective at lessening distress in the short term, but perpetuate distress in the long term.

When OCD initially develops, patients may attempt to refrain from engaging in the neutralizing behavior. However, this attempt to resist a compulsion results in increased distress, which the patient perceives as being relieved only by performing the neutralizing behavior. Over time, and after repeated failure to "defend against the obsessions and compulsions," the individual may give into them, no longer experiencing a desire to resist them, and incorporate the behaviors into his or her daily routines.

Goal-Specific Assessment Tools

- *Compulsive Activity Checklist* (Freund, Steketee, & Foa, 1987): assesses impairment of daily activities as a result of obsessions and compulsions.
- *Counting of ritual behaviors:* records the frequency and duration of compulsive rituals.

Goal-Specific Potential Interventions

- Exposure and response prevention
- Modeling
- Disrupt rituals

Exposure and Response Prevention.   Exposure and response prevention (ERP) involves *exposing* patients to their obsessions, and at the same time, *preventing* them from engaging in their neutralizing behaviors. Exposure permits habituation of the feared stimuli (i.e., obsessions), which have been previously classically conditioned. In addition, neutralizing behaviors that were previously reinforced (i.e., secondary to temporarily decreased distress) are now prevented. Thus, patients learn that their previous ways of coping with distress (i.e., neutralizing behaviors) are neither necessary nor effective. This latter aspect of ERP is imperative, as exposure without response prevention would only serve to strengthen the feared response (Foa & Franklin, 2001).

To conduct ERP, a fear hierarchy is developed, to which the patient is systematically and progressively exposed. Some obsessions are more amenable to imaginal exposure (e.g., murdering a child), whereas others can be accessed *in vivo* (e.g., washing hands after touching dirt). Where possible, treatment should include *both* types of exposure situations. For example, although it is obviously not advisable to encourage a patient to engage in behavior that is associated with the intrusive thought of killing a child (i.e., actually committing murder), the patient needs to be encouraged to *not* avoid various situations that previously served as neutralizing behaviors (e.g., not visiting a sibling's family to avoid being with a nephew). In general, the exposure is in excess of what the patient normally experiences in real life (e.g., actually rubbing dirt all over one's hands and not washing them) in an effort to enhance habituation to the feared stimuli.

It is important to note that one form of overt neutralizing behavior entails reassurance from others. That is, patients seek assurance from others that their fear will not, in fact, occur and/or that the responsibility for danger is shared. Within the context of therapy, patients may seek reassurance from the therapist regarding their safety verbally (e.g., "Will I be all right?") or behaviorally (e.g., assessing the therapist's reaction to the exposure). It is vital that the therapist pay heed to *not* provide these types of reassurances during the exposure treatment.

Modeling. In an effort to increase cooperation with ERP, the therapist may decide to model the exposure and response prevention protocol early in treatment. For example, a therapist working with a compulsive cleaner may scatter papers, books, and other items on the desk. Although modeling may facilitate engagement in ERP, it is vital that the patient quickly participate in planning and executing this technique to increase independence.

Disrupt Rituals. Before executing a response prevention protocol, it may be helpful to disrupt the patient's performance of the ritual. This may involve completing the behavior in an extremely lengthy, drawn-out manner or repeating the behavior an atypical number of times (e.g., in a series of 5 if the behavior is usually repeated in 3s). Further, the patient can be directed to postpone engaging in the ritual for a specific period of time (e.g., initially a minute, working up to several hours), after which the patient can decide if he or she would still like to carry out the neutralizing behavior. Often patients are surprised that, after waiting for a period of time, they do not feel the need to perform the ritual. This may facilitate motivation and confidence in the credence of ERP.

Goal 3: Decrease Covert Maladaptive Behaviors

OCD has been described as a type of phobia where the feared stimuli are cognitions. Unlike an object or experience, thoughts are difficult to avoid. Thus, people with OCD engage in behaviors to decrease distress associated with obsessions. However, approximately 20%–25% of patients with OCD exhibit no overt behaviors. Instead, covert maladaptive behaviors are implemented in an effort to lessen the anxiety related to the obsessions. Examples of such covert behaviors include thought suppression and bargaining thoughts (e.g., repeating prayers or counting to a certain number).

Whereas exposure and response prevention can be utilized for covert maladaptive behaviors, challenges to this procedure arise due to their inaccessibility. Further, covert avoidance can occur during exposure (i.e., patient is not really letting him or herself experience the feared obsessions). In an effort to prevent this, the patient can be asked to periodically provide a SUDS rating. If SUDS levels are not elevated to the expected level, covert avoidance may be occurring. The techniques contained in the following section may be more effective for decreasing such covert maladaptive behaviors.

Goal-Specific Assessment Tools

- *Behavioral Avoidance Tests* (BAT; Steketee, Chambless, Tran, Worden, & Gillis, 1996): assesses multi-step behavioral avoidance (e.g., thinking "bad" numbers).
- *Hierarchy of Avoidant Situations* (Leahy & Holland, 2000): allows patient to rank thoughts that are avoided according to the amount of distress predicted if confronted.

Goal-Specific Potential Interventions

- Loop tapes
- Diary of thought suppression
- Behavioral experiments

Loop Tapes. In an effort to expose the patient to his interpretation of obsessions and prevent covert maladaptive behaviors, *loop tapes* can be used (Leahy & Holland, 2000). Here, the patient verbalizes his or her feared thoughts while being audiotaped and then listens to them repeatedly in and out of session. The direct vocal stimuli engenders the act of thought suppression and other covert maladaptive behaviors difficult, allowing habituation to occur. As treatment progresses, a larger variety of fears can be recorded to increase generalizability.

Diary of Thought Suppression. Attempts to suppress a thought frequently result in an *increase* in that thought. To allow patients to experience this occurrence firsthand, a diary of thought suppression can be recorded. Here, patients are asked to try to suppress their thoughts on specified days and not to suppress them on others. They record the amount of time actually spent thinking about these thoughts, observing a significant increase on days when thought suppression occurred.

Behavioral Experiments. Behavioral experiments can be a useful intervention for symptoms of OCD. Regarding covert maladaptive thoughts, patients are asked to *try to make* the catastrophe occur by repeating their covert behaviors. For example, a patient who believes that if she does not wash her hands, her family could get sick is asked to test this hypothesis by seeing if not washing actually causes familial illness.

Additional Instrumental Outcome Goals/Treatment Target

- *Decrease General Stress.* OCD symptoms can increase in the presence of stressors. In fact, in approximately 60% of OCD cases, specific preceding stressors can be identified prior to the onset of OCD symptoms. To decrease stressors, problem-solving therapy, engendering social support, and relaxation training may be helpful.
- *Enhance Social Skills.* Given the emotional, cognitive, behavioral, and time commitment associated with OCD, numerous facets of the patient's life including social relationships can be adversely affected. Decreased social functioning is related to poorer outcomes. Thus, in OCD, treatment to enhance social relationships (e.g., communication skills training, conjoint therapy, and role-playing) can be important components of an overall intervention plan.

- *Decrease Depressive Symptoms.* As previously noted, persons with OCD are at risk for developing significant depressive symptoms. These symptoms appear to be secondary to the debilitating nature of OCD. Specifically, the perceived lack of control over thoughts results in helplessness and other depressive symptoms. To treat these symptoms, cognitive therapy, problem-solving therapy, behavioral activation, as well as other techniques discussed in Chapter 5 on depression, can be implemented.
- *Decrease "Overvalued Ideation."* "Overvalued ideation" is a term used by Foa (1979) to describe a certain subset of individuals with OCD who are convinced that their fears are realistic and that their rituals will, in fact, prevent negative events. When such strong convictions are present, patients do not benefit from ERP but require remedial therapy to address these convictions. *Danger Ideation Reduction Therapy* (DIRT; Jones & Menzies, 1998) aims to change these beliefs. DIRT includes attentional training, corrective information, cognitive restructuring, expert testimony, and evaluation of the probability of a catastrophe without exposure or relapse prevention. This treatment technique may be valuable for patients who refuse exposure or for those who did not benefit from ERP.
- *Increase Self-Efficacy.* Patients with OCD often feel unable to control their thoughts and stop their compulsions, potentially resulting in decreased self-efficacy. Cognitive therapy, guided positive imagery, coping skills training, and problem-solving therapy can help increase self-efficacy and facilitate participation in therapy.

ADDITIONAL CLINICAL CONSIDERATIONS

CBT is an effective treatment for OCD. Not only are cognitions, emotions, and behaviors altered with CBT, but studies demonstrate that biological changes occur in the brain following CBT that mirror results from psychopharmacological interventions (Baxter et al., 1992).

Relaxation can be an important component of CBT for any anxiety disorder, including OCD. Progressive muscle relaxation, diaphragmatic breathing, and guided imagery can help alleviate muscular and psychological tension. However, it is important to remember that relaxation skills should *not* be used during ERP, due to the importance of patients' exposure to their feared experiences in this intervention.

As with most psychological problems, it is important to consider *cultural features* when working with patients who appear to have OCD. For example, fear of leprosy in Africa or obsessions with cleanliness in certain Muslim cultures are more common than in European-American cultures. When working with African-American patients, it is helpful to keep in mind potential cultural influences, such as the reluctance to discuss OCD symptoms with family and therapist (Hatch, Friedman, & Paradis, 1996).

Several authors recommend the inclusion of a relapse prevention component in order to help patients better cope with the possibility of recurring obsessions (e.g., Foa & Franklin, 2001). Here, it is explained that a temporary return of OCD symptoms may occur but that it should not be interpreted as a treatment or personal failure. In addition, patients are taught to identify potential causes of relapse (e.g., stressors) and how to effectively cope with those circumstances.

REFERENCES

American Psychiatric Association. (2000). *Diagnostic and statistical manual of mental disorders* (ed. 4, text revision). Washington, DC: American Psychiatric Press.

Antony, M. M., Orsillo, S. M., & Roemer, L. (2001). *Practitioner's guide to empirically based measures of anxiety.* New York: Kluwer Academic/Plenum Publishers.

Amir, N., Freshman, M., Ramsey, B., Neary, E., & Brigidi, B. (2001). Thought-action fusion in individuals with OCD symptoms. *Behaviour Research and Therapy, 39,* 765–776.

Baxter, L. R., Jr., Schwartz, J. M., Bergman, K. S., Szuba, M. P., Guze, B. H., Mazziotta, J. C. et al. (1992). Caudate glucose metabolic rate changes with both drug and behavior therapy for obsessive-compulsive disorder. *Archives of General Psychiatry, 49,* 681–689.

Beck, J. S. (1995). *Cognitive Therapy: Basics and Beyond.* New York: Guilford Press.

Burns, G. L., Keortge, S. G., Formea, G. M., & Sternberger, L. G. (1996). Revision of the Padua Inventory of obsessive-compulsive disorder symptoms: distinctions between worry, obsessions, and compulsions. *Behaviour Research and Therapy, 34,* 163–173.

Emmelkamp, P. M., & Beens, H. (1991). Cognitive therapy with obsessive-compulsive disorder: A comparative evaluation. *Behaviour Research and Therapy, 29,* 293–300.

Foa, E. B. (1979). Failure in treating obsessive-compulsives. *Behaviour Research and Therapy, 17,* 169–176.

Foa, E. B., & Franklin, M. E. (2001). Obsessive-compulsive disorder. In D. H. Barlow (Ed.), *Clinical handbook of psychological disorders: A step-by-step treatment manual* (3rd ed.) (pp. 209–263). New York: Guilford Press.

Foa, E. B., Kozak, M. J., Salkovskis, P. M., Coles, M. E., & Amir, N. (1998). The validation of a new obsessive-compulsive disorder scale: The Obsessive-Compulsive Inventory. *Psychological Assessment, 10,* 206–214.

Foa, E. B., & Kozak, M. J. (1996). Psychological treatment for obsessive-compulsive disorder. In M. Mavissakalian & R. F. Prien (Eds.), *Long-term treatments of anxiety disorders* (pp. 285–309). Washington, DC: American Psychiatric Press.

Freund, B., Steketee, G., & Foa, E. (1987). Compulsive Activity Checklist (CAC): Psychometric analysis with obsessive-compulsive disorder. *Behavioral Assessment, 9,* 67–79.

Goodman, W. K., Price, L. H., Rasmussen, S. A., Mazure, C., Fleischmann, R. L., Hill, C. L. et al. (1989b). The Yale-Brown Obsessive Compulsive Scale. I. Development, use, and reliability. *Archives of General Psychiatry, 46,* 1006–1011.

Hatch, M. L., Friedman, S., & Paradis, C. M. (1996). Behavioral treatment of obsessive-compulsive disorder in African Americans. *Cognitive and Behavioral Practice, 3,* 303–315.

Hodgson, R. J., & Rachman, S. (1977). Obsessional-compulsive complaints. *Behaviour Research and Therapy, 15,* 389–395.

Jones, M. K., & Menzies, R. G. (1998). Danger ideation reduction therapy (DIRT) for obsessive compulsive washers: A controlled trial. *Behaviour Research & Therapy, 26,* 959–970.

Karno, M. G., Golding, M., Sorensen, S. B., & Burnam, A. (1988). The epidemiology of OCD in five U.S. communities. *Archives of General Psychiatry, 45,* 1094–1099.

Leahy, R. L., & Holland, S. J. (2000). *Treatment plans and interventions for depression and anxiety disorders.* New York: Guilford Press.

Neziroglu, F., McKay, D., Yaryura-Tobias, J. A., Stevens, K. P., & Todaro, J. (1999). The Overvalued Ideas Scale: development, reliability and validity in obsessive-compulsive disorder. *Behaviour Research and Therapy, 37,* 881–902.

Nezu, A. M. (in press). Problem solving and behavior therapy revisited. *Behavior Therapy.*

Obsessive Compulsive Cognitions Working Group. (1997). Cognitive assessment of obsessive-compulsive disorder. *Behaviour Research and Therapy, 35,* 667–681.

Overholser, J. C. (1999). Cognitive-behavioral treatment of obsessive-compulsive disorder. *Journal of Contemporary Psychotherapy, 29,* 369–382.

Salkovskis, P. M. (1985). Obsessional-compulsive problems: a cognitive-behavioural analysis. *Behaviour Research and Therapy, 23,* 571–583.

Salkovskis, P. M. (1999). Understanding and treating obsessive-compulsive disorder. *Behaviour Research and Therapy, 37*(Suppl. 1), S29–S52.

Salkovskis, P. M., Wroe, A. L., Gledhill, A., Morrison, N., Forrester, E., Richards, C. et al. (2000). Responsibility attitudes and interpretations are characteristic of obsessive compulsive disorder. *Behaviour Research and Therapy, 38,* 347–372.

Shafran, R., Thordarson, D. S., & Rachman, S. (1996). Thought-action fusion in obsessive compulsive disorder. *Journal of Anxiety Disorders, 10,* 379–391.

Steketee, G., Chambless, D. L., Tran, G. Q., Worden, H., & Gillis, M. M. (1996). Behavioral avoidance test for obsessive-compulsive disorder. *Behaviour Research and Therapy, 34,* 73–83.

Steketee, G., & Frost, R. (2001). Development and initial validation of the Obsessive Beliefs Questionnaire and the Interpretation of Intrusions Inventory. *Behaviour Research and Therapy, 39,* 987–1006.

van Oppen, P., de Haan, E., van Balkom, A. J. L. M., & Spinhoven, P. (1995). Cognitive therapy and exposure in vivo in the treatment of obsessive-compulsive disorder. *Behaviour Research and Therapy, 33,* 379–390.

11

Posttraumatic Stress Disorder

GENERAL DESCRIPTION AND DIAGNOSTIC ISSUES

Posttraumatic stress disorder (PTSD) is the fourth most common psychiatric disorder in the United States. PTSD can be extremely debilitating, resulting in significant impairment in numerous facets of a person's overall quality of life.

According to the *Diagnostic and Statistical Manual of Mental Disorders, Fourth Edition Text Revision* (DSM-IV-TR; American Psychiatric Association, 2000), the essential feature of PTSD is the development of characteristic symptoms following direct exposure to, witnessing of, or learning about a loved one experiencing an extreme traumatic stressor that involves actual or threatened death or serious injury or other threats to one's physical integrity. The person's response to the event must involve intense fear, helplessness, or horror. The characteristic symptoms resulting from the exposure include persistent reexperiencing of the traumatic event, avoidance of stimuli associated with the trauma, numbing of general responsiveness, and symptoms of increased arousal. The full symptom picture must be present for more than one month, and the disturbance must cause clinically significant distress or impairment in social, occupational, or other important areas of functioning.

Reexperiencing of the traumatic event can occur in any of the following ways: (a) recurrent and intrusive distressing recollections of the event; (b) recurrent distressing dreams of the event; (c) acting or feeling as if the traumatic event were recurring (e.g., sense of reliving the experience, dissociative flashback episodes); (d) intense psychological distress when exposed to stimuli associated with the traumatic event; and (e) physiological reactivity on exposure to internal or external cues that resemble an aspect of the traumatic event. Efforts are made by the individual with PTSD to avoid the stimuli associated with the trauma and to psychologically numb oneself by avoiding thoughts, feelings, or conversations associated with the trauma, as well as avoiding activities, places, or people that arouse recollections of the trauma. There is an inability to recall important aspects of the trauma, along with markedly diminished interest or participation in significant activities. In addition, the person with PTSD has feelings of detachment or estrangement from others, a restricted range of affect (e.g., unable to have loving feelings), and a sense of a foreshortened future (e.g., does not expect to have a normal life span). Increased arousal is manifested by difficulties falling or staying asleep, irritability or outbursts of anger, difficulty concentrating, hypervigilance, and an exaggerated startle response.

PTSD is differentiated between *acute* (i.e., symptoms last less than 3 months) and *chronic* (i.e., duration of symptoms is 3 months or more) specifications. The latter is more common. Although symptoms usually develop shortly after exposure to the trauma, a specification of "With Delayed Onset" is warranted if the onset of symptoms occurs at least 6 months following the event.

The overall prevalence rate for PTSD is 9.5%, with rates twice as high for women (11.3%) as compared to men (5.6%; Kessler et al., 1995). In civilian populations, sexual assault, physical assault, and motor vehicle accidents are the most common predecessors to PTSD (Norris, 1992). Those who assist others during traumatic events are also at increased risk for PTSD, including peacekeepers and emergency responders (e.g., police officers, emergency medical technicians and fire fighters). Additional populations are also at greater risk for developing PTSD. For example, approximately 30% of Vietnam veterans (Foy, 1992) and 31% to 57% of rape victims (Foa & Riggs, 1994) meet diagnostic criteria for PTSD.

In addition to the above diagnostic criteria, PTSD is characterized by various common associated features. Individuals with PTSD may describe painful feelings of guilt about surviving when others did not survive the traumatic event, or about the actions they performed in order to survive. Phobic avoidance of situations or activities that resemble the original trauma may interfere with interpersonal relationships, leading to marital conflict, divorce, or loss of one's job. Interpersonal relationships may be further characterized by social withdrawal, hostility, and difficulty relating to others. Further, there is a change in the individual's previous "personality," including feelings of ineffectiveness, shame, or hopelessness, a loss of previously sustained beliefs, and a sense of being constantly threatened.

Complex PTSD, also known as "Disorders of Extreme Stress," are a constellation of associated symptoms, which habitually present with PTSD. Such symptoms include impulsivity, difficulties with emotional regulation, dissociative symptoms, sexual problems, and somatic complaints. Regarding the latter, patients with PTSD are at an increased risk for poor physical health associated with increased utilization of healthcare services and higher rates of mortality (Schnurr, Friedman, Sengupta, Jankowski, & Holmes, 2000).

Not all individuals who experience a severe trauma develop PTSD. The severity, duration, and proximity of an individual's exposure to the traumatic event are the most important factors affecting the likelihood of developing this disorder. There is some evidence that individuals with preexisting psychiatric disorders, family history of psychopathology, childhood misfortunes (e.g., poverty), poor coping ability, decreased social support, and severe initial reaction to the trauma are more vulnerable to developing PTSD. However, this disorder can develop in individuals without any predisposing conditions, most notably if the stressor is particularly extreme.

Differential Diagnostic Issues

There is much symptom overlap between PTSD and other psychiatric disorders, necessitating a differential diagnosis. Similar to PTSD, *adjustment disorder* requires the presence of a stressor, however the stressor may not be as extreme or traumatic and the symptoms do not meet diagnostic criteria for PTSD. Conversely, *acute stress disorder* differs from PTSD only in its duration, with symptoms for the former developing and resolving within four weeks. If symptoms persist past four weeks, the diagnosis of PTSD is warranted. In *obsessive-compulsive disorder* and *generalized anxiety disorder*, there may be intrusive thoughts, but neither is based on reliving a trauma. *Schizophrenia* and other *psychotic disorders* are characterized by perceptual disturbances (e.g., hallucinations) in contrast to PTSD where flashbacks are based on reliving the trauma. Finally, in contrast to PTSD, *malingering* entails intentional faking of symptoms for some benefit (e.g., financial, compensation benefits).

Co-Morbidity Issues

PTSD rarely occurs in isolation. Approximately 88% of men with PTSD have co-morbid diagnoses, most frequently generalized anxiety disorder, panic disorder, simple phobia, agoraphobia, mood disorder (e.g., major depressive disorder, dysthyfmia, bipolar), and substance/alcohol abuse. Similarly, 79% of women with PTSD have co-morbid diagnoses, most commonly agoraphobia and panic disorder, major depressive disorder, alcohol and drug abuse, and conduct disorder. Premorbid psychiatric disorders are a risk factor for developing PTSD. In fact, certain psychiatric conditions (e.g., substance use and conduct disorders) may predispose the experience of a traumatic event.

ASSESSMENT OF DISORDER

PTSD is often not identified in patients. Over 60% of men and 50% of women in the United States report having experienced a traumatic event in their life, with the majority experiencing multiple traumas. Given the high rate of both traumatic experience within the general population and co-morbidity for those with PTSD, it is important to assess for PTSD in patients presenting for other anxiety, mood, and substance abuse disorders.

As can be seen by the abundant measures listed below, numerous questionnaires are available to evaluate PTSD. For ease, the self-report measures are presented according to the primary assessment of either traumatic events or PTSD symptoms (see Antony, Orsillo, and Roemer, 2001, for a review of such assessment tools).

Clinician Ratings

- *Clinician-Administered PTSD Scale* (Blake et al., 1990; Blake, Weathers, Nagy, & Kaloupek, 1995): provides for a diagnosis of PTSD.
- *PTSD Symptom Scale-Interview* (Foa, Riggs, Dancu, & Rothbaum, 1993): diagnoses and assesses symptom severity of PTSD.

- *Structured Clinical Interview for DSM-IV-TR Axis I Disorders* (First, Spitzer, Gibbon, & Williams, 2001): assesses Axis I disorders (PTSD module is sensitive and reliable).
- *Structured Interview for Disorders of Extreme Distress* (Pelcovitz et al., 1997): assesses wide range of responses to trauma (e.g., regulation of affect, relations with others, perception of self and the perpetrator, somatization).
- *Structured Interview for PTSD* (Davidson et al., 1997; Davidson, Smith, & Kudler, 1989): diagnoses and assesses symptom severity of PTSD in addition to survivor and behavior guilt.

Self-Report Measures

Events

- *Stressful Life Events Screening Questionnaire* (Goodman, Corcoran, Turner, Yuan, & Green, 1998): assesses lifetime exposure to traumatic events.
- *Traumatic Events Questionnaire* (Vrana & Lauterbach, 1994): assesses type, frequency, and severity of traumatic experiences.
- *Traumatic Life Events Questionnaire* (Kubany, Leisen, Kaplan, & Kelly, 2000): assesses exposure and reaction to traumatic events.

Symptoms

- *Crime-Related Post-Traumatic Stress Disorder Scale* (Saunders, Arata, & Kilpatrick, 1990): assesses PTSD symptoms regarding crime-related events.
- *Davidson Trauma Scale* (Davidson et al., 1997): assesses frequency and severity of PTSD symptoms.
- *Keane PTSD Scale of the Minnesota Multiphasic Personality Inventory-2* (Keane, Malloy, & Fairbank, 1984): assesses symptoms of PTSD.
- *Mississippi Scale for PTSD* (Keane, Caddell, & Taylor, 1988): assesses PTSD symptoms (e.g., reexperiencing, avoidance and numbing, and hyperarousal).
- *Penn Inventory for PTSD* (Hammarberg, 1992): assesses frequency and severity of PTSD symptoms.

- *Posttraumatic Diagnostic Scale* (Foa, Cashman, Jaycox, & Perry, 1997): diagnoses PTSD and the severity of symptoms.
- *PTSD Checklist* (Blanchard, Jones-Alexander, Buckley, & Forneris, 1996): assesses severity of PTSD symptoms.
- *Purdue PTSD Scale-Revised* (Lauterbach & Vrana, 1996): assesses frequency of each symptom in the PTSD diagnostic criteria.
- *Short Screening Scale for PTSD* (Breslau, Peterson, Kessler, & Schultz, 1999): screens for PTSD in persons who experienced a traumatic event.
- *Trauma Symptom Inventory* (Briere, Elliott, Harris, & Cotman, 1995): assesses PTSD and associated symptoms (e.g., anger/irritability, dysfunctional sexual behavior, impaired self-reference).

GENERAL THERAPY GOALS

Ultimate Outcome Goals

Given the significant impairment experienced by people with PTSD, ultimate outcome goals are geared towards enhancing overall functioning and quality of life. Specific goals include decreasing emotional, cognitive, behavioral, and physical symptoms of distress and anxiety. Enhancing social relationships and the ability to work outside the home (or go to school) are additional ultimate goals. In addition, CBT treatment seeks to decrease associated psychopathology (e.g., poor anger control) and comorbid problems (e.g., substance abuse).

Major Instrumental Outcome Goals/Treatment Targets

Major instrumental outcome goals for PTSD include:

- Decrease psychophysiological arousal
- Decrease dysfunctional beliefs
- Enhance adaptive coping skills

Goal 1: Decrease Psychophysiological Arousal

PTSD requires not only the experience (i.e., actual or vicarious) of a traumatic event, but also fear and distress that are perceived to be uncontrollable. This results in intrusive thoughts, heightened arousal, and avoidance. Learning theory posits that heightened intrusive thoughts and physiological distress are due to classical conditioning (i.e., pairing certain stimuli such as cognitive or environmental cues with negative reactions to the trauma), stimulus generalization, and second-order conditioning. In an attempt to decrease physical and psychological distress, patients with PTSD avoid exposure to stimuli associated with the trauma. This results in negative reinforcement, increasing the likelihood of further avoidance. Avoidance can be manifested in numerous ways, including thought suppression, decreased emotional processing, and staying away from people or places that remind the individual of the traumatic event.

Goal-Specific Assessment Tools

- *Impact of Events Scale* (Horowitz, Wilner, & Alvarez, 1979; Weiss & Marmar, 1997): assesses intrusion and avoidance related to a traumatic event.
- *Accident Fear Questionnaire* (Kuch, Cox, & Direnfeld, 1995): assesses anxiety related to and avoidance following a motor vehicle accident.
- *Physiological Assessment:* assesses increased arousal via autonomic functioning (e.g., heart rate, blood pressure, electromyography, Galvanic skin response).
- *Subjective Units of Distress Scale* (SUDS): assesses patients' self-reported level of physiological or psychological distress, usually on a scale from 0 (*not at all distressed*) to 100 (*the most distressed they have ever been*).
- *Behavioral Avoidance Test (BAT):* patients' individually tailored hierarchy of avoided situations; to be used in conjunction with SUDS ratings.

Goal-Specific Potential Interventions

- Prolonged exposure
- Multiple-channel exposure therapy
- Anxiety management

Prolonged Exposure.   In prolonged exposure (PE), also referred to as flooding, patients confront their feared stimuli via either *imaginal* or *in vivo* presentations, thus breaking the vicious cycle of avoidance and arousal. Patients discover that, unlike their belief that anxiety will continue to increase when confronted with the traumatic stimuli, the symptoms of distress will decrease. As a result, avoidance is no longer needed as a coping style (Taylor et al., 2003).

In PE, a fear hierarchy is developed that rank orders anxiety-provoking stimuli related to the trauma. When conducting imaginal PE, the therapist encourages the patient to recount, in the *present tense*, as many details about the traumatic event as can be remembered for approximately 45–60 minutes. The narrative should include both *external* (e.g., environmental, interpersonal) and *internal* (e.g., thoughts, physiological reactions) cues. This prolonged exposure permits the patient to habituate to the distressing experiences of the traumatic event. The narrative is recorded and the patient listens to the tapes for homework exposure until a 50% SUDS reduction. Conversely, in vivo exposure entails contact with the actual feared stimuli (e.g., avoided locations).

Virtual exposure is an alternative to imaginal exposure that incorporates computer graphics, body tracking devices, and stimulation of multiple senses (e.g., vision, auditory). For example, Vietnam veterans have been successfully treated with a virtual reality protocol (Rothbaum, Hodges, Ready, Graap, & Alarcon, 2001). Virtual exposure may be helpful for PTSD related to the September 11th terrorist attacks (Difede, Hoffman, & Jaysinghe, 2002).

Multiple-Channel Exposure Therapy. Multiple-channel exposure therapy (M-CET) was developed in response to the frequent experience of panic attacks in persons with PTSD. Falsetti and colleagues (Falsetti, Resnick, Dansky, Lydiard, & Kilpatrick, 1995) developed a model of panic in persons with PTSD that suggests that the traumatic events may have induced a panic attack. Later, external (e.g., places or sounds associated with the trauma) and internal (e.g., emotional distress, physiologic arousal, maladaptive cognitions such as "I am going crazy") cues trigger subsequent panic attacks. Specific symptoms of PTSD (e.g., hyperarousal and hyper-vigilance) further increase one's susceptibility to panic. The purpose of M-CET is to afford exposure, first to physiological sensations associated with panic attacks via interoceptive exposure. Next, patients participate in exposure to cognitive and behavioral cues of the trauma that are being avoided. This progression, thus, decreases the additional fear of experiencing panic when engaging in traditional exposure for patients with PTSD. Further, psychoeducation is provided regarding panic attacks and PTSD, in addition to cognitive restructuring, which addresses distortions. M-CET, with both patient and therapist manuals available (Falsetti & Resnick, 1997a; Falsetti & Resnick, 1997b, respectively), has demonstrated efficacy at treating women with a broad range of trauma experiences (Falsetti et al., 1995).

Anxiety Management. Anxiety management includes teaching a wide variety of techniques to address anxiety. Examples include relaxation training, diaphragmatic breathing, positive self-statements, and biofeedback. Regarding biofeedback, learning to identify and control muscular tension created by hyperarousal can facilitate a decrease in anxiety symptoms. Anxiety management training, incorporating education on identifying cognitive and physical signs of anxiety and countering anxiety-provoking scenes with relaxation, decreases the frequency and intensity of intrusive thoughts and avoidance for patients with PTSD (Pantalon & Motta, 1998).

Goal 2: Decrease Dysfunctional Beliefs

Several theories regarding the role of dysfunctional beliefs in PTSD have been developed. Ehlers and Clark (2000) highlight maladaptive information processing in PTSD. Specifically, the individual with PTSD is thought to process the traumatic experience with the interpretation that threat continues to be present. This expectation of threat results in selective attention to threatening stimuli, cognitive intrusions, physiological arousal, psychological distress, and maladaptive coping skills (e.g., avoidance). Using a cognitive constructivist paradigm, McCann and Pearlman (1990a) posit that traumatization can result in cognitive conflicts, which give rise to the intrusive thoughts, nightmares, arousal, and avoidance. Specifically, there is a disturbance of specific schema (e.g., safety, trust, independence, power, esteem, and intimacy) about themselves and others that differs from cognitive schema held prior to the trauma. Resick and Schnicke (1993) further conjecture that patients are often unable to effectively cognitively process the traumatic event within their available schema. As a result, maladaptive *assimilation* (i.e., understanding of the event is changed in order to fit into preexisting schemas) or *accommodation* (i.e., previous beliefs are modified to match the event) may ensue. Ineffective cognitive processing can result in thought intrusion, distress, and maladaptive coping.

Guilt is a prominent emotion arising from faulty cognitions. Guilt may be related to surviving (e.g., "I should have been the one who died in the car accident"), actions before the trauma (e.g., "I should never have gone over to his house"), and behavior during the trauma (e.g., "only terrible people would commit such wartime acts").

Goal-Specific Assessment Tools

- *Trauma-Related Guilt Inventory* (Kubany, Haynes, Abueg, & Manke, 1996): assesses cognitive and emotional guilt related to the experience of a traumatic event.
- *Dysfunctional Thought Record* (Beck, 1995): identifies automatic thoughts and situations that trigger them, actual automatic thoughts, emotions, adaptive counter thoughts, and emotional and cognitive consequences.

Goal-Specific Potential Interventions

- Cognitive restructuring
- Guided self-dialogue
- Behavioral experiments
- Thought stopping

Cognitive Restructuring.   The goal of cognitive restructuring is to identify and modify maladaptive cognitions. Such cognitions may include negative appraisal ("This situation is too much for me to handle;" "I cannot relate to other people"), assumptions ("No one is trustworthy;" "The world is dangerous"), and self-schema ("I am vulnerable;" "I must be a bad person to have had this happen to me"). After learning to identify dysfunctional beliefs, patients are instructed to evaluate their accuracy and recognize distortions (e.g., catastrophizing, fortune-telling, selective attention). Patients then learn to develop more adaptive cognitions.

Certain cognitions may hinder participation in treatment. For example, often patients hold maladaptive beliefs about discussing the trauma ("It is dangerous to think about the trauma, even in a safe place;" "Thinking about the traumatic event will make me live through it again;" "Experiencing anxiety will result in my losing control"). Cognitive restructuring techniques can facilitate the identification and modification of such dysfunctional beliefs, which in turn, can enhance participation in treatment.

Psychoeducation is an important component of cognitive restructuring. Patients learn common emotional (e.g., fear, anger, guilt), physiological (e.g., hyperarousal), attentional (e.g., hypervigilance), cognitive (e.g., blaming self, loss of trust in others), and behavioral (e.g., avoidance, angry outbursts) responses to traumatic events. Faulty cognitions are identified as the reason for such characteristic and maladaptive reactions.

Reliving the trauma is an intervention incorporating cognitive restructuring and exposure. Patients are instructed to vividly describe the event (either verbally or in writing) in an effort to change maladaptive cognitions. Using this intervention for rape victims, Resick and Schnicke (1993) developed *Cognitive Processing Therapy* (CPT), where patients write, in concise detail, their traumatic event and then read this narrative aloud. "Stuck points," or information that has not been effectively processed, are then identified. Stuck points often involve safety, trust, power, esteem, and intimacy schemas. Maladaptive cognitions are modified via cognitive restructuring techniques and then incorporated as patients, again, recount the trauma. CPT is especially effective in treating PTSD-associated guilt (Resick, Nishith, Weaver, Astin, & Feuer, 2002).

Guided Self-Dialogue. After maladaptive cognitions have been identified, guided self-dialogue can assist in enhancing more positive self-statements. Using this technique, patients are asked a series of questions facilitating the identification of more adaptive self-verbalizations. Specific topics include accurate identification of the probability of danger, self-efficacy regarding one's ability to cope with stressful situations, and self-reinforcement for one's hard work. Patients then repeat the positive self-statements while preparing for and confronting feared stimuli. Guided self-dialogue, thus, facilitates the employment of newly learned cognitive processing.

Behavioral Experiments. As noted previously, patients with PTSD anticipate harm. Behavioral experiments permit the individual to test hypotheses about their current level of danger. Although behavioral experiments are similar to *in vivo* exposure in that both entail patients engaging in a previously evaded activity, their purposes are somewhat different. The goal of PE is to habituate to the physiological and psychological arousal. The objective of behavioral experiments is to test maladaptive assumptions to determine their veracity. Examples of behavioral experiments for a rape victim who holds the belief that "If I go out again, I will get attacked" include going out with friends, going to public places (e.g., a restaurant) or, eventually, dating. Patients with PTSD related to a motor vehicle accident with the belief "If I return to the place of the accident, I will have another accident" is instructed to return to the accident site and assess the accuracy of their predictions. During behavioral experiments, it is important that patients not use their safety behaviors (e.g., gripping the steering wheel when driving to the place of the accident) because such actions may prevent patients from experiencing the erroneous nature of their cognitions (e.g., "I may be OK *if* I hold on tightly to the steering wheel").

Thought Stopping.   In thought stopping, the patient implements an aversive stimulus in an effort to stop intrusive and obsessive thoughts. During the course of this intervention, the procedure may progress from snapping a rubber band against one's wrist and yelling "STOP," to only the latter act, to whispering and eventually saying "STOP" silently in one's head. It is important to remember that thought stopping is not to be implemented during other techniques previously discussed, as this can prevent therapeutic experience and processing of the traumatic event.

Goal 3: Enhance Adaptive Coping Skills

Individuals with PTSD often employ maladaptive coping skills (Nezu & Carnevale, 1987). In addition to the psychological avoidance and emotional numbing discussed under the first instrumental goal, much additional maladaptive coping prevails in PTSD (e.g., social withdrawal, physical isolation, anger management problems). Adaptive coping not only enhances mood, but can augment participation in subsequent exposure interventions (Cloitre, Koenen, Cohen, & Han, 2002). Further, adaptive coping (e.g., hardiness, use of social support) appears to mediate the development of PTSD (King, King, Fairbank, Keane, & Adams, 1998).

Goal-Specific Potential Interventions

- Stress inoculation training
- Problem-solving therapy
- Affective management training

Stress Inoculation Training.   Stress inoculation training (SIT) is centered on enhancing self-monitoring during anxiety-provoking situations in an effort to implement adaptive coping skills. SIT involves education (e.g., biopsychosocial aspects of fear), skills building, and application of the learned skills. Coping skills may include relaxation, diaphragmatic breathing, thought stopping, covert rehearsal, role-playing, and guided imagery. In *covert rehearsal,* patients imagine being in, and successfully coping with, an anxiety-provoking situation. Correspondingly, the patient can practice coping skills via role-plays. Examples may include a role-play involving interactions with individuals whom the patient previously avoided. *Guided imagery* involves taking patients through an induction where they successfully implement the learned, adaptive coping skills (e.g., successfully driving to work past the scene of the car accident).

Problem-Solving Therapy.   Some patients with PTSD exhibit ineffective problem-solving skills (Nezu & Carnevale, 1987) and often feel confused, hopeless, and helpless regarding what they can do to help themselves. Social problem-solving therapy (D'Zurilla & Nezu, 1999; Nezu, in press) can address such coping deficits with which patients present. In particular, problem orientation training enhances patients' beliefs that they *can* cope effectively. Training in specific problem-solving skills can enhance patient's ability to cope with stress.

Affective Management Training. In an attempt to enhance effective coping skills in persons with PTSD, different types of affect management (e.g., addressing affective dysregulation and anger) can be helpful. Affect dysregulation (i.e., the inability to effectively cope with or endure powerful emotions) is not uncommon in persons with PTSD and can significantly hinder one's quality of life (e.g., difficulties in interpersonal relationships or psychological distress). In light of these deficient coping skills, it has been argued that exposure therapy may be too overwhelming, at least initially, for some people with PTSD (Wolfsdorf & Zlotnick, 2001). As such, training in adaptive and beneficial ways to cope with emotions may be an important initial step. Interventions to decrease affective dysregulation involve addressing cognitive distortions related to affect and attempts to increase tolerance of distress. Specific skills are taught, including identifying emotions, "self-soothing" skills, and developing a crisis plan.

Anger management may also be an important component of effectively controlling affect. Anger management problems are frequent in PTSD and result in adverse psychological, social, occupational, and/or academic functioning. When addressing problems with anger, a link is made between traumatic experiences and current anger. Patients are taught to identify the emotional, physical, cognitive, and behavioral signs of anger, to recognize the negative consequences of their current anger (e.g., interpersonally, intrapersonally, occupationally), to detect specific anger triggers, and to develop coping skills to effectively mange their anger. Such coping skills may include relaxation, exercising, problem solving, journaling, or talking out anger with a friend or therapist (see also chapter 15).

Additional Instrumental Outcome Goals/Treatment Target

- *Decrease Sleep Disturbances.* Insomnia and nightmares often prevail in PTSD, contributing to further distress and decreased functioning. Insomnia can be treated with sleep hygiene (i.e., abolishing behaviors contributing to insomnia), stimulus control (e.g., decreasing awake time in bed), and sleep restriction (e.g., patient can sleep only during specified hours, no naps). Nightmares can be addressed using a technique called *imagery rehearsal*, where patients are instructed to alter the nightmare scene, when awake, to a scenario of enhanced control and then rehearse this new, more pleasant image in their imagination (Forbes, Phelps, & McHugh, 2001).

- *Decrease "Resistance."* Individuals with PTSD often avoid therapy due to their trepidation about reliving the trauma and wanting to "move on," away from traumatic memories. It has been recommended that therapists speak with patients with PTSD on the telephone, before their initial visit, to describe the avoidance symptoms of PTSD and their maladaptive nature (Resick & Calhoun, 2001). In therapy, cognitive restructuring techniques, including psychoeducation, and affective management, may help decrease "resistance" or avoidance of therapy.

- *Enhance Interpersonal Relationships.* Problematic relationships are frequent in persons with PTSD. Given difficulties with trust and affect management, relationships are often strained or avoided. Psychoeducation on the symptoms of PTSD, including avoiding interpersonal closeness, can assist both the patients and their partners. Couples therapy may also be indicated (see chapter 14).

- *Decrease Crisis Behavior.* PTSD is often associated with destructive and suicidal behavior, as well as emotional dysregulation related to crises. Dialectic Behavior Therapy (DBT; Linehan, Cochran, & Kehrer, 2001) was developed for persons with borderline personality disorder to address these problems. It has been proposed that DBT principles (e.g., non-pejorative stance, the dialectic between acceptance and change, validation of the patient's experience, and patient-therapist collaboration) can be beneficially applied when working with patients with PTSD (Becker & Zayfert, 2001; see also chapter 12).

- *Prevent PTSD.* As noted, not all individuals who experience a traumatic event will go on to develop PTSD. CBT interventions can help *prevent* PTSD symptoms from developing (e.g., Litz, Gray, Bryant, & Adler, 2002). Specific treatment recommendations include delayed intervention (e.g., 10 or more days following the trauma), multiple sessions (e.g., 4–5), normalization of reactions to trauma, relaxation training, exposure, and cognitive restructuring. In addition, enhancing social support appears to be an important factor. Brief CBT has been found to be effective at preventing the development of PTSD (Foa, Hearst-Ikeda, & Perry, 1995).

ADDITIONAL CLINICAL CONSIDERATIONS

When working with patients with PTSD, it is important to remember that certain at-risk populations may be particularly reluctant to disclose traumatic events. For example, immigrants from war-ridden areas may fear political consequences and victims of spousal or parental-induced trauma may fear ramifications of disclosure (e.g., loss of home or financial resources). Using the techniques described under the goal to *decrease resistance* may help enhance participation.

Although rare, late onset of PTSD can occur and is most frequently associated in older adults in retirement. It has been hypothesized that development of PTSD at this time may be related to stressors that may be present (e.g., the loss of work as a distraction, health problems, the developmental stage at this time of reflecting on one's life). It is important to assess for traumatic events when working with older adults, as clinical manifestations of PTSD may be misdiagnosed as mood disorders (e.g., due to symptoms of depressed mood, agitation, insomnia, guilt, and emotional flatness).

CBT can be implemented within different milieus. The decision to treat PTSD in group versus individual milieu is often determined by practical issues (e.g., patient and therapist availability). From a theoretical standpoint, however, there are advantages and disadvantages to group treatment. Benefits include normalization of PTSD symptoms, decreasing sense of isolation, decreasing self-blame, and encouraging interpersonal interactions in a safe environment. Conversely, group therapy may be overwhelming to some, and not all patients with PTSD are appropriate candidates (e.g., suicidal, substance-abusing, unstable clients may not be suitable).

There are several multicomponent treatment protocols available for specific patient populations. For example, Trauma Management Therapy (TMT; Turner, Beidel, & Frueh, 1996; Frueh, Turner, Beidel, & Mirabella, 1996) and Trauma Focus Group Therapy (TFGT; Foy, Ruzek, Glynn, Riney, & Gusman, 2002) are comprehensive interventions for combat-related PTSD. TMT, which incorporates education about PTSD, exposure therapy, social skills training, and anger management conducted initially in individual and later within group settings, is effective in decreasing PTSD symptoms (Frueh et al., 1996). In TFGT prolonged exposure, cognitive restructuring, and coping skills training are applied in a group format. Unique to TFGT, however, is the emphasis on a developmental perspective incorporating experiences and relationships beginning before military involvement to the present. Participants are asked to write an autobiographical narrative about themselves before combat and disclose this information to the group.

In addition, specific treatments have been developed for women. Cognitive Trauma Therapy (Kubany & Watson, 2002) was developed for formerly battered women and includes cognitive restructuring for trauma-related guilt, stress management, assertiveness training, and other adaptive coping skills training. Further, as previously discussed, Resick and Schnicke (1993) developed a protocol for female rape victims (CPT) that addresses both PTSD and depressive symptoms.

Additional CBT protocols exist for other specific subpopulations of persons with PTSD. For example, there is a CBT intervention for PTSD and co-morbid cocaine-dependence (Back, Dansky, Carroll, Foa, & Brady, 2001). CBT interventions for PTSD related to work (Phillips, Bruehl, & Harden, 1997), bone marrow transplant (DuHamel et al., 2000), and motor vehicle accidents (Fecteau & Nicki, 1999) have also been developed.

Finally, it is important for therapists to be aware of *vicarious traumatization*. Vicarious traumatization refers to disturbances that can occur for the *therapist* as a result of working with victims of trauma. Hearing patients' experiences can affect the clinician's own schemas about the self and world, resulting in psychological and physiological distress. McCann and Pearlman (1990b) provide important recommendations for therapists working with trauma clients to decrease vicarious traumatization, including engendering support from other professionals, balancing these cases with other cases, recognizing one's own psychological threshold, and participating in other professional and personal endeavors.

REFERENCES

American Psychiatric Association. (2000). *Diagnostic and statistical manual of mental disorders* (ed. 4, text revision). Washington, DC: American Psychiatric Press.

Antony, M. M., Orsillo, S. M., & Roemer, L. (2001). *Practitioner's guide to empirically based measures of anxiety.* New York: Kluwer Academic/Plenum Publishers.

Back, S. E., Dansky, B. S., Carroll, K. M., Foa, E. B., & Brady, K. T. (2001). Exposure therapy in the treatment of PTSD among cocaine-dependent individuals: Description of procedures. *Journal of Substance Abuse Treatment, 21,* 35–45.

Becker, C. B., & Zayfert, C. (2001). Integrating DBT-based techniques and concepts to facilitate exposure treatment for PTSD. *Cognitive and Behavioral Practice, 8,* 107–122.

Blake, D. D., Weathers, F. W., Nagy, L. M., & Kaloupek, D. G. (1995). The development of a Clinician-Administered PTSD Scale. *Journal of Traumatic Stress, 8,* 75–90.

Blake, D. D., Weathers, F. W., Nagy, L. M., Kaloupek, D. G., Klauminzer, G., Charney, D. S. et al. (1990). A clinician rating scale for assessing current and lifetime PTSD: The CAPS-1. *Behavior Therapist, 13,* 187–188.

Blanchard, E. B., Jones-Alexander, J., Buckley, T. C., & Forneris, C. A. (1996). Psychometric properties of the PTSD Checklist (PCL). *Behaviour Research and Therapy, 34,* 669–673.

Breslau, N., Peterson, E. L., Kessler, R. C., & Schultz, L. R. (1999). Short screening scale for DSM-IV posttraumatic stress disorder. *American Journal of Psychiatry, 156,* 908–911.

Briere, J., Elliott, D. M., Harris, K., & Cotman, A. (1995). Trauma Symptom Inventory: Psychometrics and association with childhood and adult victimization in clinical samples. *Journal of Interpersonal Violence, 10,* 387–401.

Cloitre, M., Koenen, K. C., Cohen, L. R., & Han, H. (2002). Skills training in affective and interpersonal regulation followed by exposure: A phase-based treatment for PTSD related to childhood abuse. *Journal of Consulting and Clinical Psychology, 70,* 1067–1074.

Davidson, J. R., Book, S. W., Colket, J. T., Tupler, L. A., Roth, S., David, D. et al. (1997). Assessment of a new self-rating scale for post-traumatic stress disorder. *Psychological Medicine, 27,* 153–160.

Davidson, J., Smith, R., & Kudler, H. (1989). Validity and reliability of the DSM-III criteria for posttraumatic stress disorder: Experience with a structured interview. *Journal of Nervous and Mental Disease, 177,* 336–341.

Difede, J., Hoffman, H., & Jaysinghe, N. (2002). Innovative use of virtual reality technology in the treatment of PTSD in the aftermath of September 11. *Psychiatric Services, 53,* 1083–1085.

DuHamel, K. N., Ostroff, J. S., Bovbjerg, D. H., Pfeffer, M., Morasco, B. J., Papadopoulos, E. et al. (2000). Trauma-focused intervention after bone marrow transplantation: A case study. *Behavior Therapy, 31,* 175–186.

D'Zurilla, T. J., & Nezu, A. M. (1999). *Problem-solving therapy: A social competence approach to clinical intervention* (2nd ed.). New York: Springer Publishing Co.

Falsetti, S. A., & Resnick, H. S. (1997a). *Multiple-channel exposure therapy: Patient Manual.* Medical University of South Carolina.

Falsetti, S. A., & Resnick, H. S. (1997b). *Multiple-channel exposure therapy: Therapist Manual.* Medical University of South Carolina.

Falsetti, S. A., Resnick, H. S., Dansky, B. S., Lydiard, R. B., & Kilpatrick, D. G. (1995). The relationship of stress to panic disorder: Cause or effect? In C. M. Mazure (Ed.), *Does stress cause psychiatric illness?* (pp. 111–147). Washington, DC: American Psychiatric Press.

Fecteau, G., & Nicki, R. (1999). Cognitive behavioural treatment of post traumatic stress disorder after motor vehicle accident. *Behavioural and Cognitive Psychotherapy, 27,* 201–214.

First, M. B., Spitzer, R. L., Gibbon, M., & Williams, J. B. W. (2001). *Structured Clinical Interview for DSM-IV-TR Axis I Disorders, Research Version, Patient Edition. (SCID-I/P)*. New York: Biometrics Research, New York State Psychiatric Institute.

Foa, E. B., Cashman, L., Jaycox, L., & Perry, K. (1997). The validation of a self-report measure of posttraumatic stress disorder: The Posttraumatic Diagnostic Scale. *Psychological Assessment, 9*, 445–451.

Foa, E. B., Hearst-Ikeda, D., & Perry, K. J. (1995). Evaluation of a brief cognitive-behavioral program for the prevention of chronic PTSD in recent assault victims. *Journal of Consulting and Clinical Psychology, 63*, 948–955.

Foa, E. B., & Riggs, D. S. (1994). Posttraumatic stress disorder and rape. In R. S. Pynoos (Ed.), *Posttraumatic stress disorder: A clinical review* (pp. 133–163). Lutherville, MD: Sidran Press.

Foa, E. B., Riggs, D. S., Dancu, C. V., & Rothbaum, B. O. (1993). Reliability and validity of a brief instrument for assessing post-traumatic stress disorder. *Journal of Traumatic Stress, 6*, 459–473.

Forbes, D., Phelps, A., & McHugh, T. (2001). Treatment of combat-related nightmares using imagery rehearsal: A pilot study. *Journal of Traumatic Stress, 14*, 433–442.

Foy, D. W. (1992). Introduction and description of the disorder. In D. W. Foy (Ed.), *Treating PTSD: Cognitive-behavioral strategies* (pp. 1–12). New York: Guilford Press.

Foy, D. W., Ruzek, J. I., Glynn, S. M., Riney, S. J., & Gusman, F. D. (2002). Trauma focus group therapy for combat-related PTSD: An update. *Journal of Clinical Psychology, 58*, 907–918.

Frueh, B. C., Turner, S. M., Beidel, D. C., & Mirabella, R. F. (1996). Trauma Management Therapy: A preliminary evaluation of a multicomponent behavioral treatment for chronic combat-related PTSD. *Behaviour Research and Therapy, 34*, 533–543.

Goodman, L. A., Corcoran, C., Turner, K., Yuan, N., & Green, B. L. (1998). Assessing traumatic event exposure: General issues and preliminary findings for the Stressful Life Events Screening Questionnaire. *Journal of Traumatic Stress, 11*, 521–542.

Hammarberg, M. (1992). Penn Inventory for Posttraumatic Stress Disorder: Psychometric properties. *Psychological Assessment, 4*, 67–76.

Horowitz, M., Wilner, N., & Alvarez, W. (1979). Impact of Event Scale: a measure of subjective stress. *Psychosomatic Medicine, 41*, 209–218.

Keane, T. M., Caddell, J. M., & Taylor, K. L. (1988). Mississippi Scale for Combat-Related Posttraumatic Stress Disorder: three studies in reliability and validity. *Journal of Consulting and Clinical Psychological, 56*, 85–90.

Keane, T. M., Malloy, P. F., & Fairbank, J. A. (1984). Empirical development of an MMPI subscale for the assessment of combat-related posttraumatic stress disorder. *Journal of Consulting and Clinical Psychological, 52*, 888–891.

King, L. A., King, D. W., Fairbank, J. A., Keane, T. M., & Adams, G. A. (1998). Resilience-recovery factors in post-traumatic stress disorder among female and male Vietnam veterans: Hardiness, postwar social support, and additional stressful life events. *Journal of Personality and Social Psychology, 74*, 420–434.

Kubany, E. S., Haynes, S. N., Abueg, F. R., & Manke, F. P. (1996). Development and validation of the Trauma-Related Guilt Inventory (TRGI). *Psychological Assessment, 8*, 428–444.

Kubany, E. S., Haynes, S. N., Leisen, M. B., Owens, J. A., Kaplan, A. S., Watson, S. B. et al. (2000). Development and preliminary validation of a brief broad-spectrum measure of trauma exposure: the Traumatic Life Events Questionnaire. *Psychological Assessment, 12,* 210–224.

Kubany, E. S., Leisen, M. B., Kaplan, A. S., & Kelly, M. P. (2000). Validation of a brief measure of posttraumatic stress disorder: The Distressing Event Questionnaire (DEQ). *Psychological Assessment, 12,* 197–209.

Kubany, E. S., & Watson, S. B. (2002). Cognitive trauma therapy for formerly battered women with PTSD: Conceptual bases and treatment outlines. *Cognitive and Behavioral Practice, 9,* 111–127.

Kuch, K., Cox, B. J., & Direnfeld, D. M. (1995). A brief self-rating scale for PTSD after road vehicle accident. *Journal of Anxiety Disorders, 9,* 503–514.

Lauterbach, D., & Vrana, S. (1996). Three studies on the reliability and validity of a self-report measure of posttraumatic stress disorder. *Assessment, 3,* 17–25.

Linehan, M. M., Cochran, B. N., & Kehrer, C. A. (2001). Dialectical behavior therapy for borderline personality disorder. In D. H. Barlow (Ed.), *Clinical handbook of psychological disorders: A step-by-step treatment manual* (pp. 470–522). New York: Guilford Press.

Litz, B. T., Gray, M. J., Bryant, R. A., & Adler, A. B. (2002). Early intervention for trauma: Current status and future directions. *Clinical Psychology-Science & Practice, 9,* 112–134.

McCann, I. L., & Pearlman, L. A. (1990a). *Psychological trauma and the adult survivor: Theory, therapy, and transformation.* New York: Brunner/Mazel.

McCann, I. L., & Pearlman, L. A. (1990b). Vicarious traumatization: A framework for understanding the psychological effects of working with victims. *Journal of Traumatic Stress, 3,* 131–149.

Nezu, A. M. (in press). Problem solving and behavior therapy revisited. *Behavior Therapy.*

Nezu, A. M., & Carnevale, G. J. (1987). Interpersonal problem solving and coping reactions of Vietnam veterans with posttraumatic stress disorder. *Journal of Abnormal Psychology, 96,* 155–157.

Norris, F. H. (1992). Epidemiology of trauma: Frequency and impact of different potentially traumatic events on different demographic groups. *Journal of Consulting and Clinical Psychological, 60,* 409–418.

Pantalon, M. V., & Motta, R. W. (1998). Effectiveness of anxiety management training in the treatment of posttraumatic stress disorder: A preliminary report. *Journal of Behavior Therapy and Experimental Psychiatry, 29,* 21–29.

Pelcovitz, D., van der Kolk, B., Roth, S., Mandel, F., Kaplan, S., & Resick, P. (1997). Development of a criteria set and a structured interview for disorders of extreme stress (SIDES). *Journal of Traumatic Stress, 10,* 3–16.

Phillips, M. E., Bruehl, S., & Harden, R. N. (1997). Work-related post-traumatic stress disorder: Use of exposure therapy in work-simulation activities. *American Journal of Occupational Therapy, 51,* 696–700.

Resick, P. A., & Calhoun, K. S. (2001). Posttraumatic stress disorder. In D. H. Barlow (Ed.), *Clinical handbook of psychological disorders: A step-by-step treatment manual* (pp. 60–113). New York: Guilford Press.

Resick, P. A., Nishith, P., Weaver, T. L., Astin, M. C., & Feuer, C. A. (2002). A comparison of cognitive-processing therapy with prolonged exposure and a waiting condition for the treatment of chronic posttraumatic stress disorder in female rape victims. *Journal of Consulting and Clinical Psychology, 70,* 867–879.

Resick, P. A., & Schnicke, M. K. (1993). *Cognitive processing therapy for rape victims: A treatment manual.* Newbury Park, CA: Sage.

Rothbaum, B. O., Hodges, L. F., Ready, D., Graap, K., & Alarcon, R. D. (2001). Virtual reality exposure therapy for Vietnam veterans with posttraumatic stress disorder. *Journal of Clinical Psychiatry, 62,* 617–622.

Saunders, B. E., Arata, C. M., & Kilpatrick, D. G. (1990). Development of a Crime-Related Post-Traumatic Stress Disorder scale for women within the Symptom Checklist-90—Revised. *Journal of Traumatic Stress, 3,* 429–448.

Schnurr, P. P., Friedman, M. J., Sengupta, A., Jankowski, M. K., & Holmes, T. (2000). PTSD and utilization of medical treatment services among male Vietnam veterans. *Journal of Nervous and Mental Disease, 188,* 496–504.

Taylor, S., Thordarson, D. S., Maxfield, L., Fedoroff, I. C., Lovell, K., & Ogrodniczuk, J. (2003). Comparative efficacy, speed, and adverse effects of three PTSD treatments: Exposure therapy, EMDR, and relaxation training. *Journal of Consulting and Clinical Psychology, 71,* 330–338.

Turner, S. M., Beidel, D. C., & Frueh, B. C. (unpublished manuscript). *Trauma Management Therapy for chronic combat-related PTSD: A multicomponent behavioral treatment program.*

Vrana, S., & Lauterbach, D. (1994). Prevalence of traumatic events and post-traumatic psychological symptoms in a nonclinical sample of college students. *Journal of Traumatic Stress, 7,* 289–302.

Weiss, D. S., & Marmar, C. R. (1997). The Impact of Event Scale—Revised. In J. P. Wilson & T. M. Keane (Eds.), *Assessing psychological trauma and PTSD* (pp. 399–411). New York: Guilford Press.

Wolfsdorf, B. A., & Zlotnick, C. (2001). Affect management in group therapy for women with posttraumatic stress disorder and histories of childhood sexual abuse. *Journal of Clinical Psychology, 57,* 169–181.

12

Borderline Personality Disorder

GENERAL DESCRIPTION AND DIAGNOSTIC ISSUES

According to the *Diagnostic and Statistical Manual of Mental Disorders, Fourth Edition, Text Revision* (DSM-IV-TR; American Psychiatric Association, 2000), personality disorders are described as enduring and cross-situational patterns of cognitions, affect, and behavior that are inconsistent with the expectations of a person's social and cultural environment. Individuals with personality disorders are characterized by their adaptive inflexibility, that is, their limited strategies for relating to others, achieving goals, and coping with stress. Disorders that are characterized under this rubric usually emerge in adolescence, reveal characteristic response patterns that are quite pervasive and cross-situationally consistent, and continue over time, leading to significant distress.

Borderline personality disorder (BPD) is diagnosed when an individual displays a characteristic pattern of intense instability regarding his or her emotions, interpersonal relationships, and sense of identity. In addition, BPD patients often display a pattern of impulsive and self-harming behavior. It is the most common personality disorder encountered in clinical settings, with an estimated prevalence rate of 10% in outpatient settings, 15% to 20% in inpatient settings, and approximately 1% to 2% in the general population (Skodol et al., 2002). The characteristic response patterns of BPD and its associated behavioral, interpersonal, and occupational disturbance is not a direct consequence of substance abuse or specific medical conditions and is not explained by other psychiatric disorders (e.g., bipolar disorder, major depression, panic disorder, or other personality disorders), although these problems can also exist in persons diagnosed with BPD.

BPD, like all personality disorders, is defined by characteristic thoughts, feelings, and behaviors that are long term; exist prior and into early adulthood; and represent the typical way in which an individual perceives, interprets, or interacts with the world. Because of this pattern, there is a trend in the nonbehavioral literature to suggest that such problems represent strong underlying traits. The cognitive-behavioral literature, however, has suggested that although behavioral problems may be well-learned and cross-situational, the response styles characteristic of BPD probably represent a combination of temperamental vulnerability and learned cognitive, emotional, and behavioral responses (Cohen & Nezu, 1989; Linehan, 1993).

Five out of nine diagnostic criteria specified by DSM IV-TR must be met for a person to be diagnosed with BPD. These include frantic attempts to avoid abandonment, a pattern of unstable and intense emotional expression of interpersonal relations ranging from extreme idealization to devaluation, a persistent identity disturbance, impulsive and potentially self-destructive behavior patterns, recurrent suicidal or self-mutilating behavior, marked reactivity of mood, frequently involving intense and inappropriate anger, chronic perceptions of emptiness, and transient paranoid thoughts or dissociated perception when under stress.

The habituated and pervasive patterns of behavior that define this disorder have been reorganized and conceptualized by Linehan (1993) as a phenomena of emotional, behavioral, interpersonal, cognitive, and self-dysregulation in which relationships are often highly changeable and conflictual. Resulting dramatic interpersonal behavior, including that associated with the therapeutic relationship, can include frantic efforts to avoid rejection, anger over perceived abandonment, intense emotional distress, chronic feelings of emptiness, and impulsive behavior associated with these states that place the individual at high risk for self-harm. When patients engage in such parasuicidal behavior and actual suicidal acts, they create significant risk to themselves, concern to their significant others, and challenges to the clinicians with whom they work. As a result, BPD patients frequently experience repeated hospitalizations, emergency room visits, and similar crisis situations.

Long-term outcome studies of patients with BPD have documented a high rate of actual suicide completion, with reported rates of suicide among treated patients consistently found to be about 10% (Paris, 2002). This rate doubles when only people who have a documented history of parasuicidal behavior are considered (Stone, Hurt, & Stone, 1987). Moreover, approximately 60% to 80% of people diagnosed with BPD engage in some form of self-harming behavior (Linehan, 2000).

Differential Diagnostic Issues

BPD diagnostic criteria include symptoms such as mood disturbance, suspicious thinking, and hypersensitivity, that are also observed in other more acute, DSM Axis I disorders. Therefore, consideration must be given to a careful assessment of the acute versus chronic pattern of symptoms and behavior. For instance, although BPD is characterized by instability of mood, and an episode of mood disorder can appear to have many BPD characteristics, BPD should only be diagnosed after documenting that the pattern of mood instability had an early onset and a long-standing course (i.e., several years).

Although the differential diagnosis of BPD from other personality disorders is made based on the specific criteria with which it is associated as previously described, there may be clinical features and criteria that overlap with other personality disorders defined by DSM IV. For example, attention-seeking behavior and rapidly shifting emotions may be similar to behavior seen in *histrionic personality disorder*. Angry reaction to minor insults is also characteristic of *narcissistic personality disorder*. Intense fears of abandonment are often similar to fears associated with *dependent personality disorder*. Finally, impulsive acts or destructive behavior are also characteristic of *antisocial personality disorder*. Individuals with BPD will typically experience many of these features in the context of a pervasive pattern of *instability* across emotional, behavioral, cognitive, and interpersonal domains (Linehan & Kehrer, 1993). Therefore, the episodes of depression, anxiety, anger, and mistrust are usually reactive and not confined to one type of mood disorder. The behavioral expression of fear of abandonment in persons diagnosed with BPD often takes the form of feelings of emotional emptiness, rage, and demands, rather than attempts at appeasement or submissiveness than are seen in *dependent personality disorder*. Impulsive and destructive behavior is usually directed toward oneself in the form of suicidal, parasuicidal, or mutilating acts, rather than for the personal gain, profit, or power that is observed in individuals diagnosed with *antisocial personality disorder*.

Other disorders also need to be diagnostically differentiated from BPD. Emotional instability and self-destructive behavior related to substance abuse must be differentiated from similar BPD behavior patterns.

Co-Morbidity Issues

Co-morbid disorders are common in persons with BPD. Frequent co-morbidity is reported with Axis I disorders, such as mood disorders, substance abuse, and anxiety (Trull, Stepp, & Durrett, 2003). Overall, an average of about 65% of those with BPD may be expected to have an additional Axis I diagnosis of substance abuse (van den Bosch, Verheul, & van den Brink, 2001). Moreover Axis I co-morbidity is associated with poorer outcome (Skodol et al., 2002; Trull et al., 2003). Patients are often referred for therapy following a hospitalization due to emotionally intense, self-harming, or suicidal behavior. It is therefore necessary to assess for BPD in patients who present with symptoms of depression and hopelessness. One important assessment consideration is that the same co-morbid negative affective state may exist for two individuals with BPD but have different functional explanations. For example, negative affect, such as depression, may be a consequence of the disorder, may be related to the affect regulation effects of substance abuse, or may represent an independent Axis I diagnosis with overlapping diagnostic criteria (Kim & Goff, 2002). As such, a functional understanding of symptoms is important to determine diagnostic co-morbidity.

There is a high prevalence among persons diagnosed with BPD of having a history of sexual abuse. This can be associated with more severe symptoms and indicates the need to assess and target symptoms specific to a history of sexual abuse or trauma, such as dissociative reactions (Soloff, Lynch, & Kelly, 2002).

Individuals with behavior patterns that meet criteria for BPD may also exhibit additional Axis II disorders. Significant co-occurrence with BPD is observed for *antisocial, avoidant, passive-aggressive*, and *depressive personality disorders*. In addition, gender differences concerning this comorbidity is reported with *antisocial personality disorder*, being significantly more comorbid for men, and *obsessive-compulsive personality disorder*, being more comorbid for women (Grilo, Sanislow, McGlashon, 2002).

ASSESSMENT OF DISORDER

Assessment protocols to help the clinician to differentially diagnose BPD, as well as to measure the severity of relevant symptoms, include semi-structured interviews, clinician ratings, and self-report inventories.

Semi-Structured Interviews

A thorough diagnostic evaluation can be accomplished using semi-structured interviews developed specifically to assess personality disorders. The following protocols, developed in concert with DSM-IV diagnostic criteria, provide for assessment of symptoms across *all* personality disorders, and may be administered to the patient or through an interview with a significant other serving as an informed source, and may take up to two hours to administer.

- *Diagnostic Interview for Personality Disorders* (Zanarini, Frankenburg, Chauncey, & Gunderson, 1987).
- *International Personality Disorder Examination* (Loranger, 1999).
- *Personality Disorder Interview* (Widiger, Mangine, Corbitt, Ellis, & Thomas, 1995).
- *Structured Clinical Interview for DSM-IV Axis II Personality Disorders* (First, Spitzer, Gibbons, Williams, & Benjamin, 1996).

In addition, there are several semi-structured interviews that assess for criteria *specific* to BPD.

- *The Revised Diagnostic Interview for Borderlines* (Zanarini, Gunderson, Frankenburg, & Chauncey, 1989): contains subscales for various components of BPD symptoms.
- *Borderline Personality Disorder Severity Index* (Arntz et al., 2002): measures the frequency of borderline symptoms in the previous 3-month period and is an adaptation of an interview developed by Weaver & Clum (1993).

In addition to semi-structured interviews, there is a clinician rating that does not require a specific interview protocol, but is designed to be completed by the patient's therapist:

- *Personality Assessment Form* (Pilkonis, Heape, Ruddy, & Serrao, 1991).

Self-Report Inventories

- *Millon Multiaxial Inventory* (Millon, Millon, & Davis, 1994): provides scoring for DSM-IV personality disorders as well as clinical syndromes.
- *Personality Assessment Inventory* (Morey, 1991): based on the DSM-II criteria and provides a subscale for BPD, Axis I diagnoses, and validity scales.

Kim and Goff (2002) caution that individuals with BPD may experience greater psychiatric disturbance than is evident from their initial behavioral presentation. As such, they suggest that it is useful to specifically assess for the intensity of disruptive emotional states such as depression and anger, maladaptive cognitive patterns, dissociative symptoms and behavior, and interpersonal problems. These can be further measured using various self-report instruments that are relevant to these specific areas. Numerous additional instruments specific to disruptive emotional states, such as depression, anxiety, or anger, are available in the chapters of this text aimed at the treatment of these clinical problems. Suggestions for initial screening of other comorbid disruptive emotional or behavioral problems are encouraged and may include additional measures such as those listed below.

- *Brief Symptom Inventory* (Derogatis & Spencer, 1982): assesses psychiatric symptoms across a wide range of areas.
- *Michigan Alcohol Screening Test* (Selzer, 1971): a screening measure to assess for the presence of alcohol problems among psychiatric patients.
- *Eating Symptoms Inventory* (Whitaker, 1989): a self-report screening instrument for eating disorders.
- *PTSD Checklist* (Weathers, Litz, Huska, & Keane, 1991): a self-report screening measure of the presence and severity of posttraumatic stress disorder symptoms based upon the DSM criteria.

GENERAL THERAPY GOALS

Ultimate Outcome Goals

When working with patients with BPD, general ultimate outcome goals include decreasing the frequency of hospitalizations, decreasing the frequency and intensity of self-harming behaviors, improving self-regulation, and improving interpersonal relationships. In addition, because of the significant co-morbidity of other Axis I and II disorders in persons diagnosed with BPD, decreasing problems related to other psychological disorders or symptoms may represent important additional ultimate outcome goals. For example, individuals who attempt to manage their emotional instability by using alcohol or other drugs to help decrease emotional pain, or who exhibit significant symptoms of depression, anger, panic, eating disorders, or dissociation, would benefit from interventions developed to ultimately reduce the clinical targets associated with those disorders.

Possibly due to the presence of such strong co-morbid factors, as well as the level of risk involved with BPD patients, very little controlled research has been conducted with regard to outpatient treatment. As a result, the need for a clinical decision making model to help guide the case formulation and treatment design process is especially important when working with patients diagnosed with BPD (see also Cohen & Nezu, 1989; Koerner & Linehan, 1997). The few interventions that have been found to be efficacious in treating these patients have involved a variety of treatment components aimed at multiple clinical targets. *Dialectical behavior therapy* (DBT; Linehan, 1993) represents such an approach and has demonstrated efficacy in reducing episodes of parasuicidal behavior, decreasing hospitalizations, and decreased attrition from therapy (Linehan, Armstrong, Suarez, Allmon, & Heard, 1991; Linehan & Kehrer, 1993).

Major Instrumental Outcome Goals/Treatment Targets

BPD is defined by a challenging constellation of thoughts, emotions and behavior related to multiple causal paths. Although the underlying mechanisms for the hallmark symptom of emotional dysregulation is unclear, it is likely that biological factors concerning one's emotional reactivity play a role. However, the etiology of this dysregulation has been hypothesized as causally related to genetic influences, prenatal factors, and traumatic childhood events that impact the brain and nervous systems (Trull et al., 2003). Because most individuals with temperamental vulnerability do not develop BPD, a multicausal perspective suggests that specific developmental environments appear to set the stage for BPD.

One crucial developmental circumstance according to Linehan is one of an "invalidating environment" (Linehan, 1993). An invalidating environment is defined by the tendency to negate or respond unpredictably and inappropriately to an individual's private experiences, such as particular emotions and interpretation of events. An invalidating family environment, for example, is one in which an individual's cognitive emotional experiences are punished, trivialized, dismissed or disregarded and are attributed to socially unacceptable characteristics such as over-reactivity, laziness, or lack of motivation. As a function of such a social learning history, patients may learn to anticipate invalidation in future relationships and direct their limited coping efforts focused on ways to either anticipate or react to this "attack." Teaching such individuals new skills through therapy is extremely challenging as they tend to be very "rejection-sensitive" and often experience therapeutic change efforts as further invalidation of their emotional difficulties. At the same time, ignoring the need for change can be just as invalidating because it diminishes the seriousness of the person's disorganized behavioral patterns. The major instrumental outcome goals that are listed below are necessarily focused on *both* an increase in the person's perception of validation, as well as their motivation and commitment to change.

- Increase therapy adherence and motivation
- Decrease parasuicidal behavior and suicidal ideation
- Improve self-regulatory skills
- Increase cognitive accuracy
- Improve problem-solving skills
- Improve interpersonal skills

Goal 1: Increase Therapy Adherence and Motivation

The participation in therapy required of patients with patterns of emotionally volatile, impulsive, and destructive behavior requires their hard work and commitment. The behavior problems that BPD patients exhibit represents a well habituated "quick fix" for emotional dysregulation. As such, there will be many repeated incidents of self-harming thoughts and behavior even as an individual is learning the skills necessary to improve his or her life. In addition, due to the frequent hypersensitivity to rejection, many patients with BPD might view the therapist's attempts to help them change as a sign of disapproval and rejection. Therefore, specific strategies aimed at establishing and maintaining a commitment to stay in treatment and continue to work on goals may influence other instrumental outcomes, as well as the ultimate outcome goals.

Goal-Specific Assessment Tools

- *Behavioral Observation and Recording:* measures therapy attendance, promptness, and completion of homework assignments.
- *Clinical Interview:* monitor why treatment is being sought and the cost benefit to the patient for continuing to work hard toward change versus the immediate "relief" of impulsive problem solving.
- *Readiness to Change Questionnaire* (Rollnick, Heather, Gold, & Hall, 1992): a standardized motivational assessment scale frequently used for patients with addictive disorders which may be helpful in identifying changes in motivation.

One obstacle to the use of standardized assessment scales regarding motivation that are used with other populations is that persons without BPD may slowly come to accept and commit to change, whereas individuals with BPD may make intense and profound commitments initially, then experience symptoms of panic and devastation when they are unable to live up to these self-imposed expectations.

Goal-Specific Potential Interventions

- Psychoeducation
- Dialectical behavior therapy validation strategies
- Contingency management
- Acceptance and commitment therapy

Psychoeducation. The primary focus of psychoeducation is the provision of information regarding the multifaceted nature of the disorder and rationale for treatment. This educational process can be extended to partners and families. Although there are no studies to support the efficacy of this approach with individuals with BPD, the benefits of psychoeducational interventions have been described with regard to other disorders that involve serious disturbance and changes of mood, such as bipolar disorder (Craighead, Miklowitz, Frank, & Vajk, 2002).

Dialectical Behavior Therapy Validation Strategies. Dialectical behavior therapy (DBT) consists of a cognitive-behavioral protocol for the treatment of BPD in which the behavioral skill building component is balanced with techniques designed to provide acceptance and tolerance of the patient. Strategies that help to validate the patient's emotional experience include providing opportunities for emotional expression, teaching emotional observation and labeling skills, "reading" the patient's emotions, and communicating the validity of emotions (Linehan, 1993).

Contingency Management. In order to enhance motivation through contingency management, contingencies that are currently operating in the patient's environment require recognition and manipulation where adaptive behaviors are reinforced, and maladaptive, therapy-interfering behaviors are not (Comtois, Levensky, & Linehan, 1999).

Acceptance and Commitment Therapy. Integrating theoretic concepts from contextualism and behavior analysis, this therapeutic approach developed by Hayes, Strosahl, and Wilson (1999) provide techniques that focus on helping patients accept the effects of life difficulties and to move in the direction of their chosen values. Many of the techniques are aimed at overcoming the verbal barriers that contribute to avoidance and confusion that interfere with commitment to the purpose and direction of seeking therapeutic help.

Goal 2: Decrease Parasuicidal Behavior and Suicidal Ideation

According to Kim and Goff (2002), it is important to conduct a functional analysis with regard to any incidence of self-injurious behavior. For example, parasuicidal acts may follow a belief and intention that others will be better off if the patient is gone, whereas other self-harm actions may function as an expression of anger, attempt to punish oneself, struggle to regain a sense of balance, or self-distraction. These authors also recommend assessing physiologic events in order to better understand the causal factors of suicidal and parasuicidal behaviors. For example, physiologic events may serve as antecedent arousal for self-harm, as an antecedent affective state of anticipatory excitement, as a consequent analgesia or relief from pain, or a consequent reduction in arousal following self-harm.

Behaviors in which the patient attempts to engage in self-injurious behavior or actually attempt suicide are an essential instrumental variable in that suicide completion is much more likely in individuals who engage in previous suicide attempts, parasuicidal acts, and self-harm behaviors (Stone, Hurt, & Stone, 1987). In addition, as reported by Zanarini, Frankenburg, Khera and Bleichmar (2001), suicidality is predictive of the number of hospitalizations experienced by women diagnosed with BPD.

Goal-Specific Assessment Tools

- *Parasuicide History Interview* (Linehan, Heard, Brown, & Wagner, 2001): a semistructured interview measuring topography, intent, medical severity, social context, precipitating and concurrent events, and outcomes for single parasuicide episodes.

- *Self-monitoring of Parasuicidal Behavior* (e.g., Diary Cards; Linehan & Keherer, 1993): provides an ongoing record of parasuicidal behavior.
- *Hopelessness Depression Symptom Questionnaire* (Metalsky & Joiner, 1997): provides a measure of the degree of hopelessness present.
- *Visual Analogue Scale:* provides a way of recording the current intensity and severity of suicidal thinking.
- *Daily or Weekly Thought Record:* records the situational triggers and current pattern of hopeless thoughts, suicidal intention, and suicidal planning.
- *Adult Trait Hope Scale* (Snyder, 2000): provides a measure of the degree of hopefulness with regard to managing meeting individual future goals.

Goal-Specific Potential Interventions

- DBT behavioral harm reduction strategies
- Problem-solving therapy
- Cognitive restructuring
- Hope-based interventions

Dialectical Behavior Therapy Behavioral Harm Reduction Strategies. As part of the DBT approach, specific strategies are aimed at reducing parasuicidal and suicidal behavior including assessing and responding to emergencies, collaboration for a non-suicidal behavioral plan, and conducting a behavioral analysis of the high risk behavior. Conducting a careful functional analysis of the environmental, emotional, cognitive responses, and overt actions that led up to the critical behavior, provides an opportunity for the therapist to discuss alternative solutions, to underscore the negative effects of the behavior, and to reinforce nonsuicidal responses. Linehan et al. (1991) found DBT to reduce parasuicidal behavior. In another study, Turner (2000) also reported that DBT led to significant improvement in suicidal and self-harm behavior.

Problem-Solving Therapy. Problem-solving therapy (D'Zurilla & Nezu, 1999; Nezu, in press) is designed to increase one's overall coping ability when dealing with stressful situations. This approach views parasuicidal acts and suicidal behavior as ineffective attempts to solve problems and offers patients alternative strategies for solving stressful problems. Research by Schotte and Clum (1990) has consistently indicated that interpersonal problem-solving deficits are associated with suicidal behavior and feelings of hopelessness. PST is a cognitive-behavioral intervention that provides training for patients specifically designed to reduce one's negative and hopeless attributions regarding their perceived ability to cope with stressful problems. Part of this approach involves changing those cognitive factors that negatively impinge on one's *problem orientation* or general view of problems, and one's self-assessment regarding problem-solving capabilities (e.g., beliefs about why a problem occurred, attributions about who is responsible for the problem occurring in the first place, and self-efficacy beliefs).

Cognitive Restructuring. This cognitive therapy approach helps patients to identify the self-defeating thoughts, negative self-talk, and irrational beliefs that are related to hopelessness and suicidal ideation. Through cognitive restructuring, patients learn to identify their own cycles of thoughts and learn to change dysfunctional thought patterns. Many studies support the efficacy of cognitive techniques in the improvement of symptoms of depression and hopelessness (Dobson, 1989). Conceptually, cognitive restructuring can be thought of as an umbrella term that encompasses several specific therapy strategies: rational-emotive therapy (e.g., Ellis, 1994), cognitive therapy (Beck, 1995), and self-instructional training (Meichenbaum, 1985). Whereas differences among these three approaches exist, all involve helping patients to better identify and then alter maladaptive thoughts.

Hope-Based Interventions. Strategies geared to increase hope may play a major role in decreasing depressive self-thoughts (Snyder, LaPointe, Crowson, & Early, 1998), as well as negative emotional reactivity. Hopeful thoughts reflect the belief that one can find paths to desired goals and become motivated to use them. As a result, hope-based interventions can change a therapeutic intervention from trying to repair the worst things in life to building qualities that can help manage life more effectively. Snyder et al. (2000), in fact, suggests that a variety of CBT strategies are particularly well suited to enhance hope (e.g., problem-solving therapy, relapse prevention, training in subgoal production). Given this conceptualization, within the context of treatment for patients with BPD, it might be helpful to apply such CBT strategies with the reframed goal of increasing hope.

Goal 3: Increase Self-Regulatory Skills

Patients with BPD tend to experience emotions very intensely, as well as having significant difficulty controlling their affective responses (Yen,

Zlotnick, & Costello, 2002). This involves both a dispositional emotional vulnerability, as well as a perceived lack of ability to regulate emotion once it is physiologically experienced. As such, interventions based upon both lowering physiologic arousal, as well as training individuals to manage affect once experienced, may provide an increase in self-regulatory ability.

Goal-Specific Assessment Tools

- *Self-Monitoring* (Diary Cards; Record of Coping Attempts): behavioral assessment technique in which patients are taught to monitor their own behavior between outpatient sessions.
- *Physiologic Measures* (Heart Rate): Heart rate has been identified by anxiety and trauma researchers as providing a good combination of clinical utility, research, and practical functionality with regard to measurement of increased emotional sensitivity (Anthony, Orsillo, & Roemer, 2001).

Goal-Specific Potential Interventions

- Mindfulness meditation
- Stress inoculation training
- Relaxation training
- Identifying and labeling affect
- Increase pleasant events

Mindfulness Meditation.   Philosophically rooted in Eastern spiritual and meditative practices, mindfulness refers to a state of consciousness wherein a person is highly aware and focused on the reality of the present moment (including stressful events), such that he or she may bear such situations "mindfully" rather than automatically reacting to it in ways that may have been maladaptive or destructive in the past. This approach shows promise as an effective technique for a variety of anxiety and stress disorders (Kabat-Zinn, 1994), addictions (Marlatt & Kristeller, 1999), as well as BPD symptoms (Linehan, 1993).

Stress Inoculation Training.   A cognitive-behavioral approach developed by Meichenbaum (1985) to give patients a sense of mastery over their fears by teaching a variety of coping skills. The approach includes an educational component, muscle relaxation, breathing control, covert modeling, role playing, thought stopping, and guided self-dialogue.

Relaxation Training.   Relaxation skills training provides a way to calm or decrease physiologic arousal associated with negative emotional states and may include progressive muscle relaxation, autogenic training, breathing techniques, and guided imagery.

Identifying and Labeling Affect. This skill is focused on improving one's ability to observe and identify emotional states. Rather than view negative affect as an internal event to be feared, learning to identify and label negative affect can cue the patient as to where problems exist in their day-to-day life and direct their efforts toward solving them. This technique ("viewing emotions as cues") is one of the specific techniques included in Nezu and Nezu's approach to problem-solving therapy (e.g., Nezu, Nezu, & Perri, 1989).

Increase Pleasant Events. Patients with BPD may exhibit a hopeless reluctance to learn new skills because of their fears of failure. By previously having experienced invalidating or punishing reactions to their emotional expression, they not only become preoccupied with avoiding pain, but also may have lost their awareness of the positive and pleasant experiences that are available to them. Behaviorally, strategies that are focused on reinforcing behaviors that involve engaging in pleasant events or activities can counter patterns of avoidance, withdrawal, inactivity, or boredom. Strategies aimed at increasing pleasant awareness and participation in pleasant events and emotional experiences, such as joy and gratitude, have been demonstrated to be effective for depressed patients. Such techniques may provide a way for suicidal patients to increase their reasons to live without the difficult demands of trying to directly challenge suicidal thoughts (Lewinsohn & Munoz, 1992). Behavioral interventions that increase pleasant experiences, such as behavioral activation, may serve to improve a patient's ability to better manage depressive symptoms.

Goal 4: Increase Cognitive Accuracy

Core dysfunctional beliefs are self-maintaining because they structure patients' perceptions and interpretations of events and cause them to habitually react in ways that confirm their (inaccurate) beliefs. Patients with BPD frequently exhibit such negative core beliefs. For example, Arntz et al. (2002) developed a list of 20 common BPD assumptions based on the writings of Beck and colleagues (1990), as well as Young (1999). Such core beliefs reveal themes of aloneness, dependency, emptiness, "badness," interpersonal distrust, and vulnerability. In addition, the high prevalence of sexual abuse among persons diagnosed with BPD can further lead to cognitive target symptoms associated with trauma, such as fears, distrust, and dissociative symptoms (Soloff, Lynch, & Kelly, 2002). Although these criteria may not meet a formal diagnosis of PTSD, specific strategies aimed at increasing cognitive accuracy particular with regard to stressful events may be clinically indicated. Dissociative symptoms present in BPD patients with a history of childhood sexual abuse has been identified as a potentially important treatment target (Zanarini, Ruser, Frankenburg, Hennen, & Gunderson (2000).

Goal-Specific Assessment Tools

- *Dissociative Symptoms Scale* (Zanarini et al., 2000): provides identification of risk factors associated with dissociative experiences of borderline patients.
- *Borderline Personality Disorder Scale* (Butler, Brown, Beck, & Grisham, 2002): subscale developed by the authors from PBQ (Beck, Freeman, & Associates, 1990) which assesses a range of personality disorders.
- *Cognitive Diaries:* self-report of common thinking errors.

Goal-Specific Potential Interventions

- Cognitive restructuring
- Cognitive processing therapy
- Problem-solving therapy

Cognitive Restructuring.   Within Beck's cognitive therapy approach for personality disorders (Beck et al., 1990), cognitive distortions or errors in thinking are viewed as a core problem associated with the behavioral and emotional problems in BPD. The overall approach of cognitive restructuring (CT) is one of guided discovery, where the therapist and patient collaboratively engage in obtaining new data to test various assumptions. It has been suggested by Young (1999) that schema-focused CT therapy, which focuses on the early developmental cognitive-emotional learning experience of the patient, can serve as an important intervention to reduce and provide relapse of mood disturbance and increase stability of mood.

Cognitive Processing Therapy.   Cognitive processing therapy (CPT) is a therapy approach developed to treat the specific symptoms of PTSD in survivors of sexual assault (Resick & Schnicke, 1992; 1993). One unique feature is that it combines the main ingredient of exposure-based therapies for anxiety symptoms with the cognitive components found in most cognitively based approaches. It is a strategy that elicits memories of a traumatic event and then directly confronts remaining conflicts and maladaptive core beliefs about the event. CPT has been found to improve PTSD symptoms, including paranoid thoughts and dissociative symptoms.

Problem-Solving Therapy.   Problem-solving therapy (PST) provides specific therapeutic training and techniques in ways to decrease negative and distorted ways of thinking that obstruct one's problem-solving efforts. Skills designed to increase "realistic optimism" provide patients with greater cognitive flexibility (Nezu, in press).

Goal 5: Improve Problem-Solving Skills

Individuals diagnosed with BPD lack the capability to engage in adaptive responses and construct a life that is worth living (Linehan, 1993). Although there are many different skill deficits that may contribute to such maladaptive behavior patterns, problem solving has been identified as a particularly important core skill area. Problem-solving ability can be broken down into specific component areas, some of which may be similar to other instrumental outcome goals or treatment targets, such as improving cognitive accuracy. However, the integration and effective use of various problem-solving cognitive and behavioral skills, which are interrelated and interdependent, requires a specific training focus and continued practice (D'Zurilla & Nezu, 1999). These areas include: (a) the cognitive-emotional set with which one approaches a problem; (b) the skills required to define and set realistic goals; (c) the ability to generate alternative solutions; (d) the skills required to weigh decisions; and (e) the ability to commit to and implement chosen solutions.

Goal-Specific Assessment Tools

- *Social Problem-Solving Inventory-Revised* (D'Zurilla, Nezu, & Maydeu-Olivares, 2002): self-report measure of problem-solving ability.
- *Role Play of Relevant Problematic Situations:* provides for observation of problem-solving skills related to specific situations.

Goal-Specific Potential Interventions

- Problem-solving therapy
- Dialectical behavior therapy

Problem-Solving Therapy.   Problem-solving therapy teaches individuals to cope more effectively by learning how to alter the nature of the problem, changing one's reactions to it (e.g., acceptance that a goal cannot be reached), or both (Nezu, in press). Overarching goals of PST include: (a) decreasing the negative impact (e.g., emotional distress) related to the experience of both major and minor life events and problems, (b) increasing one's ability to cope more effectively with such problems, and (c) minimizing the likelihood of similar problems occurring in the future. Problem-solving therapy (D'Zurilla & Nezu, 1999) has been demonstrated to be an effective way to increase one's ability across several pertinent component skill areas, as well as one's overall problem-solving style.

Dialectical Behavior Therapy. Dialectical behavior therapy (DBT) employs problem-solving principles as a major treatment focus, both as a way for the therapist to model more effective coping, as well as the DBT basis for structured skills training techniques (Linehan, 1993).

Goal 6: Improve Interpersonal Skills

Although many patients diagnosed with BPD have social and conversational skills, their social effectiveness with regard to other behavioral-expressive areas is often deficient. Linehan (1993) recommends that the interpersonal skills listed below are best learned through both group and individual therapy formats. Consistent with a dialectic approach, the group format allows for a structured skills training experience in which the lack of individual attention is more easily tolerated by the patient. Although it is not possible to evaluate the impact of each individual skill acquisition to the overall effectiveness of DBT, the following interpersonal skill areas are included in most DBT-based interventions. As such, it may be important to assess the strengths or deficits of such skills with each individual BPD patient.

Social and interpersonal skill training programs have been effective in enabling persons with disabling mental disorders to function within their social communities. All of the skill training areas listed below draw upon learning principles and the use of techniques including role play, social modeling, coaching, prompting, feedback, in-vivo exercises, and homework assignments. Many studies support the use of such techniques for such skill acquisition in real-life settings (Kopelowicz, Liberman, & Zarate, 2002).

Goal-Specific Assessment Tools

- *Role-plays of Relevant Skill Area:* Role play of specific situations provides for observation of various interpersonal skills.

Goal-Specific Potential Interventions

- Communication skills training
- Assertiveness skills training
- Activity and leisure skills

Communication Skills Training. Individuals with BPD who have developmental experiences in which their emotions have been either punished, unrecognized, or discounted, often lack the skills to communicate their emotions in nondramatic or nondestructive ways. As a result of such a strong negative focus on their own affective states, they also are frequently challenged with regard to their ability to listen to or empathize with others. Training in basic communication skills provides education, specific techniques to improve these skills, and reinforced practice of using these new skills in their lives.

Assertiveness Skills Training. Because of a tendency to experience extremes of mood, individuals with BPD often have difficulty when attempting to express positive feelings, refuse requests, or express negative opinions in a manner that is considerate and respectful of others. Training in assertiveness skills helps teach patients to identify and rehearse appropriate assertive behaviors, as well as practice these skills in their day-to-day relationships.

Activity and Leisure Skills. Individuals with BPD have not experienced opportunities to be self-reliant and exert control over establishing their own pleasant experiences, interests, or management of time. A direct focus on building such independent activity and leisure skills with support, encouragement, and coaching, may contribute to behavioral stability.

Additional Instrumental Outcome Goals/Treatment Targets

Secondary treatment targets for BPD essentially focus on specifically addressing comorbid disorders. These include:

- *Decrease Substance Abuse.* Individuals with BPD show a high rate of comorbidity with regard to substance abuse disorders. Although there are some overlapping criteria, it has been suggested that comorbidity occurs because the two conditions share the problem of impulse control. Substance abuse in persons with BPD may represent a form of this core target of impulsivity. As such, a possible secondary treatment goal for a patient with BPD includes decreasing impulsive behaviors that are specifically related to substance abuse. Possible intervention approaches include various cognitive-behavioral strategies to reduce relapse associated with addictive behaviors (Marlatt & Gordon, 1985), social skills training, behavioral contracts, incentive programs, and community reinforcement (Finney & Moos, 2002).

ADDITIONAL CLINICAL CONSIDERATIONS

Working with BPD can arouse frustration, disappointment, and other negative affective reactions in therapists who confront frequent patterns of extreme emotional instability, suicidal and other therapy-interfering behaviors. It may be important to enlist peer supervision and support as part of the overall treatment plan to aid in awareness of one's own reactions to such challenging patients, and to help maintain an objective and scientific approach to treatment (Linehan, 1993).

REFERENCES

American Psychiatric Association. (2000). *Diagnostic and statistical manual of mental disorders* (ed. 4, text revision). Washington, DC: American Psychiatric Press.

Anthony, M. M., Orsillo, S. M., & Roemer, L. (Eds.) (2001). *Practitioner's guide to empirically based measures of anxiety.* New York: Kluwer/Academic.

Arntz, A., van den Hoorn, M. A., Cornelius, J., Verheul, R., van den Bosch, M. A., & de Bie, A. J. H. T. (2002). Reliability and validity of the borderline personality disorder severity index. *Journal of Personality Disorders, 17,* 45–59.

Arntz, A. (1996). *BPDSI. Borderline Personality Disorder Severity Index.* Maastricht, The Netherlands: The University of Limburg, Department of Medical, Clinical, and Experimental Psychology.

Beck, J. S. (1995). *Cognitive therapy: Basics and beyond.* New York: Guilford Press.

Beck, A. T., Freeman, & Associates (1990). *Cognitive therapy of personality disorders.* New York: Guilford Press.

Butler, A. C., Brown, G. K., Beck, A. T., & Grisham, J. R. (2002). Assessment of dysfunctional beliefs in borderline personality disorder. *Behaviour Research and Therapy, 40,* 1231–1240.

Cohen, N. S., & Nezu, C. M. (1989). Personality disorders. In A. M. Nezu & C. M. Nezu (Eds.), *Clinical decision making in behavior therapy: A problem-solving perspective* (pp. 267–295). Champaign, IL: Research Press.

Comtois, K. A., Levensky, E. R., & Linehan, M. M. (1999). Relationship between Borderline Personality Disorder and Axis I diagnosis in severity of depression and anxiety. *Journal of Clinical Psychiatry, 60,* 752–758.

Craighead, W. E., Miklowitz, D. J., Frank, E., & Vajk, F. C. (2002). Psychosocial treatments for bipolar disorder. In P. E. Nathan & J. M. Gorman (Eds.), *A guide to treatments that work* (2nd ed.; pp. 263–276). New York: Oxford University Press.

Derogatis, L. R., & Spencer, P. M. (1982). *Brief Symptom Inventory: Administration, scoring, and procedures manual.* Baltimore, MD: Clinical Psychometric Research.

Dobson, K. S. (1989). A meta-analysis of the efficacy of cognitive therapy for depression. *Journal of Consulting and Clinical Psychology, 57,* 414–419.

D'Zurilla, T. J., & Nezu, A. M. (1999). *Problem-solving therapy: A social competence approach to clinical intervention* (2nd ed.). New York: Springer Publishing Co.

D'Zurilla, T. J., Nezu, A. M., & Maydeu-Olivares (2002). *Social Problem-Solving Inventory-Revised (SPSI-R): Technical manual.* North Tonawanda, NY: Multi-Health Systems.

Ellis, A. (1994). *Reason and emotion in psychotherapy* (rev. ed.). New York: Birch Lane Press.

Finney, J. W., & Moos, R. H. (2002) Psychosocial treatments for alcohol use disorders. In P. E. Nathan & J. M. Gorman (Eds.), *A guide to treatments that work* (2nd ed., pp. 157–168). New York: Oxford University Press.

First, M., Gibbon, M., Spitzer, R. L., Williams, J. B. W., & Benjamin, L. S. (1997). *User's guide for the Structured Clinical Interview for DSM-IV Axis II Personality Disorders.* Washington, DC: American Psychiatric Press.

Goodman, M., & Yehuda, R. (2002). The relationship between trauma and borderline personality. *Psychiatric Annals, 32,* 337–345.

Grilo, C. M., Sanislow, C. A., & McGlashan, T. H. (2002). Co-occurrence of DSM-IV personality disorders with borderline personality disorder. *Journal of Nervous and Mental Disease, 190,* 552–554.

Hayes, S. C., Strosahl, K. D., & Wilson, K. G. (1999). *Acceptance and commitment therapy: An experiential approach to behavior change.* New York: Guilford Press.

Kabat-Zinn, L. (1994). *Mindfulness meditation for everyday life.* New York: Hyperion.

Kim, S. A., & Goff, B. C. (2002). Borderline personality disorder. In M. Hersen (Ed.), *Clinical behavior therapy: Adults and children* (pp. 16–180). New York: Wiley.

Koerner, K., & Linehan, M. M. (1997). Case formulation in dialectical behavior therapy. In T. D. Eells (Ed.), *Handbook of psychotherapy case formulation* (pp. 340–367). New York: Guilford Press.

Kopelwicz, A., Liberman, R. P., & Zarate, R. (2002). Psychosocial treatments for schizophrenia. In P. E. Nathan & J. M. Gorman (Eds.), *A guide to treatments that work* (2nd ed., pp. 201–228). New York: Oxford University Press.

Lambert, M. J., & Hill, C. (1994). Assessing psychotherapy outcomes and processes. In A. E. Bergin & S. L. Garfield (Eds.), *Handbook of psychotherapy and behavior change* (4th ed., pp. 72–133). New York: Wiley.

Lewinsohn, P. M., & Munoz, R. (1992). *Control your depression* (Rev. ed.). New York: Fireside Publishers.

Linehan, M. M. (1993). *Cognitive behavioral treatment of borderline personality disorder.* New York: Guilford Press.

Linehan, M. M. (2000). The empirical basis for Dialectical Behavior Therapy: Development of new treatments versus evaluation of existing treatments. *Clinical Psychology: Science and Practice, 7,* 113–119.

Linehan, M. M., Armstrong, H. E., Suarez, A., Allmon, D., & Heard, H. L. (1991). Cognitive-behavioral treatment of chronically parasuicidal borderline patients. *Archives of General Psychiatry, 48,* 1060–1064.

Linehan, M. M., Heard, H. L., & Armstrong, H. E. (1993). Naturalistic follow-up of a behavioral treatment for chronically parasuicidal borderline patients. *Archives of General Psychiatry, 50,* 971–974.

Linehan, M. M., & Kehrer, C. A. (1993). Borderline personality disorder. In D. H. Barlow (Ed.), *Clinical handbook of psychological disorders* (2nd ed., pp. 396–441). New York: Guilford Press.

Loranger, A. W. (1999). *International Personality Disorder Examination (IPDE).* Odessa, FL: Psychological Assessment Resources.

Marlatt, G. A., & Gordon, J. R. (Eds.). (1985). *Relapse prevention: Maintenance strategies in the treatment of addictive behaviors.* New York: Guilford Press.

Marlatt, G. A., & Kristeller, J. L. (1999). *Mindfulness and meditation.* In W. R. Miller (Ed.), *Integrating spirituality into treatment* (pp. 67–84). Washington, DC: American Psychological Association.

McNair, D. M., Lorr, M., & Dropppleman, L. F. (1992). *EdITS manual for the profile of Mood States.* San Diego, CA: Edits.

Metalsky, G. I., & Joiner, T. E. (1997). The Hopelessness Depression Symptom Questionnaire. *Cognitive Therapy and Research, 21,* 359–384.

Meichenbaum, D. M. (1985). *Stress inoculation training.* New York: Allyn & Bacon.

Millon, T., Millon, C., & Davis, R. (1994). *MCMI-III manual.* Minneapolis, MN: National Computer Systems.

Morey, L. C. (1991). *Personality Assessment Inventory: Professional manual.* Tampa, FL: Psychological Assessment Resources.

Nezu, A. M. (in press). Problem solving and behavior therapy revisited. *Behavior Therapy.*

Nezu, A. M., Nezu, C. M., & Perri, M. G. (1989). *Problem-solving therapy for depression: Theory, research, and clinical guidelines.* New York: Wiley.

Paris, J. (2002). Chronic suicidality among patients with borderline personality disorder. *Psychiatric Services, 53,* 738–742.

Pilkonis, P. A., Heape, C. L., Proietti, J. M., Clark, S. W., McDavid, J. D., & Pitts, T. E. (1995). The reliability and validity of two structured diagnostic interviews for personality disorders. *Archives of General Psychiatry, 52,* 1025–1033.

Resick, P. A., & Schnicke, M. K. (1992). Cognitive processing therapy for sexual assault victims. *Journal of Consulting and Clinical Psychology, 60,* 748–756.

Resick, P. A., & Schnicke, M. K. (1993). *Cognitive therapy for rape victims: A treatment manual.* Newbury Park, CA: Sage.

Rollnick, S., Heather, N., Gold, R., & Hall, W. (1992). Development of a short "Readiness to Change" questionnaire for use in brief opportunistic interventions. *British Journal of Addictions, 87,* 743–754.

Schotte, D. E., & Clum, G. A. (1987). Problem solving skills in suicidal psychiatric patients. *Journal of Consulting and Clinical Psychology, 50,* 690–696.

Selzer, M. L. (1971). The Michigan Alcoholism Screening Test: The test for a new diagnostic instrument. *American Journal of Psychiatry, 127,* 1653–1658.

Skodol, A. E., Gunderson, J. G., Pfol, B., Widiger, T. A., Livesley, W. J., & Siever, L. J. (2002). The borderline diagnosis I: Psychopathology, comorbidity, and personality structure. *Biologic Psychiatry, 51,* 936–950.

Snyder, C. R. (2000). The past and possible futures of hope. *Journal of Social and Clinical Psychology, 19,* 11–28.

Snyder, C. R., Ilardi, S. S., Cheavens, J., Michael, S. T., Yamhure, L., & Sympso, S. (2000). The role of hope in cognitive-behavior therapies. *Cognitive Research and Therapy, 24,* 747–762.

Snyder, C. R., LaPointe, A., Crowson, J. J., & Early, S. (1998). Preferences of high- and low-hope people for self-referential input. *Cognition and Emotion, 12,* 807–823.

Soloff, P. H., Lynch, K. G., & Kelly, T. M. (2002). Childhood abuse as a risk factor for suicidal behavior in Borderline Personality Disorder. *Journal of Personality Disorders, 16,* 201–214.

Stone, M. H., Hurt, S. W., & Stone, D. K. (1987). The PI 500: Long-term follow-up of borderline inpatients meeting DSM-III criteria. I: Global outcome. *Journal of Personality Disorders, 1,* 291–298.

Trull, T. J., Stepp, S. D., & Durrett, C. A. (2003). Research on borderline personality disorder: An update. *Current Opinion in Psychiatry, 16,* 77–82.

Turner, R. M. (2000). Naturalistic evaluation of dialectical behavior therapy-oriented treatment for borderline personality disorder. *Cognitive and Behavioral Practice, 7,* 413–419.

Van den Bosch, L. M. C., Verheul, R., & van den Brink, W. (2001). Substance abuse in borderline personality disorder: Clinical and etiological correlates. *Journal of Personality Disorders, 15,* 416–424.

Weathers, F. W., Litz, B. T., Huska, J. A., & Keane, T. M. (1991). *The PTSD checklist (PCL).* Boston: National Center for PTSD/Boston VA Medical Center.

Weaver, T. L., & Clum, G. A. (1993). Early family environments and traumatic experiences associate with Borderline Personality Disorder. *Journal of Consulting and Clinical Psychology, 61,* 1068–1075.

Whitaker, A., Davies, M., Shaffer, D., Johnson, J., Abrams, S., Walsh, B. T., Kalikow, K. (1989). The struggle to be thin: A survey of anorexic and bulimic symptoms in a non-referred adolescent population. *Psychological Medicine, 19,* 143–163.

Widiger, T. A., Mangine, S., Corbitt, E. M., Ellis, C. G., & Thomas, G. V. (1995). *Personality Disorder Interview-IV: A semi-structured interview for assessment of personality disorders. Professional manual.* Odessa, FL: Psychological Assessment Resources.

Yen, S., Zlotnick, C., & Costello, E. (2002). Affect regulation in women with Borderline Personality Disorder traits. *Journal of Nervous and Mental Disease, 190,* 693–696.

Young, J. E. (1999). *Cognitive therapy for personality disorders: A schema-focused approach (3rd edition).* Sarasota, FL: Professional Resource Press

Zanarini, M. C., Frankenburg, F. R., Chauncey, D. L., & Gunderson, J. G. (1987). The diagnostic interview for personality disorders: Interrater and test–retest reliability. *Comprehensive Psychiatry, 28,* 467–480.

Zanarini, M. C., Frankenburg, F. R., Khera, G. S., & Bleichmar, J. (2001). Treatment histories of borderline inpatients. *Comprehensive Psychiatry, 42,* 144–150.

Zanarini, M. C., Gunderson, J. G., Frankenburg, F. R., & Chauncey, D. L. (1989). The Revised Diagnostic Interview for Borderlines: Discriminating BPD from other Axis II disorders. *Journal of Personality Disorders, 3,* 10–18.

Zanarini, M. C., Ruser, T., Frankenburg, F. R., Hennen, J., & Gunderson, J. G. (2000). Risk factors associated with the dissociative symptoms of borderline patients. *Journal of Nervous and Mental Diseases, 188,* 26–30.

13

Male Erectile Disorder

GENERAL DESCRIPTION AND DIAGNOSTIC ISSUES

In general, sexual dysfunctions are characterized by disturbances in sexual desire and the psychophysiological changes associated with the sexual response cycle in men and women. According to the *Diagnostic and Statistical Manual of Mental Disorders, Fourth Edition, Text Revision* (DSM-IV-TR; American Psychiatric Association, 2000), the sexual response cycle for men can be divided into the following four phases: (a) *sexual desire*, (b) *excitement* (increase in subjective sexual pleasure accompanied by penile tumescence and erection), (c) *orgasm* (sensation of ejaculatory inevitability and actual ejaculation of semen), and (d) *resolution* (muscular relaxation and sense of general well-being).

Male sexual dysfunctions can occur in one or more of these phases. These include: *hypoactive sexual desire disorder* (a deficiency or absence of sexual fantasies and desire for sexual activity accompanying by marked distress), *sexual aversion disorder* (an aversion to and active avoidance of genital sexual contact with a sexual partner), *male erectile disorder* (difficulties achieving and/or maintaining an erection), *male orgasmic disorder* (persistent delay or absence of orgasm following normal sexual excitement), *premature ejaculation* (persistent or recurrent onset of orgasm with minimal sexual stimulation), and *dyspareunia* (genital pain associated with sexual

205

intercourse). Because of the frequency in which such problems are presented at an outpatient setting, this chapter focuses specifically on male erectile disorder (MED).

MED involves a persistent or recurrent inability to attain or maintain an adequate erection. It must also be accompanied by significant emotional distress or interpersonal difficulty. Individuals with MED vary with regard to patterns of responses. Some individuals report that they have difficulty obtaining any type of erection from the outset of a sexual encounter, whereas others report that normal tumescence occurs until attempting penetration. Others report that the erection decreases or is lost during intercourse itself. Some men indicate that they are only able to achieve an erection during self-masturbation.

MED is a common clinical complaint. Of men between the ages of 18 and 59 years old, 10.4% report some form of erectile problems during the past year (Laumann, Paik, & Rosen, 1999), although it increases dramatically with age. For example, in the Massachusetts Male Aging Study (Feldman, Goldstein, Hatzichristou, Krane, & McKinlay, 1994), 52% of men between the ages of 40 to 70 experienced erectile dysfunction, in which approximately three times as many older men experienced moderate to severe erectile problems as compared to younger males. The National Institutes of Health Consensus Conference (1993) on impotence found erectile dysfunction to be prevalent, suggesting that it affects 10–20 million men in the United States.

The increased successful use of sildenafil citrate (i.e., Viagra) in the treatment of MED has both positive and negative consequences for the outpatient CBT clinician (i.e., on the positive side it has increased awareness of the problem and slightly decreased associated stigma; on the down side, it has led to an increase in medical practitioner treatment). However, MED may not always be successfully treated by medication. For example, sildenafil does not improve libido, promote spontaneous erections, or induce erections irrespective of the individual's degree of arousal. More important, depending on the etiology of the dysfunction, this drug's efficacy ranges between 40% to 80% (Segraves & Althof, 2002), indicating significant variability depending on extenuating circumstances. Moreover, although not severe, a variety of side effects do exist (e.g., headaches, flushed face, dyspepsia).

Differential Diagnostic Issues

MED is not accounted for by another Axis I disorder (except another sexual problem), nor is it due excessively to the direct physiological effects of a substance, medication, or general medical condition. Various abused drugs, as well as certain prescribed medications (e.g., antihypertensives, antidepressants, neuroleptics) may be the cause of MED. This needs to be ruled out. If both MED and substance abuse are present, but it is judged that the sexual dysfunction is not exclusively caused by the direct physiological effects of the substance use, then *male erectile disorder, due to combined factors*, should be diagnosed.

Various medical conditions may also lead to sexual difficulties regarding penile erections. Examples include diabetes, multiple sclerosis, renal failure, peripheral neuropathy, peripheral vascular disease, spinal cord injury, and injury of the autonomic nervous system due to surgery or radiation (e.g., Marks, Friedman, DelliCarpini, Nezu, & Nezu, 1997). A complete medical exam is important and strongly advised prior to psychosocial treatment. Identifying whether nocturnal penile tumescence occurs is important to differentiate between primary MED and MED due to a general medical condition.

Co-Morbidity Issues

Erectile difficulties are frequently associated with sexual anxiety, fear of failure, performance anxiety, and decreased sexual pleasure. Such sexual problems can lead to distressed marital, interpersonal, and sexual relationships. Individuals with depression and substance abuse often report problems with sexual arousal.

ASSESSMENT OF DISORDER

A variety of measures exist that assess various general and specific sexual problems and related features. The reader is directed to a compendium of reviewed measures by Davis, Yarber, Bauserman, Schreer, and Davis (1998).

Clinician Ratings

- *Derogatis Sexual Functioning Inventory* (Derogatis, 1997): is a semi-structured interview that assesses a person's current level of overall sexual functioning.

Self-Report Measures

- *Derogatis Sexual Functioning Inventory* (Derogatis & Melisaratos, 1979): self-report inventory of overall sexual functioning.
- *Sexual Dysfunction Scale* (McCabe, 1998): self-report questionnaire that measures various sexual dysfunctions and associated factors.

GENERAL THERAPY GOALS

Ultimate Outcome Goals

Although in most cases, men enter therapy for MED with a performance-oriented goal in mind (i.e., achieve firm erections), Bach, Wincze, and Barlow (2001) suggest that goals involving increased sexual satisfaction and improved sexual relationships serve to decrease performance pressure and anxiety, factors that can impede any success in therapy. As such, it may be particularly important for the CBT clinician to discuss such goal-related issues with the patient or couple using a completed CPM and GAM (see chapters 2 and 3) prior to implementing a treatment plan.

In general, it is preferable, if one has a sexual partner, for both to undergo assessment and treatment as a couple. The partner can provide additional information and perspectives about the patient's sexual difficulties, as well as allowing the clinician to observe the actual interactions between the couple. In addition, according to Bach et al. (2001), working with a couple counters the notion that the male with erectile disorder needs to be "fixed." Further, Wylie (1997) found that male patients tended to remain in treatment if their partner attended the assessment interview, whereas Hirst and Watson (1997) found that the best predictor of outcome was whether one received treatment individually or as a couple, where couple sex therapy resulted in better outcome. This chapter is being presented with the assumption that the following precepts are applicable for both heterosexual and gay couples.

Major Instrumental Outcome Goals/Treatment Targets

- Overcome myths about male sexuality
- Decrease performance anxiety

- Decrease dysfunctional cognitions
- Improve stimulus control

Goal 1: Overcome Myths about Male Sexuality

Faulty beliefs, unrealistic expectations, and lack of information regarding physiological, anatomical, and psychological aspects of basic human sexual functioning can serve as etiological factors across sexual dysfunctions (Bach et al., 2001; Pridal, 2001). In Western society, a male may have grown up with a set of beliefs about the relationship between masculinity and sexuality, some of which can initiate and/or maintain the sexual dysfunction. Some of these myths of male sexuality include the following (see also Zilbergeld, 1998):

- A real man is not into sissy stuff like feelings and communication.
- All touching is sexual and therefore should lead to sex.
- A real man performs in sex.
- Bigger is better.
- Women won't like me if I can't "get it up."
- Real men don't have sex problems.
- I should be able to last all night.

Goal-Specific Assessment Tools

- *Sexual Opinion Survey* (Fisher, 1998): measures sexual attitudes and beliefs.
- *Semi-structured Interview*: clinician can use a list of myths (such as the preceding one) as a springboard to inquire about general and specific attitudes.

Goal-Specific Potential Interventions

Psychoeducation. Providing patients with accurate information about basic physiology, anatomy, and sexual functioning is an important treatment strategy across sexual dysfunctions. Providing such information can help to correct various myths and misunderstandings about sexual functioning. For example, Wincze and Carey (2001) suggest that various beliefs (e.g., one's erection must appear first before sexual activity to signal sexual interest) can lead to significant avoidance of sexual interactions.

Misunderstandings or lack of information regarding various risk factors are also important to ameliorate. For example, few males may realize that cigarette smoking can serve as both an indirect and direct cause of MED

(Mannino, Klevens, & Flanders, 1994; NIH Consensus Conference, 1993). Educating patients in accurate information about sex can occur in session through didactics and/or through bibliotherapy. A recent meta-analysis of bibliotherapy approaches for the treatment of sexual disorders provides ample evidence for its efficacy (van Lankveld, 1998; see also van Lankveld, Everaerd, & Grotjohann, 2001).

Goal 2: Decrease Performance Anxiety

A common theme across both earlier and contemporary psychosocial theories of erectile disorder highlights the etiological role of performance anxiety, whereby due to fears of failure, embarrassment, or "not being masculine," men may experience erectile failure. Barlow (1986) notes that negative affect specific to sexual stimuli is a central etiological feature of MED.

Goal-Specific Assessment Tools

- *International Index of Erectile Functioning* (Rosen et al., 1997): a 15-item measure of erectile functioning.
- *Subjective Units of Distress Scale* (SUDS): assesses patients' self-reported level of physiological or psychological distress, usually on a scale from 0 (*not at all distressed*) to 100 (*the most distressed they have ever been*) ratings.

Goal-Specific Potential Interventions

- Sensate focus
- Anxiety reduction

Sensate Focus.   This intervention procedure was originally developed by Masters and Johnson (1970) and is applicable for various male and female sexual disorders. Essentially, this technique teaches patients to first develop, and then focus on, a heightened awareness of sensations. The focus then shifts to such physical and emotional sensations rather than on one's performance. Performance anxiety becomes reduced as a function of working toward a goal that is immediately attainable (i.e., enjoying touching one another), as compared to striving toward the objective of sustained tumescence, which at the beginning of treatment, is unlikely. Internal pressure on oneself to "perform" becomes lessened, and the couple becomes able to enjoy each other's physicality. If implemented correctly, the couples' confidence in themselves and their relationship can increase, hence contributing further to a positive outcome. The pace of this approach should be gradual in order to reduce the psychological pressure. If relevant, instructions at the initial implementation of this procedure would be to deliberately *not* have sexual intercourse even if an erection occurs. The major goal is for the couple to learn to be more affectionate, to give and receive sexual pleasure, and to set multiple goals for sexual interactions beyond "successful intercourse." It is important that the pace at which additional activities (e.g., eventual intercourse) become part of the sexual event is agreed upon by both partners.

Anxiety Reduction. Morokoff, Baum, McKinnon, and Gilliland (1987) found that a combination of acute and chronic stress can lead to erectile failure. As such, if the patient with MED is found to experience heightened levels of anxiety symptoms prior to even attempting the sensate focus protocol, it may be important to teach him various anxiety reduction or stress management strategies, including progressive muscle relaxation, visualization, deep breathing, and autogenic training. Having the partner provide the actual relaxation induction can be particularly helpful (Nezu & Nezu, 2003).

Goal 3: Decrease Dysfunctional Cognitions

Barlow (1986) suggests that men and women with sexual disorders respond to sexual stimuli by focusing on negative self-statements and cognitions. This actually serves to distract them from erotic cues, thus interfering with their ability to become aroused. Research has documented that being distracted from erotic stimuli leads to decreased physiological arousal (e.g., Abrahamson et al., 1985). Dysfunctional thinking patterns in this context can involve both misconceptions and negative attitudes. They can also involve interfering thoughts, such as worrying about the firmness of one's erection or wondering if a sexual partner is enjoying his "technique." Wincze and Carey (2001) note that many patients, in fact, ignore or dismiss such thoughts as contributors to sexual difficulties.

Cyranowski, Aaerstad, and Andersen (1999) more recently described the concept of *sexual self-schemas*, which are cognitive generalizations regarding sexual elements of the self that represent a core component of one's sexuality. As core beliefs about sexual aspects of oneself, if positive, such schemas are likely to facilitate sexual functioning. On the other hand, when extremely negative, conflictual, or weak, such generalizations serve as potential risk factors for subsequent sexual dysfunctions.

Goal-Specific Assessment Tools

- *Sexual Self-Schema Scales* (Cyranowski, Aarestad, & Andersen, 1999): measures core beliefs about sexual aspects of oneself.

- *Thoughts Record:* self-monitoring of automatic thoughts related to sexual difficulties.

Goal-Specific Potential Interventions

- Cognitive restructuring
- Problem-solving therapy

Cognitive Restructuring.   Conceptually, sexual-dysfunction-related cognitive variables can be classified into two categories—negative attitudes (e.g., "I'm not going to be able to please my new girlfriend if I can't get it up like last time") and interfering thoughts (e.g., "I wonder how many boyfriends she has had sex with before me"). The first goal in decreasing the negative influence such cognitions have on sexual functioning is to help the patient identify when they occur. Completing a thoughts record after attempting sex can be helpful in this regard. One way to counteract self-defeating negative attitudes (e.g., "My penis isn't large—she is not going to be that excited when I take off my clothes") is to provide education and apply cognitive restructuring strategies. Conceptually, cognitive restructuring can be thought of as an umbrella term that encompasses several specific therapy strategies: rational-emotive therapy (e.g., Ellis, 1994), cognitive coping techniques from stress inoculation therapy (Meichenbaum, 1975), and cognitive therapy (Beck, 1995). Whereas differences among these approaches exist, all involve helping patients to better identify and then alter maladaptive thoughts. After learning to become more aware and recognize when such negative thoughts occur, patients are next taught how to assess the accuracy of such thoughts and to stop engaging in various cognitive errors (e.g., blaming, catastrophizing, overgeneralizing, personalizing) by replacing such maladaptive cognitions with more adaptive ones. Using Beck's cognitive therapy, patients are trained to assess and change their thinking into a more inductive and Socratic style than direct refutation or argumentative rebuttal. If the patient tends to be somewhat defensive, the more Socratic approach to cognitive restructuring may be more appropriate to apply.

Problem-Solving Therapy.   A related therapy approach to CT is problem-solving therapy (PST; D'Zurilla & Nezu, 1999; Nezu, in press) which is geared to increase one's overall coping ability when dealing with stressful situations. Part of this approach involves changing those cognitive factors that negatively impinge on one's *problem orientation* or general view of problems and one's self-assessment regarding one's problem-solving capabilities (e.g., beliefs about why a problem occurred, attributions about who is responsible for the problem occurring in the first place, self-efficacy beliefs). This approach can be adapted to help patients overcome negative thinking regarding sexual issues.

Goal 4: Improve Stimulus Control

Many couples, where one or both are experiencing sexual difficulties, often believe that sexual functioning is an automatic process that only involves a willing partner (Bach et al., 2001). Understanding what environmental and/or psychological factors either facilitate or hinder sexual desire and arousal for both partners becomes crucial, especially when attempting to enhance the effects of the sensate focus strategy previously described. Various environmental (e.g., music, lighting), temporal (e.g., time of day or night that sex is preferred), biological (e.g., presence of illness, fatigue), psychological (e.g., each member's mood), and interpersonal (e.g., physical attraction to each other) factors can impinge on the quality of a sexual interaction. Sex therapy in this context involves helping the couple to better understand their own and each other's "preferred sexual stimuli," as well as fostering their ability to engage in sex using more optimal conditions.

Goal-Specific Assessment Tools

- *Semi-structured interview:* to assess for conditions or factors that positively affect one's sexual arousal.

Goal-Specific Potential Interventions

- Stimulus control

Stimulus Control. This intervention approach entails three major steps. First, the therapist should help educate the couple that a multitude of factors can affect sexual functioning. Next, each partner is asked to create a list of conditions that are positive and negative influences on his or her sexual arousal. Last, the couple is encouraged to work towards maximizing the number of positive factors in each sexual encounter. This should be applied in tandem with the sensate focus procedure to maximize overall sensual pleasure. Because of vast differences in tastes and preferences across many of these factors (e.g., difference in tastes regarding what constitutes the "correct" mood music), it is important that the therapist help the couple to negotiate appropriately when working towards an agreement.

Additional Instrumental Outcome Goals/Treatment Targets

- *Marital distress/relationship conflict.* Simultaneous to assessing the sexual problem, it is likely that the therapist will begin to have an appreciation of the quality of the relationship per se beyond the sexual difficulties. If significant relationship conflict exists, where the sexual problems are secondary, then marital/couples treatment may be more appropriate (see chapter 14). However, if relationship problems do exist but appear to be a consequence of the frustration or tension associated with the sexual dysfunction, sex therapy can continue assuming that the couples' distress be identified as an additional treatment target (Metz & Epstein, 2002).
- *Poor Communications.* Assuming that this factor is not part of a larger relationship problem, improving the ability of each partner to communicate effectively with each other can be important. This might entail difficulties in talking about sexual issues, or problems regarding suppressed anger, resentment, or other negative feelings.
- *Mood Disturbance.* One of the most common individual risk factors for poor outcome regarding sex therapy is the presence of a psychological disorder (Hawton, 1995). For example, one of the defining characteristics of depression is the lack of interest or pleasure in activities the person previously enjoyed. Angst (1998) found that the rates of sexual dysfunction in a group of 591 men and women who were categorized as nondepressed, untreated depressed, and treated depressed was 26%, 45%, and 62%, respectively. Distress and worry are normal reactions to sexual problems. However, if a negative mood state is found to be clinically significant, then ameliorating this distress should be prioritized as a crucial treatment goal.

ADDITIONAL CLINICAL CONSIDERATIONS

The effects of age on sexual functioning is complex and often counters stereotypes. Little is known about the prevalence of sexual disorders among the elderly as a result of the lack of well-designed epidemiological studies (Fisher, Zeiss, & Carstensen, 1993), although erectile dysfunction may be the most common health disorder in older men (Godschalk, Chen, Katz, &

Mulligan, 1994). Whether the natural aging process, the greater prevalence of general health problems, or increased use of medications has any definitive or permanent effect on sexual functioning among the elderly is unknown. It is likely that the best predictor of sexual functioning among the elderly is previous sexual behavior (George & Weiler, 1981). Age-related changes are important and potentially influence sexual health, but should not be automatically viewed as the "cause" of the dysfunction (Zeiss & Zeiss, 1999). Although few outcome studies exist regarding CBT (or any other approach) for the treatment of sexual disorders among the elderly, it is likely that by adapting the above procedures on an idiographic basis, such strategies would be efficacious for treating MED in older persons (Fisher, Swingen, & O'Donohue, 1997; Zeiss & Zeiss, 1999).

Cultural factors also need to be taken into account when conducting treatment for sexual disorders. A variety of socio/ethnic/cultural factors can influence an individual's beliefs, attitudes, and actual behavior in sexual relationships. One's religious beliefs, for example, may frown upon or even prohibit activities such as masturbation or the use of sensate focus. The therapist needs to be particularly sensitive to any differences in values regarding sexual issues.

Prior sexual abuse, either as a victim or a perpetrator, may serve as a predisposing causal factor regarding one's beliefs, expectations, and desire regarding sexual activities. For example, male victims of adult-child contact are 3 times as likely to experience erectile dysfunction, whereas men who have sexually assaulted women are 3.5 times as likely to report erectile dysfunction (Laumann et al., 1999). As such, traumatic sexual acts can have significant effects on sexual functioning, even years beyond the actual event (e.g., child rape). Being alert to the possibility that such a risk factor exists for a given patient is important.

REFERENCES

Abrahamson, D. J., Barlow, D. H., Sakheim, D. K., Veck, J. G., & Athanasiou, R. (1985). Effect of distraction on sexual responding in functional and dysfunctional men. *Behavior Therapy, 16,* 503–515.

Angst, J. (1998). Sexual problems in healthy and depressed persons. *International Clinical Psychopharmacology, 13* (Suppl. 6), S1–S4.

American Psychiatric Association. (2000). *Diagnostic and statistical manual of mental disorders* (ed. 4, text revision). Washington, DC: American Psychiatric Press.

Bach, A. K., Wincze, J. P., & Barlow, D. H. (2001). Sexual dysfunction. In D. H. Barlow (Ed.), *Clinical handbook of psychological disorders: A step-by-step treatment manual* (3rd ed., pp. 562–608). New York: Guilford Press.

Barlow, D. H. (1986). Causes of sexual dysfunction: The role of anxiety and cognitive interference. *Journal of Consulting and Clinical Psychology, 54,* 140–148.

Beck, J. S. (1995). *Cognitive therapy: Basics and beyond.* New York: Guilford Press.

Cyranowski, J. M., Aarestad, S. L., & Andersen, B. L. (1999). The role of sexual self-schema in a diathesis-stress model of sexual dysfunction. *Applied & Preventive Psychology, 8,* 217–228.

Davis, C. M., Yarber, W. L., Bauserman, R., Schreer, G., & Davis, S. L. (Eds.). (1998). *Handbook of sexuality-related measures.* Thousand Oaks, CA: Sage.

Derogatis, L. R. (1997). The Derogatis Interview for Sexual Functioning (DISF/DISF-SR): An introductory report. *Journal of Sex and Marital Therapy, 23,* 291–304.

Derogatis, L. R., & Melisaratos, N. (1979). The DSFI: A multidimensional measure of sexual functioning. *Journal of Sex and Marital Therapy, 5,* 244–281.

D'Zurilla, T. J., & Nezu, A. M. (1999). *Problem-solving therapy: A social competence approach to clinical intervention* (2nd ed.). New York: Springer Publishing Co.

Ellis, A. (1994). *Reason and emotion in psychotherapy* (Rev. ed.). New York: Birch Lane Press.

Feldman, H. A., Goldstein, I., Hatzichristou, D. G., Krane, R. J., & McKinlay, J. B. (1994). Impotence and its medical and psychosocial correlates: Results of the Massachusetts Male Aging Study. *Journal of Urology, 151,* 54–61.

Fisher, J. E., Swingen, D. N., & O'Donohue, W. (1997). Behavioral interventions for sexual dysfunction in the elderly. *Behavior Therapy, 28,* 65–82.

Fisher, J. E., Zeiss, A. M., & Carstensen, L. L. (1993). Psychopathology in the aged. In P. B. Sutker & H. E. Adams (Eds.), *Comprehensive handbook of psychopathology* (2nd ed., pp. 815–842). New York: Plenum Press.

Fisher, W. A. (1998). The Sexual Opinion Survey. In C. M. Davis, W. L. Yarber, R. Bauserman, G. Schreer, & S. L. Davis (Eds.), *Handbook of sexuality-related measures* (pp. 34–37). Thousand Oaks, CA: Sage.

George, L. K., & Weiler, S. J. (1981). Sexuality in middle and late life: The effects of age, cohort, and gender. *Archives of General Psychiatry, 38,* 919–923.

Godschalk, M. F., Chen, J., Katz, P. G., & Mulligan, T. (1994). Prostaglandin E1 as treatment for erectile failure in elderly men. *Journal of the American Geriatrics Society, 42,* 1263–1265.

Hawton, L. (1995). Treatment of sexual dysfunctions by sex therapy and other approaches. *British Journal of Psychiatry, 167,* 307–314.

Hirst, J. F., & Watson, J. P. (1997). Therapy for sexual and relationship problems: The effects on outcome of attending as an individual or as a couple. *Sexual and Marital Therapy, 12,* 321–337.

Laumann, E. O., Paik, A., & Rosen, R. C. (1999). Sexual dysfunction in the United States: Prevalence and predictors. *Journal of the American Medical Association, 281,* 537–544.

Mannino, D. M., Klevens, R. M., & Flanders, W. D. (1994). Cigarette smoking: An independent risk factor for impotence? *American Journal of Epidemiology, 140,* 1003–1008.

Marks, D. I., Friedman, S. H., DelliCarpini, L., Nezu, C. M., & Nezu, A. M. (1997). A prospective study of the effects of high dose chemotherapy and bone marrow transplantation on sexual function in the first year after transplant. *Bone Marrow Transplantation, 19,* 819–822.

Masters, W. H., & Johnson, V. E. (1970). *Human sexual inadequacy.* Boston: Little, Brown.

McCabe, M P. (1998). Sexual dysfunction scale. In C. M. Davis, W. L. Yarber, R. Bauserman, G. Schreer, & S. L. Davis (Eds.), *Handbook of sexuality-related measures* (pp. 191–192). Thousand Oaks, CA: Sage.

Meichenbaum, D. H. (1977). *Cognitive behavior modification.* New York: Plenum Press.

Metz, M. E., & Epstein, N. (2002). Assessing the role of relationship conflict in sexual dysfunction. *Journal of Sex and Marital Therapy, 28,* 139–164.

Morokoff, P. J., Baum, A., McKinnon, W. R., & Gilliland, R. (1987). Effects of chronic unemployment and acute psychological stress on sexual arousal in men. *Health Psychology, 6,* 545–560.

National Institutes of Health (NIH) Consensus Conference. (1993). Impotence: NIH Consensus Panel on Impotence. *Journal of the American Medical Association, 270,* 83–90.

Nezu, A. M. (in press). Problem solving and behavior therapy revisited. *Behavior Therapy.*

Nezu, C. M., & Nezu, A. M. (2003). *Awakening self-esteem: Psychological and spiritual techniques for improving your well-being.* Oakland, CA: New Harbinger.

Pridal, C. G. (2001). Male gender role issues in the treatment of sexual dysfunction. In G. R. Brooks & G. E. Glenn (Eds.), *The new handbook of psychotherapy and counseling with men: A comprehensive guide to settings, problems, and treatment approaches* (pp. 309–334). New York: Wiley.

Rosen, R. C., Riley, A., Wagner, G., Osterloh, I. H., Kirkpatrick, J., & Mishra, A. (1997). The International Index of Erectile Function (IIEF): A multidimensional scale for assessment of erectile dysfunction. *Urology, 49,* 822–830.

Seagraves, T., & Althof, S. (2002). Psychotherapy and pharmacotherapy for sexual dysfunctions. In P. E. Nathan & J. Gorman (Eds.), *A guide to treatments that work* (pp. 497–524). New York: Oxford University Press.

van Lankveld, J. J. D. M. (1998). Bibliotherapy in the treatment of sexual dysfunctions: A meta-analysis. *Journal of Consulting and Clinical Psychology, 66,* 702–708.

van Lankveld, J. J. D. M., Everaerd, W., & Grotjohann, Y. (2001). Cognitive-behavioral bibliotherapy for sexual dysfunctions in heterosexual couples: A randomized waiting-list controlled clinical trial in the Netherlands. *The Journal of Sex Research, 38,* 51–67.

Wincze, J. P., & Carey, M. P. (2001). *Sexual dysfunction: A guide for assessment and treatment* (2nd ed.). New York: Guilford Press.

Wylie, K. R. (1997). Treatment outcome of brief couple therapy in psychogenic male erectile disorder. *Archives of Sexual Behavior, 26,* 527–545.

Zeiss, A. M., & Zeiss, R. A. (1999). Sexual dysfunction: Using an interdisciplinary team to combine cognitive-behavioral and medical approaches. In M. Duffy (Ed.), *Handbook of counseling and psychotherapy with older adults* (pp. 294–313). New York: Wiley.

Zilbergeld, B. (1998). *The new male sexuality* (rev. ed.). New York: Bantam Books.

14

Couple Distress

GENERAL DESCRIPTION AND DIAGNOSTIC ISSUES

The majority of people in the United States get married (Kreider & Fields, 2002). In 1996, 69% of men and 76% of women over the age of 15 years had been married at least once. Nevertheless, approximately 50% of marriages will end in divorce. The marital relationship tends to erode within the first 4–5 years (Bradbury, Cohan, & Karney, 1998), with the median time between marriage and separation being 6.6 years. Ten percent of couples divorce within 5 years of marriage and 20% of couples will divorce within 10 years. However, most (75%) people remarry. For the purpose of the current chapter, the term "couple" will be used to designate a significant romantic relationship between two adults, suggesting that the principles are potentially applicable to people who are not legally married or are of the same gender.

Given the high prevalence of marriages and divorces, couple distress is not uncommon. The question arises why, when it is presumed that couples form because two people like each other, does couples distress arise? One answer involves the changing nature of relationships. Dating is often characterized by excitement and novelty. However, as time elapses, certain events can occur that result in relationship distress, including "reinforcement erosion" (i.e., previously reinforcing behaviors become common and less reinforcing as they are repeatedly performed) and the emergence or recognition of incompatibilities (e.g., differences that were previously disregarded or discounted are now recognized as a disparity).

In addition, problems or stressors are inevitable and can serve to increase couple distress. For example, financial tensions, occupational stress, illness, and other major life events (e.g., childbirth) can strain a relationship. Further, stressors can highlight partners' differences in coping styles. Certain maladaptive cognitive and behavioral patterns may present during stressful times, serving to increase such distress.

Predictors of relationship problems include parental divorce, violence within the family of origin, and individual psychopathology. Gottman and colleagues (Gottman, Coan, Carrere, & Swanson, 1998) predicted approximately 80% of divorce and marital dissatisfaction by assessing variables such as a husband's rejection of his wife's influence, negative reciprocity of emotions, and lack of deescalation during conflict resolution.

ASSESSMENT OF DISORDER

Self-Report Measures

- *Areas of Change Questionnaire* (Weiss, Hops, & Patterson, 1973): assesses specific matters couples would like to see changed.
- *Conflict Tactics Scale* (Straus, 1979): assesses frequency and severity of physical aggression; can be used as a screen for the appropriateness of couple's therapy.
- *Dyadic Adjustment Scale* (Spanier, 1976): assesses distress and commitment related to the relationship.
- *Issues Checklist* (Robin & Foster, 1989): assesses sources of conflict within the relationship.
- *Marital Satisfaction Inventory-Revised* (Snyder, 1997): assesses satisfaction with marriage; includes Domestic Violence scale to assess for physical aggression.
- *Marital Status Inventory* (Weiss & Cerreto, 1980): assess likelihood of marriage dissolution.

GENERAL THERAPY GOALS

Ultimate Outcome Goals

When working with couples, ultimate outcome goals may include reducing conflict, decreasing negative conduct, and enhancing closeness and intimacy. Couples therapy is geared toward enhancing the partnership (i.e., working together to address problems effectively) and altering maladaptive patterns of interactions and contingencies in an effort to support each other through times of stress (e.g., emotionally and instrumentally), enhance a better understanding of each other, and increase caring. Emotions may be targeted, specifically by decreasing either emotional disengagement or negative emotions (e.g., anger, depressive symptoms) and by reducing negative affect reciprocity. Similarly, behaviors are targeted as ultimate outcome goals by decreasing behavioral surpluses (e.g., verbal aggression) and/or deficits (e.g., coping skills). Finally, enhancing a relationship that contributes to the well-being of each other, both in the short term (e.g., daily) and long term is desirable.

It is important to remember, however, that, rather than enhance intimacy, an ultimate goal may be to decide the best course of action for the couple. Over the course of therapy, they may mutually decide that separation is best. If so, therapy can then change goals, with ultimate outcome goals aimed at enhancing an amicable dissolution of the relationship.

Major Instrumental Outcome Goals/Treatment Targets

Major instrumental outcome goals for couple distress include:

- Enhance positive behaviors
- Improve adaptive communication and problem solving
- Decrease dysfunctional beliefs
- Enhance acceptance

Goal 1: Enhance Positive Behaviors

Social exchange theory contends that relationship satisfaction is a function of the ratio of positive to negative experiences. Further, social learning theory states that behavior is a result of environmental factors including operant and classical conditioning. Traditional behavioral marital therapy (Jacobson & Margolin, 1979) is based on these two theories and places significant emphasis on the role of behavioral exchange. Relationship dysfunction is characterized by more negative than positive interactions. In fact, it has been found that stable relationships are characterized by a ratio of negative to positive behaviors of 1:5, whereas distressed relationships are distinguished by a ratio of 0.8:1. In addition, it has been demonstrated that changing maladaptive behaviors within a partnership results in enhanced satisfaction within that relationship (Hahlweg & Markman, 1988).

The notion of reciprocity is central to traditional behavioral marital therapy (Jacobson & Margolin, 1979). Specifically, positive behaviors are more likely to occur following other positive behaviors, the same being true for punishment. Positive behaviors predict satisfaction within a relationship, whereas relationship dissatisfaction is characterized by negative behaviors.

Goal-Specific Assessment Tools

• *Spouse Observation Checklist* (Weiss, Hops, & Patterson, 1973): allows couples to assess positive behaviors performed by their partners.

Goal-Specific Potential Interventions

• Behavioral exchange
• Schedule pleasant events
• Self-regulation

Behavioral Exchange.   Given both the reciprocity and the relative increased rate of negative behaviors performed by distressed couples, the purpose of behavioral exchange is to increase positive behaviors. In behavioral exchange, individuals *independently* identify behaviors they can perform for their partner and then implement these behaviors in a variety of ways. They may be assigned to engage in a certain number of these behaviors (e.g., starting with one each week and increasing the frequency over time) without informing the partner. Alternatively, the "cookie jar technique" can be used where partners write positive acts on pieces of paper and then select the partner-pleasing activity in which they will engage. In addition, "caring days" (Stuart, 1980) can be implemented where one partner is asked to do something special for the other on that particular day.

Couples are asked to assess the benefits of their increased positive behaviors on the behaviors of their partner. Based on the concept of reciprocity, positive changes in the behavior of one partner are expected to result in similar transformations in the other.

Schedule Pleasant Events.   Distressed couples often avoid spending time together for fear of ensuing conflict. Thus, interactions are often based on discord. Scheduling pleasant events or leisure activities together can break the association between friction and time spent together. Partners are asked to identify activities that they would like to take part in (e.g., go out to dinner, go for a walk, take a short vacation). The therapist then helps the couple to plan how to implement this "date," as well as to identify and problem solve potential barriers to executing such acts (e.g., getting a babysitter to take care of the children, being certain to leave work at a specific time to ensure punctuality). Such planned events can remind couples of the joy they can collectively experience.

Self-Regulation. The premise behind self-regulation is that satisfaction with the relationship enhances when the individual makes efforts to change his or her own behaviors, thoughts, and emotions (Weiss & Halford, 1996). Thus, couples are encouraged to decrease blame and resulting behavior and increase responsibility and implementation of their own adaptive behavior. Rather than encourage engaging in positive behavior in an effort to change the other person to perform more positive actions, following a self-regulation model, the therapist assists each individual to identify ways to decrease his own problematic behavior. This approach has been found to be effective at enhancing communication and marital satisfaction (Halford, Sanders, & Behrens, 1994).

Goal 2: Improve Adaptive Communication and Problem Solving

Ineffective or destructive ways of communicating with each other, especially when attempting to work on important issues, is another characteristic of distressed couples. Rather than trying to engage in mutually cooperative problem solving, they are likely to engage in various types of coercion, such as crying, threatening, and withholding affection. Whereas initial coercion may allow one partner to be happy because she gets what she wants, it is likely to lead to increased polarization. Poor communication and conflict management skills have been found to be significant predictors of marital discontent and divorce (Gottman, Coan, Carrere, & Swanson, 1998). Communication and problem-solving training teaches the couple how to more effectively discuss and resolve problems without using destructive tactics.

Goal-Specific Assessment Tools

- *Communication Patterns Questionnaire* (Sullaway & Christensen, 1983): assesses behavioral interactions between partners.
- *Managing Affect and Differences Scale* (Arellano & Markman, 1995): assesses communication skills used by couples, particularly during conflicts.

- *Semi-structured role plays:* assesses communication and problem-solving difficulties during simulated role play regarding a particular problem area (e.g., finances, child rearing, where to live).

Goal-Specific Potential Interventions

- Communication skills training
- Emotional communications training
- Problem-solving therapy

Communication Skills Training. The enhancement of communication skills can be beneficial for couples experiencing distress. One such skill, the *speaker–listener* technique, involves specific rules for the speaker and listener. For example, the speaker is instructed to use "I" instead of "you," refrain from blaming, use "soft" emotional labels, such as "sad" or "hurt" rather than "angry," and keep statements brief. The listener is responsible for paraphrasing what the speaker says *without rebutting*. This fosters a mutual understanding that what is being *stated* by one member is actually being accurately *heard* by the other. Although this way of communicating may initially seem unnatural and strained to the couple, the therapist explains that it can be helpful because (a) it permits a more rational discussion, and (b) such "rules" will become more routine as the couple continues to practice.

Assertiveness training is another important component of communications skills. Couples learn to differentiate between aggression and assertiveness, as well as to identify effective ways to be assertive. Specifically, couples are educated in ways to make requests that are important to them, say "no" to requests that they would not like to render, and express their reactions in a non-combative manner.

Given that the occurrences of some type of conflict are inevitable, conflict resolution is another important component of communication skills. *Time out* can be a helpful technique for couples to prevent adverse effects of heightened emotional intensity (e.g., behaviors that the couple will later regret). Prior to this affective intensification, couples identify a way to stop the escalation (e.g., take 20 minutes apart to think more clearly about what each is saying). They then reconvene at a previously determined time to debrief and converse in a more rational state of mind.

Problem-Solving Therapy. Often, couples' interactions are entrenched in maladaptive coping (e.g., one person is aggressive while the other withdraws). Thus, training in problem-solving skills is an important aspect of improving communication. Problem solving emphasizes clearly defining the problem, developing alternative solutions, deciding upon the most effective option, and then implementing that solution (D'Zurilla & Nezu, 1999). It is important to remember that at times, a problem cannot be resolved by changing the situation. Rather, fostering acceptance or finding ways to decrease one's negative reaction to the problem may be more adaptive goals to set (Nezu, in press). In treating couple distress, this approach is geared to increase a dyad's ability to resolve problems together using specific problem-solving skills. Therefore, a couple is encouraged to apply the skills in tandem with the communications skills previously learned. Additional instructions include posting the mutually derived solution in a place for both individuals to view often in order to review progress towards solving the problem, setting aside a specific time and place to engage in mutual problem solving, and focusing on only one problem at a time (Wheeler, Christensen, & Jacobson, 2001).

Emotional Expression.   Because emotions are often not expressed effectively (e.g., expressing anger excessively or suppressing it), couples are taught more adaptive ways to communicate affect. *Emotion focused therapy* (Johnson, 1996) is an intervention aimed at identifying, normalizing, and expressing emotions. *Emotional Expressiveness Training* (Baucom & Epstein, 1990) facilitates the expression of emotions in a nonthreatening, non-blaming approach. Here, couples are instructed to articulate their feelings in a concise manner, to which their partner responds by paraphrasing what was said. This technique is initially implemented using positive emotions, and as the couples' skills progress, more negative emotions can be communicated.

In an effort to decrease heightened negative emotions while discussing a problem, the therapist may encourage the couple to *detach* from the problem. Borrowing a technique from integrative behavioral couple therapy (ICBT; Jacobson & Christensen, 1996), which is discussed more fully under Goal 3, detachment from the difficulty permits a rational (rather than solely emotional) examination of the problematic situation. Here, the couple discusses the problematic situation using the third person "it," instead of the second person "you." Further, an additional chair can be placed in the therapy room to represent "the problem," as an entity separate from the couple. This approach permits a neutral discussion without maladaptive emotional discharge.

Goal 3: Decrease Dysfunctional Beliefs

Decreasing dysfunctional beliefs can also improve relationship satisfaction. Baucom and colleagues (Baucom, Epstein, Sayers, & Sher, 1989) have identified five aspects of dysfunctional beliefs contributing to relationship distress. First, *distorted perceptions* can result in selective attention to a partner's negative behaviors at the expense of noticing positive behaviors. Further, couples often view negative behaviors as *linear* (e.g., husband does something wrong so wife has to react) rather that circular (e.g., both wife's and husband's behavior influence each other perpetuating maladaptive behaviors). A second component involves peoples' *attributions*. Among distressed couples, problems are often attributed to the partners' stable, negative traits, thus leading to a decline in relationship satisfaction (Bradbury & Fincham, 1990). *Expectations* for future events, both regarding the negative partners' behaviors and one's efficacy to cope, as well as unrealistic expectations about marital bliss in general (e.g., marriage means always being "in love") represents a third possible cognitive dysfunction. Fourth, discord can be caused by dysfunctional *assumptions*, which may concern one's partner (e.g., "she will never change"), as well as the relationship (e.g., "if he cared about me, he would act differently"). Finally, unrealistic *standards* about relationships (e.g., spouses should sense problems and "know" how to solve problems if they truly love their partner) can lead to couples' distress.

Goal-Specific Assessment Tools

- *Dysfunctional Thought Record* (Beck, 1995): identifies situations that trigger automatic thoughts, actual automatic thoughts, emotions, adaptive counter thoughts, and emotional and cognitive consequences.
- *Inventory of Specific Relationship Standards:* (Baucom, Epstein, Rankin, & Burnett, 1996): assesses standards held about marital relationships.
- *Marital Attitude Survey* (Pretzer, Epstein, & Fleming, 1991): assesses marital attitudes, including attributions about behaviors and expectancy for change within the relationship.
- *Relationship Attribution Measure* (Fincham & Bradbury, 1992): assesses attributions for partner's behavior.
- *Relationship Attribution Questionnaire* (Baucom et al., 1996): assesses standards for relationships and attributions for problems.
- *Relationship Belief Inventory* (Eidelson & Epstein, 1982): assesses unrealistic beliefs about relationships.

Goal-Specific Potential Interventions

- Cognitive restructuring
- Behavioral experiments
- Reframing

Cognitive Restructuring.   The goal of cognitive restructuring is to identify maladaptive cognitions and modify them to more adaptive thinking. Couples learn to identify their automatic thoughts and cognitive distortions (e.g., selective abstraction, overgeneralization, dichotomous thinking), using a dysfunctional thought record. The *downward arrow* technique can help couples identify maladaptive assumptions (e.g., "people who care about others do not get angry with them") that fuel dysfunctional beliefs (e.g., "my partner doesn't love me because he gets angry with me"). In an effort to change dysfunctional cognitions, couples are asked to identify alternative beliefs. They are instructed to then identify pros and cons to the beliefs they hold, as well as the newly identified beliefs.

Behavioral Experiments.   Following the development of alternative beliefs, couples are instructed to search for confirming or disconfirming evidence. Couples engage in behavioral experiments to determine the veracity of both their dysfunctional and newly developed cognitions. For example, a woman who previously believed her husband did not care about her stressful job develops an alternate belief that he changes the subject when she complains about work in an effort to move to a more positive topic. She may ask her husband why he changes the subject, or may express her desire to talk about her job in an effort to decrease her sense of stress. Couples are taught to weigh the evidence for and against their original and newly developed beliefs. Behavioral experiments can also be used to test maladaptive assumptions and standards.

In an effort to alter negative "tunnel vision," couples are instructed to engage in *positive tracking*. Specifically, couples are asked to pay close attention to positive behaviors produced by their partner. Such behaviors can be anything from expressing gratitude for performing a household chore to receiving a surprise gift.

Another behavioral experiment entails the use of role-plays. Specifically, couples can engage in role-plays where they discuss sources of contention, during which they are asked to verbalize thoughts and feelings that arise. This permits all parties (e.g., the therapist and both partners) to gain a better understanding of what each individual is experiencing.

Reframing.   Reframing each partner's characteristics in a more positive manner allows the couple to alter dysfunctional cognitions held about each partner. For example, the therapist teaches the couple that those characteristics that were initially viewed as attractive are often the same traits that are later perceived as problematic. For instance, spontaneity/irresponsibility and giving/squandering are pairs of attributes that are on the same continuum, the former of which is more appealing and the latter may be seen as less appealing. Using reframing, couples reconceptualize what they currently perceive as negative traits into more positive qualities.

Another form of reframing entails presenting the notion of a "collaborative set" (Jacobson & Margolin, 1979) or the shared responsibility of the individuals for the problems at hand and the ability to improve the relationship. This permits a reconceptualization of the problem as a group-effort, rather than placing blame on one's partner. Moreover, the therapist can highlight the strengths of the couple, including participating in therapy in an effort to improve their relationship. The therapist further facilitates a sense of positive hope, rather than the couple's previously held negative expectations.

Goal 4: Enhance Acceptance

Happy couples are more likely to be accepting of each other. Acceptance in this context refers to the ability of the couple to view previously irreconcilable differences in a new light so that they are tolerated and, perhaps, even appreciated. Thus, instead of trying to either change each other or to eradicate conflict, enhancing acceptance involves gaining a better understanding of the differences between each other and embracing these differences to boost empathy and compassion. Acceptance differs from resignation in that the latter term denotes resentfully giving in to one's partner, whereas the former involves "letting go" of the conflict or desire for partner change. Although related to reframing in terms of changing the interpretation of one's partner's behavior, acceptance specifically refers to accepting differences.

Some problems are "unsolvable." Thus, acceptance is particularly indicated if attempts to change one's partner's behaviors have been unsuccessful and/or are causing significant distress. Often, the demands to change actually serve to prevent change from occurring. Conversely, acceptance may result in behavior change because the pressure to change is lifted. Using joint problem-solving sessions to come to such a solution can be helpful.

Integrative behavioral couple therapy (ICBT; Jacobson & Christensen, 1996) is a protocol intervention that aims to augment acceptance in an effort to enhance the quality of the relationship. Treatment components of ICBT include case formulation, acceptance and tolerance training, and training in behavioral strategies to promote change (e.g., behavioral exchange, communications skills training, problem-solving training).

Goal-Specific Assessment Tools

- *Frequency and Acceptability of Partner Behavior* (Christensen & Jacobson, 1997): assesses frequency of problems, dissatisfaction with the relationship, and acceptance.
- *Need Fulfillment Inventory* (Prager & Buhrmester, 1998): assesses importance and achievement of needs and desires.

Goal-Specific Potential Interventions

- Case formulation
- Empathetic joining
- Tolerance building

Case Formulation.   Integral to assisting the couple in re-conceptualizing what are perceived as irreconcilable differences, the relationship case formulation entails three elements: "theme," "polarization process," and "mutual trap." A *theme* describes the source of the couple's conflict (e.g., "closeness-distance" for a couple in which one member tends to vie for more intimacy while the other struggles for greater independence). The *polarization process* describes the disparaging relations that occur as a result of attempts to change one's partner. For example, using the "closeness-distance" theme as an example, the individual who seeks greater intimacy may engage in certain behaviors trying to enhance closeness, to which the other partner reacts by withdrawing even more. Thus, a *mutual trap* develops, where the couple feels trapped and hopeless about the ability for the relationship to change. Following the assessment, which includes obtaining a clear understanding of the content and process of troublesome interactions, the couple's history (e.g., courtship, significant life events) and the level of commitment of each member, the therapist presents each component of the case formulation to the couple. Included in this formulation is the notion of a "collaborative set." This case formulation technique provides a means by which the couple is able to gain a better understanding of why each partner acts a certain way, thus facilitating acceptance for each other's behavior.

Empathetic Joining.   Empathy is an important component of acceptance. Empathetic joining is a strategy that attempts to decrease hostility and enhance compassionate unification between the couple. Specific techniques for empathetic joining include reformulation of the couple's problems and reactions to problems as normal and logical, and encouraging the use of "soft disclosures." This latter approach entails describing one's pain without blaming the other person. For example, rather than reporting emotions of anger or irritation, couples are encouraged to express feeling sad or hurt. In addition, the therapist models empathetic interpretations of each partner's behavior, permitting the individuals to learn this style of acceptance and expand their own empathy.

Tolerance Building.   In an effort to further enhance acceptance, couples are taught to build tolerance for their partners' behavior. Tolerance building can be facilitated via numerous methods. For example, the therapist may emphasize the positive aspects of the partner's behavior using reframing. Further, the therapist may highlight that the couple's traits, although different, actually complement each other, making the "whole greater than either individual partner." As an illustration, for a couple with different ideas about finances, it can be presented that if both were either frugal or lavish, additional problems would arise.

Another technique to increase tolerance involves having the partner "fake" the problematic behavior at home without initially informing the partner. The therapist explains this exercise to both partners to foster adherence. By implementing the behavior when not emotionally moved to do so, partners can assess the consequences of their actions without emotional attachment. The couple is then instructed to debrief their thoughts and feelings related to the action in an effort to enhance their understanding of the motivation for and reaction to various behaviors.

Additional tolerance training entails preparation for inevitable lapses in behavior. This serves both to normalize the occurrence of such slips, thus preventing conceptions of failure and to allow the couple to develop a plan to implement when problems occur.

Finally, because conflict is often a result of needs not being met by a partner, couples are instructed in the concept of *self-care*. Couples identify wishes that they can fulfill themselves or that other people (e.g., family, friends) can provide. This decreases the over-reliance, and subsequent stress, on the partner.

Additional Instrumental Outcome Goals/Treatment Target

- *Decrease Stress.* As previously noted, the likelihood of relationship turmoil increases during stressful events (Karney & Bradbury, 1995). Stressful events can include developmental milestones (e.g., parenthood, retirement) or emergency situations (e.g., major illness, unemployment). To decrease stressors, problem-solving therapy, engendering social support, and relaxation training can be implemented.

- *Decrease Individual Psychopathology.* Individuals with psychopathology are more likely than the general public to experience relationship difficulties and divorce. However, the direction of this relationship is unclear. The decision to engage in individual or couples therapy when psychopathology is present is idiographic and should take into consideration the severity and level of awareness of the psychopathology, as well as the partners' abilities to work together (Epstein & Baucom, 2002). It is recommended that the therapist implement CBT interventions described in other chapters in this book that correspond to the prevailing psychopathology (e.g., depression).
- *Address Ambivalence.* It is not uncommon for at least one member of the couple to demonstrate ambivalence towards therapy which can be manifested verbally or nonverbally (e.g., ignoring homework assignment). When this occurs, the ambivalence can be normalized and validated. A concise conceptualization of the motivation behind the ambivalence (e.g., feeling blamed for the distress, not really wanting to put effort into the relationship) should be developed. Interventions such as cognitive restructuring, reframing, and empathetic joining may assist in addressing ambivalence. Ambivalence can also be a sign that that individual really wants to end the relationship.
- *Enhance the Relationship.* Relationship education programs have been developed in an effort to enhance partners' satisfaction. Examples include the *Prevention and Relationship Enhancement Program* (PREP; Renick, Blumberg, & Markman, 1992; Stanley, Blumberg, & Markman, 1999) that includes training videotapes for couples (Stanley, Markman, & Blumberg, 1994) and the *Compassionate and Accepting Relationships through Empathy* (CARE; Rogge, Cobb, Johnson, Lawrence, & Bradbury, 2002) program. Overall, the emphasis of these protocols is to teach skills to improve communication, conflict management, and empathy. Such programs have demonstrated long-term beneficial effects on relationships (e.g., enhanced positive communication; Markman, Renick, Floyd, & Stanley, 1993).

ADDITIONAL CLINICAL CONSIDERATIONS

Given that violence within the relationship predicts marital problems (Rogge & Bradbury, 1999), it is vital to assess for violence when working with distressed couples. Approximately 70% of couples presenting with marital discord report the occurrence of violence within the past year (Cascardi, Langhinrichsen, & Vivian, 1992). If violence is ongoing, couples therapy is contraindicated, and the therapist must prioritize the safety and health of the victim. Individual therapy with separate therapists is often indicated. References for specific assessment of relationship violence include the Conflict Tactics Scale and Marital Satisfaction Inventory—Revised as described under "Assessment."

When working with couples, the dilemma of meeting with partners individually may arise. The protocol of ICBT, for example, stipulates that the therapist meet with each significant other individually in an effort to attain a more thorough assessment (e.g., spousal abuse). However, other therapists do not engage in such practices because there is the possibility that information will be presented to the therapist that severely manipulates the therapeutic course (e.g., desire for divorce that has not been shared with the partner). Regardless if individual sessions are held, it is vital to establish ground rules at the beginning of treatment for individual interactions with the therapist (e.g., "all information shared with me can be shared with your partner, unless you state otherwise, at which time we will discuss how to proceed").

Extramarital relationships pose an additional predicament. Because therapy requires the active participation by both partners, it is generally recommended that couples therapy not take place is there if an ongoing affair.

Couples therapy is most often implemented conjointly. However, it has been demonstrated that when a partner is unable to attend treatment despite a desire to do so (e.g., work constraints prevent therapy attendance), couples therapy involving only one partner can result in benefits to the relationship (Bennun, 1985).

It is important to consider cultural factors when working with couples, including expectations and norms, which may differ among diverse cultural backgrounds (e.g., related to ethnicity, race, socioeconomic status). For example, regarding norms, German couples not reporting relationship problems, engage in a similar level of negative verbal and nonverbal behaviors as Australian couples *presenting* with relationship complaints (Halford, Hahlweg, & Dunne, 2001).

Whereas the previous discussion can be applied to both heterosexual and homosexual relationships, a comment about gay, lesbian, and bisexual (GLB) couples is warranted. Specifically, problems including homophobia, lack of "sanctioned" role models, deficient GLB couple resources, questions about "coming out," and lack of social support from family and friends may be present and place additional strains on the relationship. Further, familiarity with norms within the GLB community is important in order to have a better understanding of what the couple may be experiencing, as well as prevent overpathologizing of symptoms and behaviors.

REFERENCES

Arellano, C. M., & Markman, H. J. (1995). The Managing Affect and Differences Scale (MADS): A self-report measure assessing conflict management in couples. *Journal of Family Psychology, 9,* 319–334.

Baucom, D. H., & Epstein, N. (1990). *Cognitive-behavioral marital therapy.* New York: Brunner/Mazel.

Baucom, D. H., Epstein, N., Daiuto, A. D., Carels, R. A., Rankin, L. A., & Burnett, C. K. (1996). Cognitions in marriage: The relationship between standards and attributions. *Journal of Family Psychology, 10,* 209–222.

Baucom, D. H., Epstein, N., Rankin, L. A., & Burnett, C. K. (1996). Assessing relationship standards: The Inventory of Specific Relationship Standards. *Journal of Family Psychology, 10,* 72–88.

Baucom, D. H., Epstein, N., Sayers, S. L., & Sher, T. G. (1989). The role of cognitions in marital relationships: Definitional, methodological, and conceptual issues. *Journal of Consulting and Clinical Psychology, 57,* 31–38.

Bennun, I. (1985). Behavioral marital therapy: An outcome evaluation of conjoint, group and one spouse treatment. *Scandinavian Journal of Behaviour Therapy, 14,* 157–168.

Bradbury, T. N., Cohan, C. L., & Karney, B. R. (1998). Optimizing longitudinal research for understanding and preventing marital dysfunction. In T. Bradbury (Ed.), *The developmental course of marital dysfunction* (pp. 279–311). New York: Cambridge University Press.

Bradbury, T. N., & Fincham, F. D. (1990). Attributions in marriage: Review and critique. *Psychological Bulletin, 107,* 3–33.

Cascardi, M., Langhinrichsen, J., & Vivian, D. (1992). Marital aggression: Impact, injury, and health correlates for husbands and wives. *Archives of Internal Medicine, 152,* 1178–1184.

Christensen, A., & Jacobson, N. (1997). *Frequency and acceptability of partner behaviors scale.* University of California at Los Angeles.

Christensen, A., & Jacobson, N. S. (2000). *Reconcilable differences.* New York: Guilford Press.

D'Zurilla, T. J., & Nezu, A. M. (1999). *Problem-solving therapy: A social competence approach to clinical intervention* (2nd ed.). New York: Springer Publishing Co.

Eidelson, R. J., & Epstein, N. (1982). Cognition and relationship maladjustment: Development of a measure of dysfunctional relationship beliefs. *Journal of Consulting and Clinical Psychology, 50,* 715–720.

Epstein, N. B., & Baucom, D. H. (2002). *Enhanced cognitive-behavioral therapy for couples: A contextual approach.* Washington, DC: American Psychological Association.

Fincham, F. D., & Bradbury, T. N. (1992). Assessing attributions in marriage: The Relationship Attribution Measure. *Journal of Personality and Social Psychology, 62,* 457–468.

Gottman, J. M., Coan, J., Carrere, S., & Swanson, C. (1998). Predicting marital happiness and stability from newlywed interactions. *Journal of Marriage and the Family, 60,* 5–22.

Hahlweg, K., & Markman, H. J. (1988). Effectiveness of behavioral marital therapy: Empirical status of behavioral techniques in preventing and alleviating marital distress. *Journal of Consulting and Clinical Psychology, 56,* 440–447.

Halford, W. K., Hahlweg, K., & Dunne, M. (2001). The cross-cultural consistency of marital communication associated with marital distress. *Journal of Marriage and the Family, 52,* 487–500.

Halford, W. K., Sanders, M. R., & Behrens, B. C. (1994). Self-regulation in behavioral couples' therapy. *Behavior Therapy, 25,* 431–452.

Jacobson, N., & Margolin, G. (1979). *Marital therapy: Strategies based on social learning and behavioral exchange principles.* New York: Brunner/Mazel.

Jacobson, N. S., & Christensen, A. (1996). *Integrative couple therapy: Promoting acceptance and change.* New York: Norton.

Johnson, S. M. (1996). *The practice of emotionally focused marital therapy: Creating connection.* New York: Brunner/Mazel.

Karney, B. R., & Bradbury, T. N. (1995). The longitudinal course of marital quality and stability: A review of theory, methods, and research. *Psychological Bulletin, 118,* 3–34.

Karney, B. R., & Bradbury, T. N. (1997). Neuroticism, marital interaction, and the trajectory of marital satisfaction. *Journal of Personality and Social Psychology, 72,* 1075–1092.

Kreider, R. M., & Fields, J. M. (2002). *Number, timing, and duration of marriages and divorces: 1996.* Washington, DC: U.S. Census Bureau.

Markman, H. J., Renick, M. J., Floyd, F. J., & Stanley, S. M. (1993). Preventing marital distress through communication and conflict management training: A 4- and 5-year follow-up. *Journal of Consulting and Clinical Psychology, 61,* 70–77.

Nezu, A. M. (in press). Problem solving and behavior therapy revisited. *Behavior Therapy.*

Prager, K. J., & Buhrmester, D. (1998). Intimacy and need fulfillment in couple relationships. *Journal of Social and Personal Relationships, 15,* 435–469.

Pretzer, J., Epstein, N., & Fleming, B. (1991). Marital Attitude Survey: A measure of dysfunctional attributions and expectancies. *Journal of Cognitive Psychotherapy, 5,* 131–148.

Renick, M. J., Blumberg, S. L., & Markman, H. J. (1992). The Prevention and Relationship Enhancement Program (PREP): An empirically based preventive intervention program for couples. *Family Relations: Journal of Applied Family and Child Studies, 41,* 141–147.

Robin, A. L., & Foster, S. L. (1989). *Negotiating parent-adolescent conflict: A behavioral-family systems approach.* New York: Guilford Press.

Rogge, R. D., & Bradbury, T. N. (1999). Till violence does us part: The differing roles of communication and aggression in predicting adverse marital outcomes. *Journal of Consulting and Clinical Psychology, 67,* 340–351.

Rogge, R. D., Cobb, R. M., Johnson, M., Lawrence, E., & Bradbury, T. N. (2002). The CARE program: A preventive approach to marital intervention. In A. S. Gurman & N. Jacobson (Eds.), *Clinical handbook of couple therapy (3rd ed.)* (pp. 420–435). New York: Guilford Press.

Snyder, D. K. (1997). *Marital satisfaction inventory-revised.* Los Angeles: Western Psychological Services.

Spanier, G. B. (1976). Measuring dyadic adjustment: New scales for assessing the quality of marriage and similar dyads. *Journal of Marriage and the Family, 38,* 15–28.

Stanley, S. M., Blumberg, S. L., & Markman, H. J. (1999). PREP: Helping couples fight for their marriage. In R. Berger (Ed.), *Preventative approaches in couple's therapy.* New York: Brunner/Mazel.

Stanley, S. M., Markman, H. J., & Blumberg, S. L. (1994). *Fighting for your marriage: Videotape series for couples.* Denver, CO: PREP: Educational Videos, Inc.

Straus, M. A. (1979). Measuring intrafamily conflict and violence: The Conflict Tactics (CT) Scales. *Journal of Marriage and the Family, 41,* 75–88.

Stuart, R. B. (1980). *Helping couples change: A social learning approach to marital therapy.* New York: Guilford Press.

Sullaway, M., & Christensen, A. (1983). Assessment of dysfunctional interaction patterns in couples. *Journal of Marriage and the Family, 45,* 653–660.

Weiss, R. L., & Cerreto, M. C. (1980). The Marital Status Inventory: Development of a measure of dissolution potential. *American Journal of Family Therapy, 8,* 80–85.

Weiss, R. L., & Halford, W. K. (1996). Managing marital therapy: Helping partners change. In V. B. van Hasselt & M. Hersen (Eds.), *Sourcebook of psychological treatment manuals for adult disorders* (pp. 489–537). New York: Plenum.

Weiss, R. L., Hops, H., & Patterson, G. R. (1973). A framework for conceptualizing marital conflict, a technology for altering it, some data for evaluating it. In L. A. Hamerlynck & L. C. M. E. J. Handy (Eds.), *Behavioral change: Methodology, concepts, and practice.* Champaign, IL: Research Press.

Wheeler, J. G., Christensen, A., & Jacobson, N. S. (2001). Couple distress. In D. H. Barlow (Ed.), *Clinical handbook of psychological disorders: A step-by-step treatment manual* (3rd ed., pp. 609–630). New York: Guilford Press.

15

Anger Problems

GENERAL DESCRIPTION AND DIAGNOSTIC ISSUES

Although problems with anger and aggressive behavior are frequently encountered in clinical settings, there are no formal diagnostic categories that adequately capture anger-related problems. The construct of anger has not received as much attention as other mood disorders in the diagnostic and treatment literature (Deffenbacher & Stark, 1992), despite the fact that anger and hostility are often central features of clinical referral problems including verbal and physical aggressive behavior, domestic violence, family and marriage dysfunction, child abuse, criminal behavior, and a range of health-related concerns, such as heart disease. Anger has been defined by DiGiuseppe and colleagues as "an internal, mental, subjective feeling state with associated cognitions and physiologic arousal patterns" (DiGiuseppe, Eckhardt, Tafrate, & Robin, 1994, p. 241). These authors and others have underscored the importance of expanding the construct of anger to extend beyond a sole focus of aggressive behavioral acts as it tends to underestimate the prevalence of anger problems that may be in need of therapeutic intervention.

One diagnostic category in which anger-related symptoms are the focus in the *Diagnostic and Statistical Manual of Mental Disorders, Fourth Edition, Text Revision* (DSM-IV-TR, American Psychiatric Association, 2000) is

235

intermittent explosive disorder. This Axis I disorder is characterized by discrete episodes of failure to resist aggressive impulses that result in serious assault or acts and destruction of property. However, the problematic anger experienced by many individuals who might be seen for treatment may not meet diagnostic criteria for this disorder. For example, although anger may negatively impact upon a person's physical and psychological well-being, actual aggressive acts or violent behavior may not always accompany anger episodes. Anger may be expressed in other ways, such as verbal anger expressions, critical remarks, "dirty looks," angry withdrawal, or passive-aggressive sabotage. Thus, this diagnosis has been criticized by many as failing to define anger and fully capture the scope of this mood disorder.

Co-Morbidity Issues

Few DSM-IV diagnoses even mention anger, much less describe the individual who has anger problems at the core of his or her dysfunction (Eckhardt, 1999). Many clinicians tend to attribute problems with anger diagnostically to other disorders. These include personality disorders (e.g., *borderline, narcissistic,* and *antisocial personality disorders* in adults, *oppositional-defiant and conduct disorders* in children), as well as other Axis I disorders. In addition, the DSM-IV-TR describes "sudden spells" of anger as occasionally present within the context of other mood disorders, such as *depressive disorders* and *panic disorder*; however, there is little information that addresses the high prevalence of anger problems in Axis I diagnostic groups. For example, Fava and Rosenbaum (1999) report that the prevalence of anger attacks in depressed patients is 30% to 40%. In addition, Mammen, Shear, Pilkonis, Kolko, and Green (1999) found that 60% of an outpatient sample of female psychiatric patients reported experiencing anger episodes. Other studies have shown that anger episodes in patients with Axis I affective disorders can lead to serious impairment such as job loss, legal trouble, and loss of friends (Gould et al., 1996).

Additional diagnoses in which irritability, anger episodes, and aggressive outbursts are common include *substance intoxication/withdrawal, posttraumatic stress disorder* in war veterans (McFall, Wright, Donovan, & Raskind, 1999), as well as some *dementias.*

DiGiuseppe et al. (1994) make a strong case for identifying anger as a core diagnostic problem and suggest that a disorder of anger is present when the patient experiences excessive and intense angry feelings for a period of greater than six months during which time the experience of anger is associated with stressful life events, minor hassles, thwarted goals, physical discomfort, perceived insult, rejection, or criticism. In addition, they suggest that it is important to consider if the anger expressed is consistent with relevant cultural norms and that it does not occur in the course of psychosis, organically-induced confusion, or intoxication. Finally, as part of the overall diagnostic picture, these authors suggest that it is important to assess whether such anger episodes adversely impact one's general functioning, causing impairment in occupational, academic, and interpersonal areas.

Given the interpersonal nature of society, significant social impairment is prevalent in persons with anger problems. Social relationships can be strained, and there is an increased risk of injury for the patient and others. Academic and occupational functioning is often affected negatively, and the risk of physical health problems can become increased (Edmondson & Conger, 1996).

Anger may have a profound role in domestic violence (DiGiuseppe et al., 1994), where the growing incidence of such behavior has been conceptualized as a major public health issue. With regard to physical illness and health, the relationship between anger and medical illness is strongly suggestive that anger and hostility are associated with hypertension, coronary heart disease, and ventricular arrhythmias (Dembroski, MacDougall, Williams, Haney, & Blumenthal, 1985; Jain et al., 1998).

In sum, co-morbid disorders are almost always present with regard to anger problems. Because there is no formal diagnostic category for anger, it is usually considered part of the symptom picture present for personality disorders, dementing conditions, depression, anxiety disorders, interpersonal aggressive behavior, domestic violence, and criminal offense.

ASSESSMENT OF DISORDER

Concerning assessment, it is useful to have a clear definition of the specific constructs of interest. DiGiuseppe et al. (1994) provide the following definitions of these constructs (p. 241):

- *Anger:* an internal, mental, subjective feeling state with associated cognitions and physiologic arousal patterns.
- *Aggression:* the overt behavior enacted with intent to do harm or injury to a person or object.

- *Hostility:* a cross-situational pattern or trait of angry affect in combination with verbal physical aggression (not stimulus bound).

There appears to be consensus within the cognitive-behavioral literature with regard to these definitions in that anger represents a subjective mood state, whereas verbal and physical aggression are behavioral acts that have a high degree of co-variation with this mood state, and hostility represents a chronic tendency or vulnerability to experience anger.

Assessment protocols that are designed to help the clinician identify and assess problems of anger, hostility, and aggression, as well as to measure the severity of relevant symptoms, include clinician ratings, behavioral observation, and self-report measures.

Clinician Ratings

- *Interpersonal Hostility Interview* (Haney et al., 1996): structured interview, originally designed to assess *Type A* behavior, the *IHAT* has become a standard method for the interview of hostility.

Behavioral Assessment

- *Behavioral Role-Play Response to Anger Vignettes* (Tescher, Conger, Edmondson, & Conger, 1999): role-play methods in which the participant is asked to respond to audiotaped anger-provoking situations. Other role-play situations may require the participant to engage in acting out responses to a provocative situation.

Self-Report Measures

- *Anger Situation Questionnaire* (van Goozen, Frijda, Kindt, & van de Poll, 1994): developed to measure anger-proneness in women (experienced emotion, intensity, and action readiness).
- *Anger Symptom Scale* (Deffenbacher, Demm, & Brandon, 1986): self-report measure of a range of anger symptoms.

- *Brief Anger-Aggression Questionnaire* (Maiuro, Vitaliano, & Cahn, 1987): a brief, six-item measure developed for rapid screening and identification of anger and aggression levels in violence-prone men.
- *Buss-Durke Hostility Inventory* (Buss & Durke, 1957): an inventory designed to measure traits related to anger, hostility and aggression.
- *Cook-Medley Hostility Scale* (Cook & Medley, 1954): was originally derived from the Minnesota Multiphasic Personality Inventory (MMPI) and is a 50-item self-report of hostility.
- *Novaco Anger Scale* (Novaco, 1975; 1994): assesses the situational and contextual determinants of anger. One part of the scale focuses on psychological vulnerabilities toward anger and aggression, whereas a second part prompts the individual to describe anger experiences related to particular situations.
- *Self-Expression and Control Scale* (Van Elderen, Maes, Komproe, & van der Kamp, 1997): a 40-item self-report inventory that includes subscales to assess internalized, expressed, and controlled anger.
- *State-Trait Anger Expression Inventory* (Spielberger, 1996, 1999): assesses both *trait* anger (temperamental tendency) and *state* anger (angry feelings experienced by an individual at any given time, accompanied by physical reactions). Additional subscales provide a profile of experience, expression, and control of anger.

GENERAL THERAPY GOALS

Ultimate Outcome Goals

When working with patients with anger problems, general ultimate outcome goals include decreasing the frequency and intensity of anger episodes and increasing alternative interpersonal (non-angry) coping skills. In addition, addressing the usefulness and functionality of anger that may occur in this population is important. Specifically, anger may result in maladaptive behaviors (e.g., aggression, destructive incidents), which then leads to harmful consequences for others and increases the social isolation or possible social sanctions of the person who is angry.

In addition, depending on the individual, other ultimate goals may be important to delineate. Given the significant co-morbidity of anger with other diagnostic groups, decreasing problems related to other psychological disorders or symptoms may be an ultimate goal. For example, individuals who "fuel" their anger triggers through alcohol or other drug use would benefit from interventions to address substance abuse. Because of the interpersonal focus of anger symptoms, relationships can be strained as a consequence. Thus, enhancing significant relationships (e.g., marriage or family) may be an ultimate goal. The vulnerability toward anger is often part of a pervasive way people have come to interact with the world, and as such, may be part of an overall symptom picture consistent with diagnostic criteria regarding a personality disorder, such as *borderline personality disorder*. If such patterns and characteristic interactional problems are found to exist, the reader is referred to chapter 12.

Finally, the consequences of anger episodes can result in feelings of guilt and self-reproach. As such, anger episodes are often associated with other mood disorders, such as depression. Referring to chapter 5 on depression may be especially helpful when ultimate outcomes for any individual include decreasing significant depressive symptoms.

It is important to note that completely suppressing or eradicating anger should not be an ultimate goal. Individuals with a tendency to suppress their anger and who lack the skills to manage and cope with anger effectively are more likely to engage in withdrawal, paradoxically manifesting greater physiologic arousal and experiencing increased risk for physical illness, such as cardiovascular disease (Mayne & Ambrose, 1999). Reducing the destructive consequences of anger and learning to manage anger more effectively are more healthy overall goals.

Major Instrumental Outcome Goals/Treatment Targets

Major instrumental outcome goals for anger reduction include:

- Decrease heightened physiologic arousal
- Decrease cognitive distortions
- Improve interpersonal skills

Goal 1: Decrease Heightened Physiologic Arousal

Physiologic arousal is a hallmark of the aggressive behavior associated with angry mood states (Deffenbacher, 1999). The individual experience of anger involves neurological, endocrine, and other physiologic processes (e.g., increased heart rate, flushed face, muscle tension) in response to situational anger triggers. Research concerning the neuropsychological mechanisms involved in anger activation indicates that it is possible for anger to be activated without individuals knowing they are angry (Mayne & Ambrose, 1999). Interventions designed to target this anger state, training the patient to lower the emotional arousal and increase an overall sense of physiologic calm and control when confronted with anger triggers, can be effective in addressing this instrumental goal.

Goal-Specific Assessment Tools

- *Subjective Rating of Anger:* patients' self-reported level of anger arousal, usually on a scale from 0 (*not at all angry*) to 100 (*the most angry you have ever been*).
- *Physiologic Measures:* Diastolic blood pressure, electromyography, blood pressure, galvanic skin response, and heart rate variability have all been shown to provide somatovisceral manifestations of anger (Edmondson & Conger, 1996; Jain et al., 1998).

Goal-Specific Potential Interventions

- Relaxation training
- Exposure
- Mindfulness Meditation

Relaxation Training. This approach includes a wide range of behavioral stress management strategies geared to specifically reduce a patient's symptoms of heightened physiologic arousal. It also aims to substitute a new conditioned response (relaxation) for the previously conditioned response to trigger situations (anger, autonomic arousal). Hormones (e.g., epinephrine and norepinephrine), which are released in arousal states, can directly influence cognition and behavior. Therefore, relaxation may be especially effective because of its indirect effects on other instrumental outcomes, as well as its direct effects on physical arousal. Arousal reduction strategies include progressive muscle relaxation, autogenic training, and visualization. Meta-analytic studies have indicated that CBT treatments that contain a relaxation component can be especially effective in improving anger management across a wide range of populations (Beck & Fernandez, 1999).

Exposure Therapy. Exposure therapy is frequently included in CBT treatments for other mood disorders (e.g., anxiety disorders) and is directed toward extinguishing a conditioned mood response to relevant stimuli.

Treatment packages including an exposure component for other disorders, such as anxiety and panic disorder, have been demonstrated to be very effective (Barlow, Craske, Cerny, & Kolosko, 1989). Based on a conceptualization of anger as a mood disorder that involves a significant physiologic arousal component, exposure procedures have been recommended as important potential techniques for reducing heightened arousal and aggressive behavior (DiGiuseppe, Tafrate, & Eckhardt, 1994). DiGiuseppe and his colleagues recommend exposure techniques for persons with anger problems based upon the following rationale: (a) the similar physiologic phenomena of anger to other mood states such as anxiety; and (b) the effect size of successful anger treatments that included an exposure component (see also Tarfrate, 1995). From a learning theory perspective, aggressive responses can be partially maintained and negatively reinforced by the reduction of heightened arousal (e.g., verbally attacking a supervisor when criticized). Exposure techniques are effective because they activate automatic biases for a long enough period of time to produce an habituation effect and reduce the automatic link between a given stimulus and the perception of threat (Eckhardt, 1999). In other words, the patient learns "not to react to" certain real-life situations by unlearning the association of anger-prone situations and aggressive behavioral reactions.

Mindfulness Meditation. Eastern meditative techniques that are rooted in Buddhist philosophy are becoming increasingly integrated into CBT treatment packages (Leifer, 1999; Nezu & Nezu, 2003). Mindfulness meditation techniques can foster a patient's understanding and awareness of the presence of their internal anger responses, as well as an understanding of the destructive results of anger. Through use of mindfulness meditative techniques, patients can develop an increased ability to self-monitor their own arousal triggers, by remaining focused in the present moment. Recent studies support the potential usefulness of mindfulness meditation as useful techniques to decrease heightened arousal and the automatic behavioral responses observed in anger episodes (DiGiuseppe, 1999).

Goal 2: Decrease Cognitive Distortions

Dysfunctional cognitions and distortions involving blame, unfairness, and suspiciousness operate in anger experiences. For example, "He ruined my presentation by asking stupid questions; he probably wants to get me fired," is an example of how an individual who is prone to episodes of anger may think when confronted with a poor work performance. When this cognitive tendency represents a pervasive way of thinking, even benign situations may be interpreted within the context of a hostile schema (e.g., "Why are you asking me that, why are you always on my case?"). Although there are few empirical studies that support this association concerning adults, research with adolescents has strongly documented the relationship between hostile interpretations and aggressive behavior (Dodge, Price, Bacoworowski, & Newman, 1990). Such beliefs can enhance anger and arousal, increase the urge to verbally or physically attack the perceived perpetrator of one's well-being, and thus perpetuate a vicious cycle. Some researchers posit that such dysfunctional beliefs are at the core of anger problems (Dryden, 1990). In addition, beliefs about the experience of anger itself (e.g., "I am right to get angry" and "It's good to let out my anger") may serve as motivational obstacles to treatment (DiGiuseppe, Tafrate, & Eckhart, 1994). When such beliefs exist, focusing on changing cognitions serves to increase motivation, as well as to decrease anger.

Deffenbacher and colleagues (e.g., Deffenbacher, Dahlen, Lynch, Morris, & Gowensmith, 2000), as well as Novaco (e.g., Robins & Novaco, 1999), suggest that extreme standards of judging others, suspiciousness concerning the insulting or harmful intent of others, rigid and righteous beliefs about how others "should" act, overgeneralization, and personalization, all can be strong factors that serve to maintain angry or aggressive episodes within the context of an overall systems approach to understanding the construct of anger.

Another theory invoking a cognitive conceptualization proposes that anger and aggression emerge as a way to resolve the discrepancy between one's high self-opinion or high self-esteem when confronted with the reality that such high self-esteem in not warranted or perceived by others (Bushman & Baumeister, 1998). Contrary to the popular myth that angry people have low self-esteem, this framework suggests that persons with high self-esteem, who are also highly narcissistic, are at significant risk for disorders related to anger.

Finally, maladaptive cognitions appear to be related to the problems of establishing a therapeutic alliance in persons with anger problems.

Goal-Specific Assessment Tools

- *Self-Monitoring of Anger Episodes:* Self-observation and report of situational anger triggers, and anger-related thoughts, images, and behavior.

Goal-Specific Potential Interventions

- Cognitive restructuring
- Problem-solving therapy
- Forgiveness skills
- Humor

Cognitive Restructuring. Conceptually, anger-related cognitive variables can be classified into several categories: *hostile anticipation of events* (e.g., "Here comes Bob, he wants to brag and show me what a loser I am"), *distorted interpretation of events* (e.g., "She said she was sorry that she was unable to help, but she didn't really care") and *dysfunctional schemas of others* ("Everyone's out to get me"). Intervention strategies to modify cognitive factors are based on cognitive restructuring principles. Conceptually, cognitive restructuring can be thought of as an umbrella term that encompasses several specific therapy strategies: rational-emotive therapy (e.g., Ellis, 1994), cognitive coping techniques from stress inoculation therapy (Novaco, 1975; Meichenbaum, 1975), and cognitive therapy (Beck & Emery, 1985). Whereas differences among these approaches exist, all involve helping patients to better identify and then alter maladaptive thoughts. When treating cognitive dysfunctions in persons with anger problems, individuals are asked to recognize their negative automatic patterns in reaction to situational triggers. Patients are next taught how assess the accuracy of these thoughts or the use of various cognitive errors (e.g., blaming, catastrophizing, overgeneralizing, personalizing) and then replace such maladaptive cognitions with more adaptive ones.

In Beck's cognitive therapy, patients are trained to assess and change their thinking in a more inductive and Socratic style than the more didactic approach that has been used in most of the CBT studies of anger treatment. All types of cognitive restructuring strategies that have been evaluated appear effective when combined with relaxation strategies in reducing trait-like anger (Deffenbacher, Dahlen, Lynch, Morris, & Gowensmith, 2000).

Problem-Solving Therapy. Problem-solving therapy (PST; e.g., D'Zurilla & Nezu, 1999; Nezu, in press) is geared to increase one's overall coping ability when dealing with stressful situations. Part of this approach involves changing those cognitive factors that negatively impinge on one's *problem orientation* or general view of problems and the self-assessment regarding one's problem-solving capabilities (e.g., beliefs about why a problem occurred, attributions about who is responsible for the problem occurring in the first place, and self-efficacy beliefs). PST has been identified as an important component of a CBT program to reduce aggression in children (Lochman, 1992) and problem-solving deficits have been proposed as important cognitive mediators in anger and aggression in adults (Basquil, Nezu, Nezu, & Klein, in press; DiGiuseppe, Tafrate, & Eckhardt, 1994).

Forgiveness Skills. Several authors have suggested that the incorporation of forgiveness interventions may contribute to helping change the cognitive component of anger. Forgiveness appears crucial to the reduction of anger because patients' angry thoughts are often focused on the wrongs that others perpetrate against them (DiGiuseppe, 1999). The psychotherapy literature with regard to training in forgiveness suggests that people experience difficulty forgiving because of their belief in commonly held myths (e.g., "Forgiving is the same as excusing or forgetting the insult ever happened"). Several studies provide support concerning the potential importance of incorporating specific training in forgiveness with regard to anger reduction (Enright & Fitzgibbons, 2002).

Humor.   Deffenbacher (1999) has recommended using techniques involving humor as a way to decrease angry cognitions. An example provided by this author is to create a comical character or drawing from a hostile label or verbally aggressive thought that can create a comical image to bring to mind when the patient engages in such labeling. Because both humor and anger responses involve arousal, it seems possible that using such images may help patients reframe their own arousal.

Goal 3: Improve Interpersonal Skills

People exhibit anger patterns because of the function anger serves. This function often includes ways to reduce arousal, increase perceptions of control or actual control over others, and avoid acknowledging one's lack of more adaptive and sophisticated coping abilities. Frequently, patients with anger problems lack such appropriate interpersonal skills with which to solve problems effectively, manage disappointments or frustrations, and effectively manage physical states of arousal. As such, lack of skills can serve to increase the usefulness or functionality of anger. Avoidance of such situations also serves to limit opportunities to learn such skills developmentally. In addition, long-term patterns of physical or verbal aggression may have created a self-fulfilling prophesy in which people with anger problems have created patterns which other people avoid or fear the individual.

Goal-Specific Assessment Tools

- *Clinician observations:* in-session role plays that center on relevant social situations can be important tools for assessing specific interpersonal skills deficits.
- *Personal Assertion Inventory* (Hedlund & Lindquist, 1984): an inventory that provides ratings of passive, aggressive, and assertive behavior.

- *Conflict Resolution Inventory* (Hartwig, Dickinson, Anderson, 1980): a self-report of approaches to conflict resolution.
- *Conflict Tactics Scale* (Straus, 1979): measures conflict resolution tactics, including verbal and physical aggression among positive family member dyads.

Goal-Specific Potential Interventions

- Communication skills training
- Assertiveness skills training
- Conflict management skills training
- Problem-solving therapy
- Social skills training
- Positive attitude training
- Group therapy

Communication Skills.   Interventions designed to increase adaptive interpersonal behavior are based upon observations that individuals with anger difficulties are deficient in verbal and nonverbal communication skills. Training includes a wide variety of skill areas such as empathy, listening, eye contact, or learning how to clearly state needs and requests. Such skills are typically included in CBT anger management programs and considered an important treatment target to include in an overall therapy protocol.

Assertiveness Skills Training.   Individuals with anger difficulties often reveal deficits in assertive behavior (Fine & Olson (1997). This includes their inability to express positive feelings, refuse requests, or express negative opinions in a manner that is considerate and respectful of others. Training in assertiveness skills involves teaching patients to identify specific behavioral deficits, rehearse appropriate assertive behaviors, and apply these newly learned behaviors to "real-life" situations.

Problem-Solving Therapy.   In addition to the focus of PST in changing the cognitive and emotional worldview with which people view problems and their own ability to effectively solve them, a central part of this approach involves improving the way in which people actually solve day-to-day problems. PST includes techniques designed to increase specific component skills, such as defining problems clearly and accurately, brainstorming alternative solutions to problems, effective personal decision-making, and decreasing avoidant or impulsive response styles (D'Zurilla & Nezu, 1999). Improving such skills have been associated with reductions in sexually aggressive behavior (Nezu, Nezu, & Dudek, 1998).

Conflict Management Skills.   Learning to more effectively manage anger episodes that occur within an interpersonal context requires skills that specifically address coping with differences of opinion or conflicting goals between people. Conflict management skills include training patients to engage in a process of bargaining, trade off, or compromise, such that each party may achieve partial success with their goals (Goldstein & Keller, 1987). Training people in such negotiation skills can increase the likelihood of a mutually satisfactory compromise being reached. In addition to negotiation skills, behavioral contracting skills can be taught so that people learn to take responsibility for their behavior and how to follow through with a compromise plan of action. Such strategies are supported by research in which negotiation and contracting has led to improvement in such skills for married couples (Jacobson, 1977).

Social Skills Training.   Social learning theories of aggression provide a rationale for social skills training with regard to anger and aggression. Similar to training in rational problem-solving skill training, social skills training teaches patients appropriate skills for managing anger more effectively in social situations. Social skills training specific to anger management would include: (a) identifying frequently encountered stressful and anger-prone situations; (b) providing information and psycho-education with regard to individual anger reaction chains; (c) providing planful and effective alternative ways to respond to their anger triggers; (d) offering opportunities for rehearsal of new skills; and (e) providing positive feedback for any behavioral change which demonstrates such skills in "real-life" situations.

Anger Inoculation Skills.   This specific type of social skills training is designed to provide a structured rehearsal of new coping thoughts to replace anger-prone thinking in response to imagined anger trigger situations in a systematic way. Similar to stress inoculation (Meichenbaum, 1975; Novaco, 1975), the patient is asked to create a hierarchy of imaginary scenarios that are likely to elicit a range of anger responses from mild to unbearable anger. The scenes are elicited and then paired with a previously learned relaxation response and coping self-statements. The imaginary scenes are gradually increased in terms of the original hierarchy, such that a calm state is paired with increasingly intense anger trigger scenes. During this performance-based intervention, the patient is engaged in cognitive-reframing, relaxation training, imagery, modeling, and role-playing (Beck & Fernandez, 1998).

Positive Attitude Training.   The rationale that supports the use of positive attitude training (e.g., joy, gratitude, patience, tolerance) is that positive emotions can broaden an individual's thought-action repertoire and build enduring personal resources to combat stress situations (Frederickson, 2000). Moreover, training in such skills focus specifically on adopting attributes such as patience, acceptance, tolerance, and forgiveness (Brack & Thoresen, 1996) and have been included in programs that led to reduced hostility (Williams & Williams, 2001).

Group Therapy. In general, providing treatment in a group setting may be particularly beneficial for some patients in terms of enhancing anger management and other interpersonal skills. Treatment outcome studies typically employ small group formats which have been found to be effective regarding the treatment of anger and aggression. Other authors have underscored the importance of focusing treatment on individual motivational obstacles as important ways to increase a patient's readiness to change (Brondolo, DiGiuseppe, & Tafrate, 1997). Although there are no clear, empirically demonstrated benefits of individual versus group psychotherapy formats, one potential benefit of a group treatment approach is that such an approach permits an opportunity for social feedback, modeling, normalization, peer encouragement, and reinforcement of skills attained.

Additional Instrumental Outcome Goals/Treatment Target

Secondary treatment targets for anger problems may include:

- *Decrease General Stress.* Individuals with anger report experiencing a high level of stress and may perceive themselves as frequently under attack by others. As such, a possible secondary instrumental outcome goal for a patient with anger includes decreasing overall general stress levels. Possible intervention approaches include various behavioral stress management strategies to reduce stress-related anger arousal, as well as coping skills training strategies, such as Problem-Solving Therapy, to help the patient manage stressful negative life events more effectively.
- *Improve Partner and Family Relationships.* If anger problems have led to significant impairment in partner and family relationships, then improving such relationships may need to be targeted as a meaningful therapy goal. Family member concerns and fears of the patient's behavior, as well as their own behavior as potentially rein-

forcing, may need to be therapeutically addressed through improving communication and functional behavioral sequences between various family members.

- *Address Drug and Alcohol Abuse.* Substance use can serve as a learned reaction to block out or avoid anger experiences or can result in a disinhibiting effect, lowering a patient's threshold for engaging in aggressive or destructive acts when in an angry state. As such, harm reduction strategies that are focused on improved management of substance use can serve to decrease aggressive episodes.

ADDITIONAL CLINICAL CONSIDERATIONS

Angry patients are often coerced into treatment by spouses, employers, or the legal system. A specific focus on motivational issues will often be an important treatment consideration for such individuals. Many people with anger problems hold strong beliefs that reducing their anger will make them weaker and more vulnerable. In addition, because anger does engender empathy from others, one way to foster a therapeutic alliance is to validate the angry patient's sense of transgression or hurt (DiGiuseppe, 1999). Another strategy reported as helpful to increase the patient's motivation in this context is to reinforce his or her positive values (e.g., fairness, caring, or integrity), while framing therapy as a way to help them change ineffective patterns of how they try to uphold their values (Brondolo, Di-Giuseppe, & Tafrate, 1997).

Different cultures may vary considerably with regard to the expression, acceptability, description, and gender-related characteristics of anger. For example, male aggression may be more socially sanctioned in some cultural contexts. Therapists need to be aware of prevailing cultural views regarding anger, as well as how consistent an individual or family view compares with its cultural system. Cultural considerations are particularly important with regard to setting therapeutic goals and developing alternative cognitive and behavioral scripts for managing anger more effectively (DiGiuseppe et al., 1994).

Meta-analyses of gender differences in physical aggression to heterosexual partners indicate that women are more likely than men to use one or more act of physical aggression. On the other hand, men are more likely to inflict actual physical injury. Overall, 62% of those injured in such relationships are women (Archer, 2000). However, it is important not to minimize the impact of anger among women in relationship problems. For example, due to social condemnation of aggressive or violent behavior, women may develop a wider range of behavioral anger expression.

Diversity considerations regarding anger include consideration of the particular assessment needs of developmentally disabled persons. Recently, there has been a growing trend to focus on improving the anger management abilities of persons with mental retardation via psychosocial protocols, as compared to more restrictive procedures, such psychotropic medication or environmental control. Associated with this need to adapt cognitive-behavioral strategies for this population is the need to develop effective assessment tools. For example, *The Anger Inventory* (Benson & Ivins, 1992) was developed for individuals with mental retardation. Interventions using such CBT strategies described above that include a combination of arousal reduction and skills acquisition have been found to be effective in reducing aggression for persons with mental retardation (Rose, 1996). Consideration, however, should be given to adapting any intervention strategy to the appropriate developmental level.

Another special population may include individuals with criminal histories who present a high risk of harm to others. Such individuals can be very resistant to treatment. This focus on the behavioral control of a criminal offender may pose specific conflicts between a therapist and other systems (e.g., law enforcement) with regard to confidentiality or the degree of restrictions that serve to increase stress and anger triggers toward others.

Treatment of anger in criminal offenders may require additional consideration regarding psychopathic characteristics, particularly those that involve social rank and shame. Specifically, humiliated anger is related to desires to retaliate, seek revenge, and dominate others (Morrison & Gilbert, 2001). Another important issue, when treating sexually aggressive offenders, is to understand those factors that serve to maintain sexual deviance (Marshall, Anderson, & Fernandez, 1999).

REFERENCES

American Psychiatric Association (2000). *Diagnostic and statistical manual for mental disorders* (ed. 4, text revision). Washington, DC: American Psychiatric Press.

Archer, J. (2000). Sex differences in aggression between heterosexual partners: A meta-analytic review. *Psychological Bulletin, 126,* 651–680.

Barlow, D. H., Craske, M. G., Cerny, J. A., & Klosko, J. S. (1989). Behavioral treatment of panic disorder. *Behavior Therapy, 20,* 261–282.

Basquil, M., Nezu, C. M., Nezu, A. M., & Klein, T. L. (in press). Aggression-related hostility bias and social problem-solving deficits in adult males with mental retardation. *American Journal on Mental Retardation.*

Beck, A. T., & Emery, C. (1985). *Anxiety disorders and phobias: A cognitive perspective.* New York: Basic Books.

Beck, R., & Fernandez, E. (1999). Cognitive-behavioral therapy for the treatment of anger: A meta-analysis. *Cognitive Therapy and Research, 22,* 63–74.

Benson, B., & Ivins, J. (1992). Anger, depression and self concept in adults with mental retardation. *Journal of Intellectual Disability Research, 36,* 169–175.

Bracke, P. E., & Thoreson, C. E. (1996). Reducing Type A behavior patterns: A structured group approach. In R. Allan & S. Scheidt (Eds.), *Heart and mind: The practice of cardiac psychology* (pp. 255–291). Washington, DC: American Psychological Association.

Brandolo, E., DiGiuseppe, R., & Tafrate, R. C. (1997). Exposure-based treatment for anger problems: Focus on the feeling. *Cognitive and Behavioral Practice, 4,* 75–98.

Bushman, B., & Baumeister, R. (1998). Threatened egotism, narcissism, self-esteem, and direct and misplaced aggression: Does self-love or self-hate lead to violence. *Journal of Personality and Social Psychology, 75,* 219–229.

Buss, A. H., & Durkee, A. (1957). An inventory for assessing different kinds of hostility. *Journal of Consulting Psychology, 2,* 343–349.

Chemtob, C. M., Novaco, R. W., Hamada, R. S., & Gross, D. M. (1997). Cognitive-behavioral treatment of severe anger in post-traumatic stress disorder. *Journal of Consulting and Clinical Psychology, 65,* 184–189.

Cook, W. W., & Medley, D. M. (1954). Proposed hostility and pharisaic-virtue scales for the MMPI. *Journal of Applied Psychology, 38,* 414–418.

Deffenbacher, J. L. (1999). Cognitive-behavioral conceptualization and treatment of anger. *Journal of Clinical Psychology/In session: Psychotherapy in Practice, 55,* 295–309.

Deffenbacher, J. L., Dahlen, E. R., Lynch, R. S., Morris, C. D., & Gowensmith, W. N. (2000). An application of Beck's cognitive therapy to general anger reductions. *Cognitive Therapy and Research, 6,* 689–697.

Deffenbacher, J. L., & Stark, R. S. (1992). Relaxation and cognitive-relaxation treatments of general anger. *Journal of Counseling Psychology, 39,* 158–167.

Dembroski, T. M., MacDougall, J. M., Williams, R. B., Haney, T. L., & Blumenthal, J. A. (1985). Components of Type A behavior hostility and anger in relationship to angiographic findings. *Psychosomatic Medicine, 47,* 219–233.

DiGiuseppe, R. (1999). End piece: Reflections on the treatment of anger. *Journal of Clinical Psychology/In Session: Psychotherapy in Practice, 55,* 365–379.

DiGiuseppe, R., Echardt, C. I., Tafrate, R. C., & Robin, M. (1994). The diagnosis and treatment of anger in a cross-cultural context. *Journal of Distress and the Homeless, 3,* 229–261.

DiGiuseppe, R., Tafrate, R. C., & Echardt, C. I. (1994). Critical issues in the treatment of anger. *Cognitive and Behavioral Practice, 1,* 11–132.

Dodge, K. A., Price, J. M., Bacoworowski, J., & Newman, J. P. (1990). Hostile attribution biases in severely aggressive adolescents. *Journal of Abnormal Psychology, 99,* 385–392.

Dryden, W. (1990). *Dealing with anger problems: Understanding your anger and aggression.* Odessa, FL: Professional Resources Exchange.

D'Zurilla, T. J., & Nezu, A. M. (1999). *Problem-solving therapy: A social competence approach to clinical intervention* (2nd ed.). New York: Springer Publishing Co.

Eckhardt, C. I. (1999). The depressing consequences of anger arousal: Behavioral treatment of anger-related depression. *Cognitive and Behavioral Practice,* 279–284.

Edmondson, C. B., & Conger, J. C. (1996). A review of the treatment efficacy for individuals with anger problems: Conceptual, assessment, and methodological issues. *Clinical Psychology Review, 16,* 251–275.

Ellis, A. (1994). *Reason and emotion in psychotherapy* (Rev. ed.). New York: Birch Lane Press.

Enright, R. D., & Fitzgibbons, R. P. (2000). *Helping clients forgive: An empirical guide for resolving anger and restoring hope.* Washington, DC: American Psychological Association.

Fava, M., & Rosenbaum, J. F. (1999). Anger attacks in patients with depression. *Journal of Clinical Psychiatry, 60, Supplement 15,* 21–24.

Fine, M. A., & Olson, K. A. (1997). Anger and hurt in response to provocation: Relationship to psychological adjustment. *Journal of Social Behavior and Personality, 12,* 325–344.

Frederickson, B. L. (2000). Cultivating positive emotions to optimize health and well-being. *Prevention and Treatment, 3.* Article 1.

Goldstein, A. P., & Keller, H. (1987). *Aggressive behavior: Assessment and intervention.* New York: Pergamon Press.

Gould, R. A., Ball, S., Kaspi, S. P., Otto, M. W., Pollack, M. H., Shekhar, A., & Fava, M. (1996). Prevalence and correlates of anger attacks: A two site study. *Journal of Affective Disorders, 39,* 31–38.

Haney, T. L., Maynard, K. E., Houseworth, S. J., Scherwitz, L. W., Williams, R. B., & Barefoot, J. C. (1996). Interpersonal hostility assessment technique: Description and validation against the criterion of coronary heart disease in the Framingham Study III. Eight-year incidence of coronary heart disease. *American Journal of Epidemiology, 3,* 36–58.

Hartwig, W. H., Dickson, A. L., & Anderson, H. N. (1980). Conflict Resolution Inventory: Factor analytic data. *Psychological Reports, 46,* 1009–1010.

Hedlund, B. L., & Lindquist, C. U. (1984). The development of an inventory for distinguishing among passive, aggressive, and assertive behavior. *Behavioral Assessment, 6,* 379–390.

Jacobson, N. S. (1977). Problem solving and contingency contracting in the treatment of marital discord. *Journal of Consulting and Clinical Psychology, 45,* 92–100.

Jain, D., Shaker, S. M., Burg, M. M., Wackers, F. J., Soufer, R. S., & Zaret, B. L. (1998). Effects of mental stress on left ventricular and peripheral vascular performance in patients with coronary artery disease. *Journal of American College Cardiology, 31,* 1314–1322.

Leifer, R. (1999). Buddhist conceptualization and treatment of anger. *Journal of Clinical Psychology, 55,* 339–351.

Lochman, J. E. (1992). Cognitive-behavioral intervention with aggressive boys: Three-year follow-up and preventative effects. *Journal of Consulting and Clinical Psychology, 60,* 426–432.

Mammen, O. K., Shear, M. K., Pilkonis, P. A., Kolko, D. J., Thase, M. E., & Greeno, C. G. (1999). Anger attacks: Correlates and significance of an unrecognized symptom. *Journal of Clinical Psychiatry, 60*, 633–644.

Marshall, W. L., Anderson, D., & Fernandez, Y. (1999). *Cognitive behavioural treatment of sexual offenders.* West Sussex, England: Wiley.

Mauro, R. D., Vitaliano, P. P., & Cahn, T. S. (1987). A brief measure for the assessment of anger and aggression. *Journal of Interpersonal Violence, 2*, 166–178.

Mayne, T. J., & Ambrose, T. K. (1999). Research review on anger in psychotherapy. *Journal of Clinical Psychology, 55*, 353–363.

McFall, M. E., Wright, P. W., Donovan, D. M., & Murray, R. (1999). Multidimensional assessment of anger in Vietnam veterans with posttraumatic stress disorder. *Comprehensive Psychiatry, 40*, 216–220.

Meichenbaum, D. H. (1975). *Stress inoculation training.* New York: Pergamon Press.

Morrison, D., & Gilbert, P. (2001). Social rank, shame, & anger in primary and secondary psychopaths. *The Journal of Forensic Psychiatry, 12*, 330–356.

Nezu, A. M. (in press). Problem solving and behavior therapy revisited. *Behavior Therapy.*

Nezu, C. M., & Nezu, A. M. (2003). *Awakening self-esteem: Psychological and spiritual techniques for improving your well-being.* Oakland, CA: New Harbinger.

Nezu, C. M., Nezu, A. M., & Dudek, J. (1998). A cognitive-behavioral model of assessment and treatment for intellectually disabled sexual offenders. *Cognitive and Behavioral Practice, 5*, 25–64.

Novaco, R. W. (1975). *Anger control: The development of an experimental treatment.* Lexington, MA: Heath.

Novaco, R. W. (1994). Anger as a risk factor for violence among the mentally disordered. In J. Monahan & H. Steadman (Eds.), *Violence and mental disorder: Developments in risk assessment.* Chicago: University of Chicago Press.

Robins, S., & Novaco, R. W. (1999). System conceptualization and treatment of anger. *Journal of Clinical Psychology/In Session: Psychotherapy in Practice, 55*, 325–337.

Rose, J. (1996). Anger management: A group treatment program for people with mental retardation. *Journal of Developmental and Physical Disabilities, 8*, 133–149.

Spielberger, C. D. (1996). *State-Trait Anger Expression Inventory: Professional manual.* Odessa, FL: Psychological Assessment Resources, Inc.

Spielberger, C. D. (1999). *State-Trait Anger Expression Inventory-2: Professional manual.* Odessa, FL: Psychological Assessment Resources, Inc.

Straus, M. A. (1979). Measuring intrafamily conflict and violence: The Conflict Tactics (CT) Scales. *Journal of Marriage and the Family, 41*, 75–88.

Tafrate, R. C. (1995). Evaluation of treatment strategies for adult anger disorders. In H. Kassinove (Ed.), *Anger disorders: Definition, diagnosis, and treatment* (pp. 109–128). Washington, DC: Taylor & Francis.

Tescher, B., Conger, J. C., Edmondson, C. B., & Conger, A. J. (1999). Behavior, attitudes, and cognitions of anger-prone individuals. *Journal of Psychopathology and Behavioral Assessment, 21*, 117–139.

Van Elderen, T., Maes, S., Komproe, I., & van der Kamp, L. (1997). The development of an anger expression and control scale. *British Journal of Health Psychology, 2*, 269–281.

Van Goozen, S. H. M., Frijda, N. H., Kindt, M., & van de Poll, N. E. (1994). Anger proneness in women: Development and validation of the anger situation questionnaire. *Aggressive Behavior, 20,* 79–100.

Williams, R. B., & Williams, V. P. (2001). Managing hostile thoughts, feelings, and actions: The LifeSkills approach (pp. 137–153). In C. R. Snyder (Ed.), *Coping with stress: Effective people and processes.* New York: Oxford.

Appendix A

Quick Guide
to Treatment Targets

ANGER PROBLEMS

Primary Treatment Targets/Instrumental Outcome Goals

Goal 1: Decrease Heightened Physiological Arousal and Aggressive Behavior

Goal-Specific Potential Interventions

- Relaxation training
- Exposure
- Mindfulness meditation

Goal 2: Decrease Cognitive Distortions

Goal-Specific Potential Interventions

- Cognitive restructuring
- Problem-solving therapy
- Forgiveness skills
- Humor

Goal 3: Improve Interpersonal Skills

Goal-Specific Potential Interventions

- Communication skills training
- Assertiveness skills training
- Problem-solving therapy
- Conflict management skills training
- Social skills training
- Positive attitude training
- Group therapy

Secondary Treatment Targets

- Decrease general stress
- Improve partner and family relationships
- Address drug and alcohol use

BORDERLINE PERSONALITY DISORDER

Primary Treatment Targets/Instrumental Outcome Goals

Goal 1: Increase Therapy Adherence and Motivation

Goal-Specific Potential Interventions

- Psychoeducation
- Dialectical behavior therapy validation strategies
- Contingency management
- Acceptance and commitment therapy

Goal 2: Decrease Parasuicidal Behavior and Suicidal Ideation

Goal-Specific Potential Interventions

- Dialectical Behavior Therapy (DBT) Behavioral Harm Reduction Strategies

- Problem-Solving Therapy (PST)
- Cognitive Restructuring
- Increase Hope

Goal 3: Improve Self-Regulatory Skills

Goal-Specific Potential Interventions

- Mindfulness meditation
- Stress inoculation training
- Relaxation skills training
- Identifying and labeling affect
- Increase pleasant events

Goal 4: Increase Cognitive Accuracy

Goal-Specific Potential Interventions

- Cognitive therapy
- Cognitive processing therapy
- Problem-solving therapy

Goal 5: Improve Problem-Solving Skills

Goal Specific Potential Interventions

- Problem-solving therapy
- Dialectical behavior therapy

Goal 6: Improve Interpersonal skills

Goal-Specific Potential Interventions

- Communication skills training
- Assertiveness skills training
- Activity and leisure skills

Secondary Treatment Targets

- Decrease substance abuse

COUPLES' DISTRESS

Primary Treatment Targets/Instrumental Outcome Goals

Goal 1: Enhance Positive Behaviors

Goal-Specific Potential Interventions

- Behavioral exchange
- Schedule pleasant events
- Self-regulation

Goal 2: Improve Adaptive Communication and Problem Solving

Goal-Specific Potential Interventions

- Communication skills training
- Emotional communications training
- Problem-solving therapy

Goal 3: Decrease Dysfunctional Beliefs

Goal-Specific Potential Interventions

- Cognitive restructuring
- Behavioral experiments
- Reframing

Goal 4: Enhance Acceptance

Goal-Specific Potential Interventions

- Case formulation
- Empathetic joining
- Tolerance building

Secondary Treatment Targets

- Decrease stress
- Decrease individual psychopathology

- Address ambivalence
- Enhance the relationship

DEPRESSION

Primary Treatment Targets/Instrumental Outcome Goals

Goal 1: Decrease Dysfunctional Thinking

Goal-Specific Potential Interventions

- Cognitive restructuring
- Problem-solving therapy

Goal 2: Improve Problem-Solving Ability

Goal-Specific Potential Interventions

- Problem-solving therapy

Goal 3: Improve Self-Control Skills

Goal-Specific Potential Interventions

- Self-control therapy
- Problem-solving therapy

Goal 4: Improve Rates of Positive Reinforcement

Goal-Specific Potential Interventions

- Coping with depression course
- Behavioral activation

Goal 5: Enhance Social/Interpersonal Skills

- Social skills training

Secondary Treatment Targets

- Decrease suicidal ideation
- Improve marital relationship
- Improve overall physical health
- Decrease relapse

GENERALIZED ANXIETY DISORDER

Primary Treatment Targets/Instrumental Outcome Goals

Goal 1: Alter Maladaptive Metacognitions

Goal-Specific Potential Interventions

- Cognitive restructuring
- Problem-solving therapy
- Mindfulness therapy

Goal 2: Decrease Intolerance of Uncertainty

Goal-Specific Potential Interventions

- Problem-solving training
- Self-monitoring
- Stimulus control

Goal 3: Decrease Avoidant Behavior

Goal-Specific Potential Interventions

- Exposure
- Behavioral experiments
- Interpersonal strategies

Goal 4: Decrease Physical Symptoms of Anxiety

Goal-Specific Potential Interventions

- Relaxation training
- Self-control desensitization
- Sleep hygiene training

Secondary Treatment Targets

- Enhance time management skills
- Decrease general life stress
- Increase self-efficacy
- Decrease need for benzodiazepines

MALE ERECTILE DISORDER

Primary Treatment Targets/Instrumental Outcome Goals

Goal 1: Overcome Myths About Male Sexuality

Goal-Specific Potential Interventions

- Psychoeducation

Goal 2: Decrease Performance Anxiety

Goal-Specific Potential Interventions

- Sensate focus
- Anxiety reduction

Goal 3: Decrease Dysfunctional Cognitions

Goal-Specific Potential Interventions

- Cognitive restructuring
- Problem-solving therapy

Goal 4: Improve Stimulus Control

Goal-Specific Potential Interventions

- Stimulus control

Secondary Treatment Targets

- Marital distress/relationship conflict
- Poor communications
- Mood disturbance

OBSESSIVE-COMPULSIVE DISORDER

Primary Treatment Targets/Instrumental Outcome Goals

Goal 1: Decrease Appraisal of Intrusive Thoughts

Goal-Specific Potential Interventions

- Cognitive restructuring
- Pie chart
- Problem-solving therapy

Goal 2: Decrease Overt Neutralizing Behaviors

Goal-Specific Potential Interventions

- Exposure and response prevention
- Modeling
- Disrupt rituals

Goal 3: Decrease Covert Maladaptive Behaviors

Goal-Specific Potential Interventions

- Loop tapes
- Diary of thought suppression
- Behavioral experiments

Secondary Treatment Targets

- Decrease general stress
- Enhance social skills
- Decrease depressive symptoms
- Decrease "overvalued ideation"
- Increase self-efficacy

PANIC DISORDER AND AGORAPHOBIA

Primary Treatment Targets/Instrumental Outcome Goals

Goal 1: Decrease Catastrophic Interpretations of Arousal

Goal-Specific Potential Interventions

- Cognitive restructuring
- Interoceptive exposure
- Focused cognitive therapy

Goal 2: Decrease Physiological Arousal

Goal-Specific Potential Interventions

- Distraction
- Relaxation
- Respiratory control

Goal 3: Decrease Safety Behaviors

Goal-Specific Potential Interventions

- Exposure
- Safety signal perspective
- Guided mastery therapy
- Behavioral experiments
- Self-instructional training

Secondary Treatment Targets

- Enhance interpersonal relationships
- Decrease stress
- Schedule activities
- Prevent relapse

SPECIFIC PHOBIAS

Primary Treatment Targets/Instrumental Outcome Goals

Goal 1: Decrease Heightened Arousal

Goal-Specific Potential Interventions

- Exposure
- Flooding
- Applied relaxation

Goal 2: Decrease Vasovagal Reaction

Goal-Specific Potential Interventions

- Exposure
- Applied tension
- Respiratory control

Goal 3: Decrease Dysfunctional Beliefs

Goal-Specific Potential Interventions

- Cognitive restructuring
- Cost-benefit analysis
- Guided positive imagery

Secondary Treatment Targets

- Improve medical health
- Increase self-efficacy
- Improve social relationships
- Decrease general stress
- Enhance performance at work
- Decrease relapse

POSTTRAUMATIC STRESS DISORDER

Primary Treatment Targets/Instrumental Outcome Goals

Goal 1: Decrease Psychophysiological Arousal

Goal-Specific Potential Interventions

- Prolonged exposure
- Multiple-channel exposure therapy
- Anxiety management

Goal 2: Decrease Dysfunctional Beliefs

Goal-Specific Potential Interventions

- Cognitive restructuring
- Guided self-dialogue
- Behavioral experiments
- Thought stopping

Goal 3: Enhance Adaptive Coping Skills

Goal-Specific Potential Interventions

- Stress inoculation training
- Problem-solving therapy
- Affective management training

Secondary Treatment Targets

- Decrease sleep disturbances
- Decrease "resistance"
- Enhance interpersonal relationships
- Decrease crisis behavior
- Prevent PTSD

SOCIAL ANXIETY

Primary Treatment Targets/Instrumental Outcome Goals

Goal 1: Decrease Heightened Physiological Arousal

Goal-Specific Potential Interventions

- Exposure therapy
- Flooding
- Relaxation training

Goal 2: Decrease Dysfunctional Beliefs

Goal-Specific Potential Interventions

- Cognitive restructuring
- Problem-solving therapy

Goal 3: Enhance Interpersonal Skills

Goal-Specific Potential Interventions

- Social skills training
- Social effectiveness training
- Group therapy

Secondary Treatment Targets

- Decrease general stress
- Improve specific social skills deficits
- Decrease focus on bodily sensations
- Address co-morbid disorders

Appendix B

Description of Selected Cognitive-Behavioral Strategies

ACCEPTANCE AND COMMITMENT THERAPY

Acceptance and commitment therapy (ACT) is a contextual behavioral psychotherapy approach that is based in relational frame theory. This approach has recently been developed to address a wide range of psychological problems including mood disorders, substance abuse, and chronic disorders. The underlying theory proposes that human verbal behavior (language) is based upon the ability to arbitrarily relate events, mutually and in combination, and to transform the stimulus functions of one event based on its relation to another. The treatment that results from this perspective identifies the unique characteristics of human language and cognition as an explanation for how psychological and emotional reactions to painful past experiences or events can be continually brought into the present. ACT strategies were developed based upon the observation that as human beings attempt to avoid such painful thoughts and feelings, they often engage in a type of experiential avoidance. It is this avoidance that results in the symptoms for which they seek psychological treatment. As such, ACT strategies are designed to reduce the narrowness and inflexibility of behavioral repertoires that arise from attempts at experiential avoidance. The general clinical goals of ACT are to undermine the hold of verbal content and cognition that leads to this avoidance behavior and to help people construct alternative contexts so that their behavior is in greater alignment with their values.

ACT therapists engage patients in non-confrontational forms of verbal interaction, such as metaphor, paradox, and experiential exercises, in order to "loosen the entanglements of thoughts and self." A central therapeutic aim is to undermine the literal impact of verbal events and to help alter patients' contexts such that value-oriented actions are likely to occur while avoidance actions are reduced.

There are several specific therapy domains of ACT and each has its own specific methodology, exercises, homework, and metaphors. These areas include the following: initiating creative hopelessness (identifying strategies that the patient has used that are not working); viewing control as the problem and not the solution; developing acceptance as an alternative life agenda; developing a transcendent sense of self (the ability to experience events in the here and now without engaging in evaluation); learning how to defuse language and cognition; and committing to valued actions.

Recommended Readings

Hayes, S. C., Strosahl, K. D., & Wilson, K. G. (1999). *Acceptance and commitment therapy: An experiential approach to behavior change.* New York: Guilford.
Hayes, S. C., Masuda, A., & De Mey, H. (in press). Acceptance and commitment therapy and the third wave of behavior therapy. *Gedragstherapie* (Dutch Journal of Behavior Therapy).

APPLIED TENSION

In contrast to other specific phobias, fainting can be common in blood–injection–injury (BII) phobia. This fainting response appears to be a result of decreased blood to the brain (i.e., decreased blood pressure). The goal of applied tension, therefore, is to increase blood pressure to prevent fainting from occurring in a person with a BII phobia.

When teaching applied tension, the therapist instructs patients to tense muscle groups in their arms and legs for 5-second intervals. Imagery, such as "Imagine the increased tension from squeezing a ball in your hands" can be provided to encourage isometric contractions. Instruction is facilitated by the therapist modeling the procedure. Patients practice this technique, first in a controlled environment, and then when facing situations involving the feared stimulus. This technique can, thus, be applied within a larger exposure therapy framework.

Recommended Readings

Bodycoat, N., Grauaug, L., Olson, A., & Page, A. C. (2000). Constant versus rhythmic muscle tension in applied tension. *Behaviour Change, 17,* 97–102.

Öst, L. G., & Sterner, U. (1987). Applied tension: A specific behavioral method for treatment of blood phobia. *Behaviour Research and Therapy, 25,* 25–29.

AUTOGENIC TRAINING

Autogenic training (meaning "self-generated") is a technique geared to help patients reduce fatigue, tension, and anxiety by teaching them to generate feelings of heaviness and warmth in their extremities. It also has been found to be helpful for patients experiencing chronic pain. Unlike progressive muscle relaxation, there is no physical activity involved in this procedure. In essence, autogenic training encourages the blood flow to the extremities and allows one's feet and hands to feel warmer. The induction provided by the therapist first directs the patient to focus on various muscles groups (e.g., right hand, left hand, right foot, left foot). The patient is then asked to repeatedly state a series of directions slowly to him or herself while breathing slowly. These include: "My right hand is heavy. My right hand is heavy and warm. My right hand is letting go." The focus then shifts to the other hand, as well as the two feet. Additional muscle groups may be part of the protocol for patients with chronic pain problems (e.g., shoulders, chest). Autogenic training can also be paired with various positive images to enhance the relaxation effect.

Recommending Readings

Davis, M. E., Eschelman, E., & McKay, M. (1995). *The relaxation and stress reduction workbook* (4th ed.). Oakland, CA: New Harbinger.

BEHAVIORAL ACTIVATION

Behavioral activation (BA) is a treatment approach for depression that is geared to increase sources of positive reinforcement in order to counter patterns of avoidance, withdrawal, and inactivity that often engender or exacerbate depressive symptoms. The major goal of BA is to help a depressed individual identify which behaviors and activities will be idiographically reinforcing in order to disrupt the cycle among depressed mood, decreased activation/withdrawal/avoidance, and worsened depression. Treatment goals are collaboratively established between the therapist and patient, a functional analysis is conducted to better understand the unique contextual and environmental triggers of depressive symptoms, and various activation strategies are taught to the patient in order to enhance the reinforcing nature of his or her life.

Activation strategies include (a) *focused activation* (i.e., engaging in those activities that have been specifically identified as reinforcing based on the previous functional analysis), (b) *graded task assignment* (i.e., assigning increasingly more difficult tasks), (c) *avoidance modification* (i.e., fostering motivation to "avoid" avoidance behaviors), (d) *routine regulation* (i.e., establishing a regular routine for basic life activities), and (e) *attention to experience* (i.e., fostering the patient's ability to better understand the *function* of depressive ruminations as a means of decreasing their frequency). In addition, the BA therapist helps to identify various obstacles to successful treatment, such as low motivation or poor compliance with homework assignments.

Recommended Readings

Jacobson, N. S., Martell, C. R., & Dimidjian, S. (2001). Behavioral activation treatment for depression: Returning to contextual roots. *Clinical Psychology: Science and Practice, 8,* 255–270.

Martell, C. R., Addis, M. E., & Jacobson, N. S. (2001). *Depression in context: Strategies for guided action.* New York: Norton.

COGNITIVE PROCESSING THERAPY

Cognitive processing therapy (CPT) is an intervention originally developed to treat the specific symptoms of Posttraumatic Stress Disorder (PTSD) in survivors of sexual assault. The treatment is grounded in information processing theories of PTSD that propose two conditions as necessary for reduction of fear: (a) activation of the fear memory; and (b) learning new information that is incompatible with current fear structures. Fear reduction occurs through the process of habituation. This learning experience involves systematic exposure to the traumatic memory in a safe environment.

A unique feature of CPT, however, is that is combines the main ingredient of exposure-based therapies with a pronounced cognitive component found in most cognitive therapies. The addition of this component is based upon the theory that although activation of fear schemas in a safe environment may sufficiently alter a person's perception of danger and fear, there may be no change in their other emotional reactions. Examples of other reactions include the tendency of some survivors to blame themselves and feel shame, anger, disgust, or confusion. These cognitive and emotional patterns may reflect themes in addition to fear, such as self-esteem, competence, and intimacy. CPT therefore provides treatment modules focused on faulty thinking patterns and identifying cognitive "stuck points" in addition to exposure-based modules.

The treatment challenges specific cognitions that are most likely to have been disrupted by the cycle of trauma. Patients are given homework assignments at each session and much of the therapeutic work is carried out between sessions. CPT includes an education phase, specific guidance regarding how to identify thoughts and feelings, and exposure strategies in which patients write about an event in detail and read the account to themselves daily. Patients also read their accounts aloud during sessions where the therapist helps them to label their feelings and identify relevant targets for cognitive change.

Recommended Readings

Resick, P. A., & Calhoun, K. S. (2001). Posttraumatic Stress Disorder. In D. H. Barlow (Ed.), *Clinical handbook of psychological disorder: A step-by-step treatment manual* (pp. 60–113). New York: Guilford Press.
Resick, P. A., & Schnicke, M. K. (1993). *Cognitive processing therapy for rape victims: A treatment manual.* Newbury Park: CA: Sage.

COGNITIVE RESTRUCTURING

Cognitive restructuring (CR) can be thought if as an umbrella term for a variety of cognitive-based approaches aimed at reducing negative automatic thoughts and ameliorating maladaptive schemas. The basic assumption underlying these perspectives is that cognitive factors (e.g., beliefs, attitudes, perceptions) influence people's emotions and behavior. In other words, it is not an event per se that determines what individuals feel, but rather their *perception* of the situation. Psychopathology, such as depression and anxiety, then, results from distortions in such cognitive factors. Three levels of cognitive dysfunctions are commonly described in cognitive models: (a) distorted or negative automatic thoughts (e.g., "I'm boring," "I'm a failure"); (b) maladaptive assumptions or faulty guiding principles (e.g., "I must get everyone's approval," "I must be loved by everyone"); and (c) dysfunctional schemas or sets of core beliefs (e.g., "I'm inadequate," "I'm stupid").

Whereas various models of CR therapy exist, all are geared to help patients to (a) identify these types of negative thinking patterns, (b) understand how such cognitions influence their emotional and behavioral responses to stressful situations, and (c) change such negative thinking by replacing the negative beliefs with more adaptive and healthy ones. Some approaches use direct refutation to challenge the logic or rationality of such thinking, whereas others engage in a collaborative relationship with the patient in an effort to mutually explore the soundness of various cognitive distortions. Additional cognitive change techniques include examining the logic of one's thoughts, conducting an analysis of the evidence "for" and "against" a particular belief, encouraging individuals to "test out" various faulty assumptions, positive reframing, and using role plays.

Recommended Readings

Beck, A. T., Emery, G., & Greenberg, R. L. (1985). *Anxiety disorders and phobias: A cognitive perspective.* New York: Basic Books.
Beck, J. S. (1995). *Cognitive therapy: Basic and beyond.* New York: Guilford Press.

DEEP BREATHING AND RESPIRATORY CONTROL

Anxiety is often accompanied by shallow and rapid breaths. Such breathing leads to decreased carbon dioxide in the blood, which results in feelings of dizziness and lightheadedness. These symptoms may trigger panic (e.g., for patients with PD/PDA) or fainting (e.g., for patients with blood-injection-injury phobias). The purpose of breathing retraining is to prevent this hyperventilation by promoting slow, controlled, relaxing inhalations and exhalations. Simply put, one cannot be anxious (e.g., breathing rapidly) and relaxed (e.g., breathing calmly) at the same time. As such, breathing retraining helps facilitate relaxing breaths.

Breathing retraining exercises combine deep breathing and respiratory control. The former refers to principally using the diaphragm to achieve slow, deep breaths. When teaching patients *diaphragmatic breathing*, the therapist models the procedure. One hand is placed on one's upper chest and the other over the diaphragm (i.e., above the navel). The therapist instructs and demonstrates that, upon inhalation, the hand over the diaphragm elevates significantly more than the upper hand. Inhalation and exhalation are slow and prolonged (e.g., to a count of 5). The therapist may provide the client with imagery, such as picturing the diaphragm, like a balloon, filling with air upon the inhalation and deflating upon exhalation. The patient is instructed to continue to breathe in this calming manner for five minutes. Patients practice this technique twice a day, progressing to engaging in deep breathing without the feedback of their hands in a controlled environment. Finally, patients learn to utilize this technique, when they are feeling anxious, as a means of counteracting the anxiety.

Respiratory control incorporates diaphragmatic breathing into a more comprehensive psychoeducational technique. First, patients experientially learn the effects of hyperventilation by taking quick breaths for two minutes, after which they are asked to describe the experience (e.g., emotions, physical sensations, thoughts of anxiety). This discussion, directed by the therapist's use of guided discovery, permits patients to appreciate the maladaptive effects of hyperventilation (e.g., heightening psychological distress). The patient is next instructed in diaphragmatic breathing, which is eventually applied during stressful situations.

Recommended Readings

Antony, M. M., & Swinson, R. P. (2000). Exposure-based strategies and social skills training. In M. M. Antony & R. P. Swinson (Eds.), *Phobic disorders and panic in adults: A guide to assessment and treatment* (pp. 191–238). Washington, DC: American Psychological Association.

Clark, D. M., Salkovskis, P. M., & Chalkley, A. J. (1985). Respiratory control as a treatment for panic attacks. *Journal of Behavior Therapy and Experimental Psychiatry, 16*, 23–30.

EXPOSURE THERAPY

In an effort to decrease both physiological and psychological distress, patients often avoid feared stimuli. Avoidance becomes negatively reinforced when this behavior pattern leads to a decrease in negative arousal. In addition, avoidance prevents patients from experiencing the natural decrease in distress that occurs over time when continual contact is maintained with a feared stimulus. Thus, the purpose of exposure therapy (ET) is to allow the patient to habituate to stimuli (e.g., objects, places, activities, thoughts) that induce or are strongly associated with anxiety.

ET begins with educating the patient to better assess his or her level of distress or anxiety (i.e., Subjective Units of Distress Scale [SUDS]). Patients then learn to identify a diverse group of idiographically stressful situations, ranging from those that create minimal arousal (e.g., SUDS of 20 out of 100) to the most stressful situation they can imagine (e.g., SUDS of 100). Each situation is vividly described to encompass diverse sensory stimuli (e.g., sights, sounds, smells, touch, physical sensations experienced). Patients are reminded that such scenes do not have to be realistic (e.g., an individual fearful of spiders may be most afraid of having spiders crawling all over him or her, although this is rather unlikely to happen in real life).

The actual exposure technique can occur either via *imagination* or *in vivo*, with patients directed to experience progressively more distressing scenes (e.g., starting with an event rated as producing a SUDS of 20 and progressively working up to the scene predicted to cause a SUDS of 100). Regarding imaginal exposure, the patient listens to the therapist vividly describe the feared scene in detail. For in vivo exposure, the patient is encouraged to actually experience the feared and previously avoided stimulus (e.g., someone with OCD who fears dirt may be asked to touch dirt without engaging in hand washing; a patient with PTSD related to a car accident is asked to drive by a particular street that had been avoided). During exposure, the patient is asked to periodically provide a SUDS rating. Contact with the feared stimulus (either imagined or in vivo) may cease only after the patient's SUDS rating has reduced to at least 50% of its original value. It is important that the therapist ensure that (a) patients are experiencing the predicted elevated SUDS at the beginning of the exposure session (e.g., not avoiding the experience of the stressor), and (b) patients understand the importance of not stopping exposure until *after* the SUDS has dropped to the pre-determined level (i.e., to permit one's body to learn and experience the natural decrease in arousal). Cessation before such habituation occurs will only serve to strengthen the arousal and avoidance associated with that particular stimulus.

Recommended Readings

Barlow, D. H. (Ed.). (2001). *Clinical handbook of psychological disorders: A step-by-step treatment manual (3rd ed.).* New York: Guilford Press.

Barlow, D. H., & Craske, M. G. (2000). *Mastery of your anxiety and panic: Client workbook for anxiety and panic.* San Antonio, TX: Psychological Corporation.

FLOODING

Flooding is similar to exposure therapy, with the identical goal of habituation to previously fearful stimuli. The difference, however, centers on the sequence of contact with the feared stimulus. Specifically, unlike exposure where patients progressively experience more distressing stimuli, flooding entails immediately experiencing a highly distressing stimulus.

Flooding begins with educating the patient to better assess one's level of distress or anxiety (i.e., Subjective Units of Distress Scale [SUDS], where 0 = no anxiety or distress at all to 100 = extremely distressing). Patients then identify diverse situations that are highly distressing. Each situation is vividly described and encompasses diverse sensory stimuli (e.g., sights, sounds, smells, touch, physical sensations experienced). Patients are reminded that such scenes do not have to be realistic (e.g., an individual fearful of public speaking in front of an audience of 1,000 people all scorning and ridiculing the patient).

The actual flooding technique can occur either via *imagination* or *in vivo*, with patients experiencing being exposed to highly distressing situations. With regard to imaginal flooding, the patient listens to the therapist vividly describe the feared scene in detail. Concerning in vivo flooding, the patient actually experiences the highly feared and previously avoided stimulus. During flooding, the patient is asked to periodically provide a SUDS rating. Contact with the feared stimulus (either imagined or in vivo) may cease only after the patient's SUDS rating has reduced to at least 50% of its original value. It is important that the therapist ensure that (a) patients are experiencing the predicted elevated SUDS at the beginning of the session (e.g., not avoiding the experience of the stressor), and (b) patients understand the importance of not stopping the flooding exposure until after the SUDS has dropped to the pre-determined level (i.e., to permit one's body to learn and experience the natural decrease in arousal). Cessation before such habituation occurs will only serve to strengthen the arousal and avoidance associated with that particular stimulus.

Recommended Readings

Barlow, D. H. (Ed.). (2001). *Clinical handbook of psychological disorders: A step-by-step treatment manual (3rd ed.)*. New York: Guilford Press.
Gelder, M. (1991). Psychological treatment for anxiety disorders: Adjustment disorder with anxious mood, generalized anxiety disorders, panic disorder, agoraphobia, and avoidant personality disorder. In W. Coryell & G. Winokur (Eds.), *The clinical management of anxiety disorders* (pp. 10–27). London: Oxford University Press.

MINDFULNESS STRATEGIES (MEDITATION)

"Mindfulness" can be defined as a flexible state of mind that includes an openness to novelty where one is sensitive to context and perspective and "situated in the present." Being mindful is to be *guided,* rather than *directed,* by rules and routines. As a philosophical perspective, it has been initially adopted from Eastern (e.g., Buddhist) religions as a particular type of meditation protocol. In *mindfulness meditation*, the individual attempts to attend to and focus upon all stimuli in one's internal and external environment, but not in a judgmental fashion and does not engage in rumination regarding any particular stimulus. It is often referred to as an "opening-up" form of meditation practice, as compared to, for example, transcendental meditation, where the individual is directed to focus specifically on a particular mantra.

As a meditative procedure, mindfulness meditation has been found to be an effective stress management and anxiety reduction strategy. As a function of this type of success, several researchers and clinicians have attempted to integrate such a philosophical framework with traditional cognitive and behavioral therapies as a means of enhancing their efficacy. For example, a mindful cognitive therapy for a depression program has been recently developed; both dialectic behavior therapy and acceptance and commitment therapy have included this perspective in their overall protocols, and others who are attempting to integrate spirituality with cognitive-behavior therapy view mindfulness as a central tenet in fostering attainment of *positive* goals (e.g., hope, forgiveness, acceptance).

Recommended Readings

Nezu, C. M., & Nezu, A. M. (2003). *Awakening self-esteem: Psychological and spiritual techniques for improving your well-being.* Oakland, CA: New Harbinger.

Segal, Z. V., Williams, J. M. G., & Teasdale, J. D. (2002). *Mindfulness-based cognitive therapy for depression: A new approach to preventing relapse.* New York: Guilford Press.

PROBLEM-SOLVING THERAPY

Problem-solving therapy (PST) provides training in a systematic model of real-life problem solving as a means to foster one's ability to cope with stressful situations. Contemporary models of problem solving identify two major component processes: problem orientation and problem-solving style. *Problem orientation* is the set of relatively stable cognitive-affective schemas that represent a person's generalized beliefs, attitudes, and emotional reactions about problems in living and one's ability to successfully cope with such problems. If negative (e.g., problems are viewed as threats, ability to solve problems is viewed as ineffective), it can engender negative affect and avoidance motivation, which can later serve to inhibit or disrupt subsequent problem-solving attempts.

Problem-solving style refers to those core cognitive-behavioral activities that people engage in when attempting to cope with problems in living. Three differing styles have been identified, the first being *rational problem solving.* This adaptive style involves the systematic and planful application of various skills, including (a) accurately defining the problem and setting realistic goals, (b) generating multiple options to attain such goals, (c) conducting a sound cost-benefit analysis in order to make effective decisions regarding which alternative solutions are likely to be successful, (d) making a commitment and carrying out a solution plan, and (e) monitoring the outcome in order to determine if continued problem solving is required to adequately cope with the stressful situation. In contrast, two maladaptive styles exist: *impulsive/careless style* (i.e., impulsive, hurried, and careless attempts at problem resolution) and *avoidant style* (i.e., avoidance of problems via procrastination, passivity, and over-dependence on others).

Specific therapy objectives of PST are to (a) enhance one's positive orientation, (b) decrease one's negative orientation, (c) improve one's rational problem-solving skills, (d) decrease one's impulsive/careless style, and (e) decrease one's avoidance style. This is accomplished through a series of didactic explanations, skills training activities, role-play exercises, and homework assignments. In addition to fostering actual skill acquisition, PST attempts to foster generalized application of such skills across a multitude of intrapersonal and interpersonal problems as a means of improving overall coping ability and decreasing psychological distress.

· Recommended Readings

Nezu, A. M., Nezu, C. M., Friedman, S. H., Faddis, S., & Houts, P. S. (1998). *Helping cancer patients cope: A problem-solving approach*. Washington, DC: American Psychological Association.
Nezu, A. M., Nezu, C. M., & Perri, M. G. (1989). *Problem-solving therapy for depression: Theory, research, and clinical guidelines*. New York: Wiley.

PROGRESSIVE MUSCLE RELAXATION

The goal of progressive muscle relaxation (PMR) is to decrease muscular tension and physiological arousal. PMR can be an adaptive coping technique to decrease physiological and psychological distress by relaxing one's body and mind. This stress management approach entails three steps, all of which are initially practiced under the therapist's supervision. However, as the patient becomes proficient, the latter two and, eventually, just the third stage, are performed. During the first step of the PMR induction, patients are instructed to contract (tense) and relax various muscle groups throughout the body. The specific areas may vary according to the prominent regions of tension, but often include: face, neck, shoulders, arms, hands, stomach, back, legs, and feet. Patients maintain an isometric contraction for approximately 3–5 seconds before relaxing the specific body part.

After the contract-relax portion, patients are instructed to focus on the same order of muscle group regions. However, in this second phase, only relaxation is employed. Thus, patients are instructed to focus on and further relax each of the muscle groups. Finally, the third step entails relaxing the entire body. Here, patients are instructed to scan their bodies, identify any areas of tension, and release the tense muscles. The PMR induction is conducted during sessions and audiotaped for practice as homework between sessions.

Recommended Readings

Davis, M. E., Eschelman, E., & McKay, M. (1995). *The relaxation and stress reduction workbook* (4th ed.). Oakland, CA: New Harbinger.

Smith, J. C. (1999). *ABC relaxation training: A practical guide for health professionals.* New York: Springer Publishing Co.

SELF-CONTROL DESENSITIZATION

Self-control desensitization is a variant of systematic desensitization (SD), which is an anxiety reduction procedure that entails having a deeply relaxed individual imagine a graded series of increasing distressing situations. SD first teaches the individual to become more aware of his or her anxiety levels by learning to use a *SUDS* scale (i.e., Subjective Units of Discomfort, where 0 = no discomfort or anxiety at all to 100 = extremely anxious). Similar to imaginal exposure, the therapist reads a series of increasingly more anxiety-provoking situations that were previously identified as relevant for a given patient. Unlike exposure, however, SD first includes teaching the patient relaxation skills (e.g., progressive muscle relaxation). While the patient is in a relaxed state, he or she is then directed to imagine one of the scenes from the hierarchy beginning with less anxiety-provoking ones. When the patient feels distress, the therapist then directs him or her to once again engage in self-relaxation. This continues until the situation no longer elicits anxiety. The procedure then proceeds up the hierarchy. Theoretically, the anxiety is "counterconditioned" or extinguished.

Self-control SD conceptualizes the procedure as training in coping skills. According to this perspective, the patient experiencing anxiety learns to relax when distressed. As such, the SD protocol provides practice in coping with anxiety. One major procedural difference regarding the self-control variation is the emphasis placed in the use of relaxation as a coping skill, whereby patients are taught to use such skills in real-life situations, in addition to SD sessions in the therapist's office.

Recommended Readings

Goldfried, M. R., & Davison, G. C. (1994). *Clinical behavior therapy* (expanded edition). New York: Wiley.

SENSATE FOCUS

Sensate focus (SF) is one of the basic treatment strategies in sex therapy. In essence, this procedure emphasizes a heightened awareness of, and focus on, the pleasurable sensations associated with sexual activities. SF teaches individuals to pay more attention to the process of sexual intimacy (e.g., touch, smell), rather than the outcome of a sexual interaction (e.g., erection, orgasm). As such, it reduces one's performance anxiety and concerns.

Initially, the couple in sex therapy is directed to deliberately avoid having sexual intercourse in order to reduce one's negative expectations and pressures (e.g., "Am I going to be able to have an erection?"). Sexual interactions initially, then, focus more on giving and receiving sensual pleasure. A first step might be to have a couple engage in mutual touching, fondling, and caressing, but not in areas related to the breast or genitals. They are restricted to this set of exercises, even if the male partner achieves a full erection. The couple is directed to explore each other bodies, focusing on how giving and receiving sexual pleasure feels, and to experiment. Initial exercises might even entail having the couple touch each other with their clothes on.

Assuming that both partners enjoyed the initial exercises, the next step involves a continuation of mutual touching, but now includes the genital area. A third step involves "vaginal containment," where, regardless if the penis is flaccid or erect, both partners insert the penis into the vagina. Actual intercourse is not yet to take place. Once both partners feel relaxed and enjoy this phase, they then move on to actual intercourse. The couple continues to be advised to focus on the sensuality and pleasure of the act and not on the outcome (e.g., sustained erection, orgasm).

Recommended Readings

Masters, W. H., & Johnson, V. E. (1970). *Human sexual inadequacy.* Boston: Little, Brown.

Wincze, J. P., & Carey, M. P. (2001). *Sexual dysfunction: A guide for assessment and treatment* (2nd ed.). New York: Guilford Press.

SOCIAL SKILLS/ASSERTIVENESS TRAINING

"Social skills" is an umbrella term that encompasses a wide range of skills and competencies necessary for effectively interacting with others. These include assertiveness skills, communication skills, nonverbal skills (e.g., avoiding versus maintaining eye contact), conversational skills, dating skills, and so forth. Social skills are learned, usually vicariously, and are influential in soliciting reinforcement from one's social environment. If effective, social skills are likely to be responsible for one's academic, work, and relationship success. On the other hand, deficient social skills may be responsible for a wide range of distress and psychological problems.

Skill deficits may be a function of (a) knowledge deficits, (b) proficiency deficits, (c) motivational deficits, and/or (d) discrimination deficits (i.e., person is unable to determine the conditions in which certain behaviors are appropriate or inappropriate). Social skills training, therefore, needs to first assess which of these problems exist. Training, then, should focus on any or all of the above etiological factors. Actual intervention strategies entail psychoeducation, modeling, behavioral rehearsal, feedback, and discrimination training. If the person appears to lack the motivation, the therapist should assess whether this avoidance is fear related.

Assertive training is a specific form of social skills training and is geared to help the individual be able to obtain what one is entitled to in social situations without impinging on the rights of others. Examples include asking for what one is entitled to (e.g., a deserved raise), standing up for one's rights (e.g., asking someone not to get ahead in a line for the movies), refusing unreasonable requests (e.g., saying "no" to a co-worker's request to borrow money), expressing one's opinion appropriately (e.g., giving an unpopular opinion), and expressing various appropriate requests (e.g., telling a friend how you feel about him or her).

Assertive training is helpful for individuals who are consistently *unassertive* in order to help them increase their ability to obtain deserved positive reinforcement, as well as those who typically are *aggressive* in social situations, as a means of decreasing the negative impact they have on others. Assertive and aggressive behaviors may result in the same objective, but the latter usually involves violating the rights of someone else. In addition to the skill deficit-related etiological factors described above, unassertiveness may also be caused by various cognitive distortions (e.g., "I don't deserve to get a raise because I'm not that good," "It's okay if that person gets ahead of me in line—he probably has more important things to do"). As such, assertiveness training can take the form of overcoming knowledge or proficiency deficits, as well as ameliorating the faulty assumptions.

Recommended Readings

Linehan, M. M. (1993). *Skills training manual for treating borderline personality disorder.* New York: Guilford Press.

Paterson, R. J. (2001). *The assertiveness workbook: How to express your ideas and stand up for yourself at work and in relationships.* Oakland, CA: New Harbinger.

VISUALIZATION AND GUIDED IMAGERY

Visualization and guided imagery are behavioral stress management and anxiety reduction strategies that focus on the use of one's imagination or "mind's eye." These strategies foster feelings of relaxation by having individuals develop soothing and pleasant images in their mind. By providing an induction that entails diverse stimuli that engage all five senses (e.g., sight, smell, touch, taste, hearing), the therapist can enhance feelings of relaxation. For example, the patient can create a safe, relaxing, and calming place to go "on a vacation in one's mind." Common safe and relaxing places include the beach, a cabin in the country, or lying on a sailboat. The therapist helps the patient to create a very vivid image by using a soothing voice and providing details to guide and enhance the sensory experience (e.g., "feel the cool breeze gently touching your face, as you slowly inhale and smell the salt air," "touch the soft pine needles on the ground as you hear the songs of birds off in the distance"). The therapist can audiotape record the induction and encourage the patient to use the tape and practice creating a "safe place" to induce a state of relaxation outside of sessions.

Visualization can also be used to enhance motivation by creating future scenes of successfully coping with stressful situations or living without negative symptomatology. It has also been found to be effective in helping patients reduce their own pain (e.g., "imagine how the pain is melting away") or to cope more effectively with various medical disorders, such as cancer (e.g., "imagine little tiny soldiers battling the cancer cells").

Recommended Readings

Naparstek, B. (1995). *Staying well with guided imagery.* New York: Warner Books.

Index

Springer Publishing Company

Problem-Solving Therapy, *Second Edition*

A Social Competence Approach To Clinical Intervention

Thomas J. D'Zurilla, PhD and Arthur M. Nezu, PhD

"There is much to recommend in this book. A major strength is its careful explication of the theoretical and empirical basis for problem-solving applications in mental health....The problem-solving manual is easy to read and will be very useful to clinicians who are setting up their own problem-solving groups."
—Child and Family Behavior Therapy

The book includes a treatment manual which provides general guidelines for the use of PST as a treatment or prevention method with a goal of increasing adaptive coping and behavioral competence, and reducing daily stress. It also includes a review of empirical studies on the outcome of PST for a variety of different target populations including those with psychiatric disorders, depression, suicidal ideation, social phobias, substance abuse problems, marital and family problems, and health problems.

Contents:

Part I: Theoretical and Empirical Foundations
- Introduction and Historical Development
- The Social Problem-Solving Process
- A Prescriptive Model of Social Problem Solving
- Measures of Social Problem-Solving Ability
- Role of Emotions in Social Problem Solving
- A Relational/Problem-Solving Model of Stress
- Social Problem Solving and Adaptation

Part II: Clinical Applications
- Problem-Solving Training Manual
- Case Illustrations
- Outcome Studies
- New Directions, Cautions, and Conclusions

1999   272pp   0-8261-1266-8   hardcover

536 Broadway, New York, NY 10012
Order Toll-Free: 877-687-7476 • Order On-line: www.springerpub.com